W   E

BHINNEKA TUNGGAL IKA

Republic of
INDONESIA

S

PHILIPPINE ISLANDS

Manila

Celebes
Sea

TALAUD

SANGI

SIAU

Menado

MOROTAI

HALMAHERA

WAIGEO

BATJAN

BANGGAI

OBI

SULA

MOLUCCA'S

CERAM

JAPEN

IRIAN
(NEW GUINEA)

SULAWESI
(CELEBES)

BURU   AMBON

Makassar   BUTUNG

Banda Sea

KAI

ARU

SALAJAR

Sea

SOLOR   ALOR   WETAR

MOA

BABAR

TANIMBAR

FREDERIK
HENDRIK

KOMORAN

FLORES

TIMOR

SUMBA

Timor Sea

Arafura Sea

AUSTRALIA

INDONESIA:
Land of Challenge

INDONESIA:
Land of Challenge

BHINNEKA TUNGGAL IKA

By Margueritte Harmon Bro

HARPER & BROTHERS PUBLISHERS
. NEW YORK .

Library of Congress catalog card number: 54-10077

To my husband
ALBIN CARL BRO
who kept his head while I roamed around Indonesia
and his sense of humor while I ground out my notes,
who read version after version with an eye to accu-
racy and constantly reminded me of the importance
of the people among the facts, this book is gratefully
dedicated.

CONTENTS

CONTENTS

ILLUSTRATIONS

The following photographs appear in a group following p. 112:

ILLUSTRATIONS

INTRODUCTION

B Y THE TIME I ENTERED FIRST GRADE I WAS already well introduced to the Far East, for my mother had two beautiful cousins who had gone out as missionaries, one to Japan and the other to China, and who came home on furlough to our house bringing their children, their quaint costumes, scripts, idols, shoes, silverwork; their hairbreadth escapes from famines, pestilence and brigands; and the needs of their hospitals, kindergartens, schools. Throughout our school days we children had saving banks for our favorite Oriental students and patients; we wrote and produced plays to make money for our projects; we sent toys and clothes; we learned geography without trying. Through our college days it was the same, with an ever-widening circle of Eastern friends, and a growing understanding that friendship means mutual exchange. In my graduate days I learned a smattering of Chinese and took courses in Eastern religions. And so there was nothing surprising about our going to China, my husband and I, for six years of work in a boys' senior middle school and considerable travel during vacations. We came home with our three China-born children and a yen to go back. But we became absorbed in other interests, including finding schools in America for our young Oriental friends, not a few of whom came to the college of which my husband was later president.

Finally in 1950 my husband turned eastward again, this

time to act as cultural officer in Korea under our Department of State. I did not get to join him there but when he was transferred to Djakarta, Indonesia, again as cultural attaché, I was free to follow. So I got out the atlas, a prewar edition which showed Indonesia as the Dutch East Indies and Djakarta as Batavia, and studied up on Java, Sumatra, Borneo, Celebes, Bali, the spice islands, the tin islands and some of the rest of the three thousand which festoon the equator for a distance greater than the spread of the United States.

Our youngest son, Andy, left college to be my fellow traveler and we sailed from New Orleans on a Danish freighter bound for Japan. We were the only passengers. My mind kept swinging back to my first trip across the Pacific on a Japanese ship with a Filipino orchestra; they hobnobbed in those days, the Filipinos and the Japanese. Japan's Twenty-one Demands on China were our chief international complication; we had finished the only World War the earth was ever to know; poison gas and the highly maneuverable airplanes had made wars too dangerous; besides, we felt friendly toward everybody.

The current scene seemed more involved, what with the wreckage of World War Two strewn about the earth and communist aggression adding to the uncertainties of nations. However, insulated from our problems by the vast sea about us and by a time cushion of three months on shipboard, we savored each day. And that is an excellent way to get into the mood of Indonesia.

Then, too, we had a kind of briefing on Southeast Asia in spending several days each in Japan, Formosa, Hong Kong, the Philippines, Indochina, Siam and Malaya; later augmented by visits to India, Ceylon, Pakistan. So we got to know something of the context of Asia in which Indonesia lives, fears, hopes. We were fortunate in having friends along the way, not only in embassies and missionary circles but among the nationals. Also I could speak enough Chinese to feel my way into the tension which marks Southeast Asia. Although our time was limited, our insights were not so casual as if we had been circumscribed by impressive official credentials.

This book is the sum of my impressions gathered from our year and a half in Java and from rather wide travel among the islands. I wish I could name the many Indonesians to whom I am gratefully indebted, but I know that it would be an embarrassment to some who helped me most if I so much as mention their help. There are Americans, too, without whose courtesy, friendliness and generosity I could never have assembled the statistical data. All of these friends know that this book is our joint effort.

Wainwright House
Rye, New York

INDONESIA:
Land of Challenge

. I .

Djakarta

DJAKARTA IS AS MUCH A STATE OF MIND AS A locality—a state of mind compounded of hustle and honk and hang-out-the-train-windows, but at the same time of an inner unhurriedness, of folk tunes and gamelan orchestras, of openhearted geniality and adolescent chip-on-the-shoulder, of diplomatic savvy and a kind of cosmic patience. However, it is a mistake to write off Djakarta—or Indonesia—as only a state of mind, something seething somewhere in the South Pacific, because the seething is being done by a nation that is now sixth largest in the world. Just on the ground of weight and mass it is important for the rest of the world to know the facts about these 80,000,000 people and their land. Probably nothing in life is more immediately important for all of us than the ability to read the figures and surmise the total before the sum is cast. Unfortunately there is scarcely a spot left on the map which we dare overlook.

Djakarta is situated on the northwest tip of Java facing into the Java Sea. Its harbor is Priok, or Tanjung Priok, a name synonymous with congestion and insecurity so far as shipping is concerned, but when we first arrived the wharves seemed only mill-run, dusty, bustling, hot. As months went by, though, and we became habituated to Priok with the wharf-life in sharper focus, we saw what the term "insecurity" meant: mild-mannered stevedores ripping open cases of cookies and distributing them to the harbor police; wheat flour piled high as a house, dumped by wharf coolies who needed the sacks for making shirts; barbed wire enclosing tons of freight stacked in the open because warehouses were too jam-packed to be sorted out. If an outsider could understand the intricacies of Priok he could probably understand the predicament of Indonesia. Maybe we took a dim view of the harbor our first day because we were not met. Our cablegram had not got through and we were on our own to get into the city if we could. We could. In one of the larger taxis, which had only five springs popping through the seat, we started off. Even now, looking back on Java with fond eyes, I see nothing enticing about that trip from the harbor.

Between the harbor and the city lie some five miles of flat, dull countryside, a wide canal with a few rusty dredges, cars and trucks plying a hot asphalt road, soldiers at the gates to the harbor areas halting all vehicles to probe, check, question. By and by the city, crowded and humid. Throughout the Chinese section stores, houses, stalls, huddle against each other, little awnings making patterns of shade. Most impressive, the number of *people*.

Once out on the fine wide palm-lined streets we found modern stucco houses appearing more solidly set up than in most parts of Asia. Verandas are more like open living rooms partially screened by bamboo blinds. Roof tile are laid together without cement, for Djakarta seldom has any kind of tropical storm; indeed, seldom a wind or even a breeze, and the rain, though it pours in torrents, comes straight down. In the Dutch times these stucco houses were inexpensive and practically every Dutchman had as much house as he wanted, while practically all Indonesians lived in bamboo-and-mat huts in the *kampongs*, those clusters of native houses of which there are hundreds inside the city. Nowadays these brick and stucco houses are very expensive to buy and incredibly difficult to rent because the Indonesians themselves insist on living in them. That is, the upper-bracket government employees, clerical personnel, executives and sub-executives, teachers, doctors, lawyers, army officers and the like all insist upon houses and the government insists on houses for them. This new order of housing discomfits the Dutch but, while it has not produced many new houses as yet, it is probably one of the best indications of the dignity of the new republic as well as of its intention and determination to take on adult status.

Before World War II Djakarta had half a million population, now grown to nearly three million with little additional housing. A house which appears from the outside to be a modest one-family dwelling usually provides quarters for at least three families, one family to each bedroom, with the kitchen and bath used jointly. In these augmented households there is a surprising surface equanimity, but after one gets to know the members one senses the city-wide neurosis of crowding. A new suburb, Kebajoran, has added close to 10,000 new homes in the past five years, relieving some of the pressure at the upper levels.

Hundreds of thousands of Indonesians still live in the kampongs—laborers, servants, vendors, *betjak* drivers, minor clerks, with their families, connections and connections of connections who have fled to the city for work or safety. These kampongs are tucked into all sorts of side streets, gullies, odd corners, half hidden by trees, moated by sluggish open canals or mere ditches which serve for sewage disposal or, if the water is high enough, as places for washing clothes, vegetables and people. The larger houses, made of matting with high roofs that usually leak in the rainy season, are divided into four rooms by low walls, each room housing a family; thus everyone shares the smoke, mosquitoes, odors and chatter of the twenty to fifty persons who live under the same roof. A kampong hotel may have only one large room in which space for sleeping mats is sold at a good price. The wonder is that people emerge from these crowded quarters looking spruce, clean and cheerful. There is no wonder about the increasingly high rate of tuberculosis.

Kampongs differ sharply in custom, language, foods, dances, music, even in their odors, depending upon the regional background of their inhabitants. Passing by, one hears the light, gay laughter of the Sundanese from west Java, the gamelan orchestras from Djogja, the hymns which distinguish the Christian districts of Minahassa in north Celebes or the Bataks of central Sumatra, the sharp dialect of Minangkabaus. But of course no foreigner picks up the nuances which make kampong life warm, friendly, joyous, sad, frustrating, a thing to be escaped from and returned to. Here in the kampongs is the real life of Indonesia; the country people transplanted to the city, adjusting to modern days and ways on the surface but still rooted in their ancient culture. The Republic rises or falls on the understanding and cooperation of the workers and peasants, and the kampongs of Djakarta are the ganglia from which afferent and efferent nerves carry impressions to all parts of the body politic and back again.

Later, after eight months of living in the neighboring city of Bandung and commuting those 130 miles, we were lucky and with plenty of pull got an apartment in Djakarta—four rooms in an old building across the railway tracks from

Tjikini market where hundreds of merchants in tiny stalls attract thousands of bargaining buyers. Between the market and us, long suburban trains (not trolleys) screeched their whistles and shook our building at ten-minute intervals so that an evening with guests was a strange affair of lapse and try again. Windows, of course, could never be closed since every chance breath of air was precious. Our second-floor quarters, which were the largest in the building, consisted of a moderate-sized living-dining room off of which opened a thin slice of balcony; a tiny back hall opening into two bedrooms and kitchen. One end of our closetless bedroom was screened, a room within a room; the windows opened onto a kitchen courtyard full of chattering wash *babus* and all the other servants of all the other families. The kitchen was eight by ten feet, had a sink but no water, a three-holed gas plate, a set of shelves, no table. Luckily the servants liked to wash dishes on the floor; they were clean if not hygienic and they never broke one dish in eighteen months. The bathroom had no window, no tub, no shower, no washbowl; the porcelain toilet had no lid and the water for flushing had to be dipped from an open vat which was filled each morning by water boys carrying buckets. There were enormous cockroaches in the bathroom; DDT bombs, powders, boiling water with lye and the servants' best "spells" never fazed them. Moreover, the roaches ran toward and not away from an intruder.

Djakarta has its share of hotels. The Hotel des Indes, an institution in Southeast Asia, is a two-story affair spreading over an area covering at least three city blocks. Before the war its food was famous with fabulous rice-tafel lunches served by twenty boys in a row, each bearing a different dish. There is still rice-tafel but lacking the dash of the old day. Hotel

Wilhelmina serves vegetables from Australia. The Jacatra has an especially obliging management. So down the line. Every hotel is always full. When a visiting fireman from Washington arrives unannounced (cablegram astray again), it is sometimes impossible to find him a bed, in which case he may have to take off by air for Bandung where there are two fairly good hotels. In any country, experiences are relative to the total pattern of daily life, and to overemphasize crowded housing and the lack of modern standards is to seem to underemphasize the will to provide better housing, the immense difficulty of finding construction experts or even adequate building materials, the scarcity of land, the whole transportation problem, the need for an improved police system.

Here in Djakarta are the government buildings. President Soekarno's home, formerly the palace of the Governor General of the Indies, is a beautiful high-pillared mansion; the Parliament Building is a dignified affair, formerly an exclusive club. The various ministries are quartered in one-story, rambling, colonnaded layouts, or in two- or three-storied buildings of the high-ceilinged, wide-corridored style of the earlier Dutch. Spotting the city with medical aid are excellent modern hospitals, second-rate semimodern hospitals, third, fourth and sixteenth-rate unmodern hospitals and clinics, besides nursing homes over which trained and not-so-trained midwives preside. Also offices of UNICEF and World Health Organization and of hundreds of Chinese *tukang gigi* or teeth artisans. Large, many-storied buildings which house the wealthy Dutch shipping and oil companies, warehouses of Indonesian, Dutch, Chinese import-export firms, jostle all sorts of shops catering to the city's sophisticated trade. And then scores of small shops offering furniture

made on the place; solid, beautifully contrived tin candle-
sticks, vases, tea sets; picture frames; Chinese objets d'art;
handmade leather purses, luggage, shoes; imported foods;
Indian shops displaying lovely French, Chinese and Japanese
silks and metallic tapestries alongside cottons from India,
Britain, the United States. The huge railway station is here,
the airport and all the offices pertaining to both. Likewise the
embassies of many nations; the spreading homes of wealthy
Chinese; imposing homes of foreign business people; new
homes of new-rich Indonesians; a few big clubs, guildhalls,
mosques and churches.

Chief thoroughfares are a restless mosaic of traffic. Streets
are paved, some of them very wide indeed, some with park-
ways, some with canals down the center; some are narrow,
some twist and turn, some are bordered by sidewalks.
Thousands of bicycles wind in and out, racing their cousins
the betjaks—a modern version of the *jinrikisha* pushed from
behind by a man on a half bicycle, a most convenient arrangement for the driver since he can jump off nimbly in a jam and
let the passenger take the brunt of it. Motorized betjaks are
fewer, fortunately, because they have a speed of forty miles
an hour. Carts drawn by small, discouraged horses bounce
alongside huge trucks. Every kind of conveyance makes its
weaving way at varying speeds—and let the pedestrian cross
a street if he can.

Djakarta's canals, known as *kalis,* are, of course, a Dutch
importation but also an inheritance of the village Indonesians. Besides being used for bathing and washing clothes they
serve as open toilets. Defecation in the kali is said to date
back 2,500 years and probably roots in the fact that the
rushing mountain streams afforded a convenient method of
excreta disposal besides enriching the rice fields into which

the water is diverted. But also perhaps the custom derives from an ancient taboo against making any part of the body or its products available to the enemy, who could use excreta as well as hair or fingernails to effect a disastrous magic spell. When the Dutch arrived in Java the population numbered some three million for the whole country and the open kali toilets were advantageous, for every family had an available stream; but now the cities are congested and the water in many of the kalis moves slowly. Along a twenty-meter stretch of a main canal I have seen men swimming, women bathing, washing their hair and the family clothes, children and adults standing in the water brushing their teeth, and people squatting over a stone embankment of the canal defecating, letting the excrement fall into the water. I watched a boy with violent diarrhea relieving himself as he squatted on the edge of the canal, using it as his stool while he called back and forth to his playmates who were bathing in the same canal less than two meters downstream. This, too, is Djakarta. A city of contrasts, we often commented riding past the unsavory canal to an Indonesian home of elegance to listen to a concert of chamber music or a particularly fine gamelan. On such an occasion one can easily be misled by the earmarks of modernity and by the preoccupation with global political concerns which mark the higher echelons.

History fans out around one in the capital. Still standing are tall, narrow houses of early Dutch settlers whose owners once closed their windows against the night air to ward off malaria; the old bank in which many a fortune in Dutch guilders was counted out; the narrow-windowed stone bastions of the early import-export trade; sections of the old city wall overlooking cobblestoned streets.

On our first New Year's Day we drove to the old part of

the city to an early Dutch church now used by an Indonesian congregation. There was a very old pipe organ whose pipes lay horizontally. Andy and I took turns playing and pumping the bellows, recalling the stiffly dressed Dutch colonists who had moved down these aisles to music from that organ. We met the Indonesian pastor, whose joy-and-sorrow face reflected his recent experience in the revolution. Then we went on to the Amsterdam Gate in the Old City and out to the Holy Cannon, a primitive bronze affair captured from the Portuguese by the Dutch around 1640. Magic powers are now imputed to the cannon; for a would-be mother to lay her hand upon it enhances, if not assures, her heart's desire. Young mothers kept coming with flowers—carnations, roses, gladioli, marigold, cosmos, lilies, African daises, marguerites—many of them carried down from the hills by vendors, a colorful hobnobbery of immigrant and native blossoms. The gentle-faced mothers had no notion of the patience and application with which Dutch scientists had acclimated and developed some of those flowers.

The unseen behind the seen. That, too, is Djakarta. Legend crowding the scientific spirit; political compulsions and historical obligations jostling each other; nationalism challenging tradition, tradition withstanding assault; practicalities defeating ambition; determination outrunning frustration. Over all hope, like a banyan tree with its wide branches casting forth fresh roots into the ancient soil.

· 2 ·

Indonesians on Location

A T THE END OF A WEEK IN DJAKARTA WE TOOK
to the hills—no room for us in the inn. Definitely the
housing authorities could do without additional foreigners,
and the American ambassador operated on the theory that
if he overlooked the fact that a man had a family it was
equivalent to his having no family, which often proved true.
But my husband had found us a sweet flimsy cottage hid in a
handsome tangle of weeds on the edge of the city of Bandung,
population a mere million, 130 miles southeast of Djakarta,
up in the mountains where the weather was blanket-cool at
night. Andy and I settled in, phrase book in hand, while my
husband commuted week ends—but not for rest; he was
always surveying schools to spot an occasional teacher who
might qualify for an American grant.

On our trips back and forth to Djakarta by car and plane I
never could credit the population statistics. The country
appears to be made up of wide open spaces. Rice fields spread
out checkerboard fashion across the lowlands and then climb
the mountainsides, tier above tier. Moreover, there are endless miles of plantations heavily wooded with cinchona, teak,
tea, rubber, and then the jungles stretching off to the edge of
the world. But after a few months one discovers that under

the palms there are thousands of people living in space where scores might be expected, and likewise that the *desas,* or country villages, are so jam-packed that an American tenement district appears roomy by contrast.

For the whole of Indonesia the population density is only 102 persons to the square mile, twice that of the United States. But practically all of the islands—certainly all of the large islands—have rugged skeletons with a backbone consisting of a series of volcanoes. People cannot live on volcanoes (although many try), nor in jungles, nor yet in salt marshes. So they huddle along the coasts and on the tablelands. Java is the most crowded. Relatively the size of Illinois, it has only 7 per cent of the archipelago's total land area but 76 per cent of the cultivated land, and almost three-fourths of the people —around 55,000,000. They average 1,400 to the square mile, but of course considerable land is uninhabitable and thus the actual concentration is terrific. I used to wonder if one reason the people are so gentle, so sunny, so reasonable, might not be because they would kill each other off if they went temperamental at such close quarters.

Sumatra, lying northwest of Java, is more than three times its size and comes second in population and development of its natural resources. It has a mere 12,000,000 people, roughly 61 to the square mile. Off its east coast lie the small tin islands of Bangka and Billiton. Borneo is the largest of the islands, close to 300,000 square miles, but the British-governed territories of the north account for slightly more than a quarter of the area; the Indonesian section, renamed Kalimantan, has around 13 people to the square mile. Celebes, renamed Sulawesi, is the orchid-shaped island lying east of Borneo, its northernmost petal flipped west-east with a final curl to the north, bringing it directly south of Mindanao,

southernmost large island of the Philippines. Some 70 people
to the square mile. New Guinea, now known as Irian and the
center of the current Indonesian-Netherlands dispute, is a
shade larger than Borneo; Australia controls the eastern half.
Off the eastern tip of Java lies the famous little island of Bali
with lofty Gunung Agung, "navel of the world," towering
at its center while lesser mountains and foothills step down
toward the coast. Bali's concentration is some 600 persons to
the square mile. Bali and Lombok, its closest neighbor, with
Timor, Flores, Sumba, Sumbawa and a few others, make up
the Lesser Sundas. The sparsely settled Moluccas, famous
in the early spice trade, lie directly east of the northern peninsula of Celebes and northwest of New Guinea. To their south
are Ceram and Ambon. And then come the hundreds of
smaller islands.

With such varied topography the climate is naturally varied
also: warm, hot, hotter, hottest. Actually it is the humidity
which makes the heat of the lowlands seem insufferable.
Djakarta's temperature averages in the low eighties but its
average mean relative humidity is about the same. Those who
can, make for the mountains. For every 400 feet of rise the
temperature drops roughly one degree—and the disposition
improves by geometric ratio as one climbs out of the heat.

June the year around. With a stirring of ancestral memory
some deciduous trees lose their leaves at regular intervals,
even attempting faint autumn colors, but most trees merely
stand quiescent for a while and then burst again into bloom.
To keep the days from running together in a year-long
montage, there are alternating monsoons which blow in the
rains and then blow them out again. Actually the winds are
more discernible as dotted lines on the weather map than as

something felt on the cheek or heard in the palms, for there is seldom a stiff breeze in any weather.

Most of the rain falls between November and January, but the rainy season is not one long downpour. The year we lived in Bandung we had only one day without sunshine and never more than eleven days without a shower. However, the rainfall is temperamental and seems to favor certain localities. It also varies by the year, some dry seasons lasting so long that the streams dry up, water power shortage becomes acute, electricity is cut to a minimum, factories close down.

Throughout the archipelago the scenery is magnificent. As the months went by I folded up my adjectives, pocketed my sighs and just looked. A vista of sea glimpsed through palm trees, a curling beach line of white sand, sharply etched rocks along a precipitous coast, steep mountain passes, serene peaks. Rivers. Whoever said that every man should have a river in his life would have liked living in Indonesia. Almost every Indonesian has a river: a wide sweeping river, a swift deep river, or at least a mountain stream. Every sort of vegetation grows along the river banks. Jungles as primitive as when the world was new, enormous trees reaching up, up into the sunlight, impenetrable bushes often bearing immense white blossoms fluted like five-pointed stars, pines with sparse needles like pin feathers on a molting goose; everything bound together with vines, hung with moss, draped with delicate parasitic ferns and epiphytic orchids. Groves of great gray-trunked nutmeg trees, often 150 feet high, with monkeys chattering in their branches. Acres of rubber trees in even rows so that whether one looks down the endless aisles horizontally, vertically, or diagonally, the trees march in perfect formation. Miles of coconut, betel or oil palm. Clove trees with their scented buds, banana palms with their fruit growing *up*, varieties of shining-leafed *djeruk*, meaning any kind of orange or lemon. Fields of sweet citronella grass.

The wonder is that the Indonesians do not become jaded with beauty. But proof that the beauty about them makes its imprint upon them lies in the exquisite design which marks the handwork of the various islands. Rice, tall and golden and heavy in the head, has furnished many a pattern; and marsh grass and bamboo and palm. Delicate butterfly and leaf patterns on batiks; small birds, wave-imprinted sea sand, pineapples, seashells, curious fish, jaunty reptiles, pheasants and birds of paradise, a thousand contours from nature transferred to articles of wearing apparel and household utensils. Indonesians and their habitat seem inseparable. Americans are American wherever one meets them: assertive, resourceful, openhanded, parochial, not too quick to ask the other fellow's point of view. The British are also British wherever one meets them, and are seldom mistaken for Dutch, Scandinavian or American, even though they may have the same general appearance. An Indonesian also maintains his personality in strange surroundings, but at home he seems to draw both strength and beauty from his own earth as if there were an osmotic play between him and the land which bears him.

But the Indonesian land is not always kind, nor the scenery enthralling when broken down into homestead patches, nor the picturesque jungles primarily the habitat of orchids. Volcanoes as neighbors can be terrifying. Take Krakatau, situated in the narrow Sunda Strait between south Sumatra and west Java. In 1883 it produced the world's largest eruption; an estimated 30,000 persons were killed; volcanic dust filtered into the atmosphere the earth around. Then for forty years the volcano was thought extinct; new vegetation appeared on its sides. In 1927 it took on new life, sputtering and threatening and in January, 1928, one of the world's biggest babies was born—a crater island known as Anak Krakatau, child of Krakatau. Later the new cone disappeared, apparently worn down by the action of the surf, but still later it rose again and since 1940 has remained a quarter mile high, with a sizable eruption in 1952. Navigation except by special orders is forbidden within the circle of Krakatau.

Other volcanoes also intermittently burst their lava plugs, throwing hot ashes and steam into the air to form destructive mud streams down the mountain. Sometimes wide cultivated areas are scorched, sometimes whole villages flee their location, often volcanic ash sifts throughout the countryside. Volcanoes may be picturesque but they do not make chummy neighbors.

Neither are the salt marshes friendly, nor the tangled torrid jungles, nor the old worn-out fields used by many generations, denuded of topsoil. Nor the rocky coasts where the rocks have worked their way up-country for a matter of miles. Nor the sharply cragged mountains where leopards roam. Nor the Sumatran forests with their tigers, wild elephants, huge bears, wild pigs, monkeys, orangutans. (The word itself is Malay—*orang* for *man* and *utan* for *wood*).

The longer we lived in Indonesia the more deeply I felt the interplay of land, men and destiny. Of course no one can live in an agricultural society and not feel the immediate dependence of man upon earth, weather, natural forces and supernatural credences.

But it is not only their closeness to their earth which gives the people their character. They are also a handcraft people. Although they are currently industrializing in the accepted twentieth century mode, still they remain a handcraft people.

They carry the habits and attitudes of the handcrafts into industry—to its detriment but not necessarily to their detriment. It is their ability to create with their hands which maintains the resilience they now need. A handcraft people has a certain advantage in that their culture has living roots and we expect living roots to produce a unique bloom. But perhaps the unique production is not the main point; it could be the act of producing which matters. Living among a handcraft people one begins to doubt if a high degree of originality is common. My experience was that few show real freshness of approach. In Bali I saw 10,000 carved deer lying in the same position, Bali-heads of all sizes but with the same headdress, smile and turn of neck; in Java whole villages making the same batik pattern; in Macassar the same delicate designs in silver filigree; in Borneo identical motifs on basketry and sleeping mats—except that I did occasionally find the star and crescent of Islam or the cross of Christianity woven into traditional Hindu designs of the tree of life. Native pottery presents no more variety; on the whole it is poor, scarce, and shows small ingenuity in workmanship and very little improvement over the centuries. But the fact that there is little originality in relation to the immense amount of handwork turned out does not mean that the craftsmen are not immensely skillful and ingenious; they *can* mold, paint, carve or otherwise work their material with originality, but they prefer to stay by the ancient, or at least the accepted, patterns. If handcrafts go by the board under the pressure of modern life, the first-handedness of participation in the creation of beauty will go underground, to reappear, perhaps, in the self-conscious cultivation of a later generation, but in the interim a dryness would lie upon the souls of the people.

Perhaps it is the people's patient artistic handwork which makes them so at ease with life. Their nature is at once pliant and self-contained, characteristics which mark their supple dignity of movement and give them superb carriage. They seem open and simple but only in the way a mountain lake is nothing-withholding to the sun. Dive as deep as you may, you will always come up with fresh treasures, not hid from view by intent but by a natural unostentation. One would expect them to be a musical people and they are.

Spiritually, music is the marrow of their bones. Its plaintive strains mark the first celebration of the newborn and the last rites of the dead, as well as all intermediate ceremonies, feasts and festivities. More, music permeates the every-days and the long sweet evenings. Indonesian music cannot be reduced to words nor approximated on Western instruments. Nor can records or wires reproduce it any more than a photograph can capture the autumn splendor of northern woods, for in a picture the tang of the crisp fall air is missing, and the fragrance of the pines, the call of a loon, the odor of wood smoke from the last campfire. And in a recording of gamelan music the scent of jasmine, the spicy odor of Indonesian food cooking not too far off, the verve of the players, the intent receptive faces of those who sit and listen—all of these elements from which the music rises are missing. Indonesian music is the animus of the people manifest in sound.

Some music is traditional, passed on from director to director, which means from drummer to drummer because the chief drummer both sets the pace and indicates the theme of an orchestral composition. An orchestra may die down for a period of years to be brought back to life under a new conductor, although customarily each musician trains his understudy, who may be a child. Thus a community has a school of music, the more so because the musicians learn the various instruments from one another. A good xylophone player, for instance, can often pick up the flute or man the cymbals. Whether playing or composing, the achievement is communal. A drummer in the process of composing is not a man alone with his thoughts; he is a composer with a theme which he beats out to his fellow musicians, indicating their parts, while they in turn improve upon his suggestions.

Gathering together the instruments of a fine orchestra is no light task. The great gongs come from Semarang in Java where the last famous makers of gongs lived; metallophones can be made locally but their frames, as the frames in which the gongs hang, are expensive, often made of teawood covered with pure gold leaf. Individuals seldom own their instruments; they belong to the village, which keeps them in a special music house or covered bandstand. An orchestra leader is treated with marked respect. To be sure, he may be a chauffeur or a carpenter by day, but if he has hands to beat the drum in the dynamic and demanding fashion of an orchestra leader, he is a marked man. At rehearsal even a prince takes direction from him and does not sit above him as would be his prerogative on other occasions. Formerly all the great princes as well as many of the princely Chinese had their own orchestras. The Sultan of Djogja still has one of the best orchestras in Java. But instruments are relatively more expensive and princes have relatively less money, so that if traditional music is to survive it has to be a passion of the people—as indeed it has always been.

Some gamelan music is accompanied by, or embroidered by, a solo voice or a chorus, but most of the singing seems to be folk melodies, some of them very old. I noted that a well-traveled Indonesian knows at once from what area the melody coming over a kampong wall derives and the musically sophisticated can tell which of the two prevalent tonal systems is being used. Some of the airs and rhythms are very lovely even to a Western ear. Almost all Indonesians appear to know many folk songs, but they are not a people who go singing down the street or who sing on their way to work as, say, the Italians do. I heard more singing in Minahassa, North Celebes, and in Sumatra than anywhere else, but that may be because these groups have the habit of singing together at church once or twice a week and also because they like the new part music. All through Minahassa I heard women singing at their work and met boys and girls on the roads singing as they went off to school. In Menado I stayed with a Dutch friend who lived in an old Japanese teahouse on the edge of a river. Across from us was a Christian village given to singing the old hymns, but one young man had a more modern contribution to offer and he offered it every evening just at five. He would come down to the river directly opposite the house, walk out into the water raising his sarong gracefully to toss it on the bank as is the modest custom, and then sing in a fine tenor voice, "Now is the hour."

Whether Western music will become acclimatized in Indonesia outside the Western-trained minority is a difficult guess. Possibly the upsurge of creativity which marks painting and literature also will produce a new kind of modern music.

The dance in Indonesia is as characteristic as the music from which it is inseparable. Both the sophisticated stylized dances and the spontaneous dancing of peasants turned performers at village festivals are facets of Indonesian personality, at once tradition-bound and spontaneous. Certainly no one class patronizes the dance more than another; in the palaces of princes and in the humblest kampong, if there is celebration then there is dancing.

The first time I saw Indonesian dancing in a kampong I was certainly an uninvited guest. We had lived on the edge of Bandung for perhaps a month when Pearl Cheng, a Chinese girl educated in America, came to spend a week end. Beginning at sundown we heard the beating of drums, insistent, rhythmic, compelling. Beyond our house lay woods which led on up into the hills and in the woods were the kampongs. The times being marked by considerable insecurity, foreigners just did not venture afield at night, but these drums could not be too far off and it seemed to me that any nearby village would be glad to have newcomers in the neighborhood pay their respects. About nine o'clock we hazarded a stroll down the road, turning up a path through the woods. Out of the nowhere a Sundanese peasant joined us and Pearl asked what the celebration might be. The hundred days' birthday of a baby, he said. Would we be welcome at the party? He thought we would; at least we could ask. So we went back home for presents and he waited to show us the way. It was good he waited, for in spite of the moonlight the path was dark under the trees, the hillside steep and as we approached a cluster of houses the dogs barked madly. Our guide was an invited guest so he knocked at the door and asked the host about us. The host was very cordial.

We entered a sizable room and found some thirty women with small children huddled into one corner watching the dancing. They moved over to share their section of the floor as we presented our presents and exchanged small talk, my share being very small indeed. An orchestra of seven men with drums, three-stringed violins, and flutes was backed against the wall opposite and in the middle of the floor a farmer boy was dancing: a Balinese. He wore ordinary white trousers, a shirt with tails out, a headdress of brown figured cloth—and he danced like one possessed, whirling, posturing, leaping into the air. The drummers speeded their beat, introducing the most intricate rhythms; men and boys around the room began to accent the rhythm with clapping of hands and staccato calls; the young man danced faster, appearing to remain in the air for seconds. I was almost afraid to breathe. He danced on for half an hour and then fell in a heap, seeming unconscious, his muscles twitching. I thought he was dying but no one else seemed concerned. One man forced a cigarette between his lips; another brought coffee and a third propped him up and made him drink. Then they pulled him into a corner, where he continued to twitch convulsively. All at once he came to and in ten minutes was joining in the rhythmic clapping which accentuated the drumbeat for the next dance. With variations the dance was repeated by others, solo or duo, until by midnight we were exhausted and took our leave with deep appreciation for the evening. An aunt of the baby insisted upon accompanying us home and at our door lifted a sizable stalk of bananas from the fold of her skirt and presented them to me.

Most Indonesian dancing does not depend upon foot action, as did this first sample, but is primarily a dance of body movement, particularly of the arms, hands, head, and neck, a kind of rhythmic posturing. At first a Western observer may find the movements monotonous, but as he learns the meaning of the symbolic posturing, gives himself to the music, and understands the Hindu stories which lie behind the dance, he finds himself caught up in a new kind of experience. Javanese dances stem from the Hindu period and have probably changed but little in a thousand years.

Some critics call them decadent and at times they do appear over-precious as if the dancer's entire attention were absorbed in reproducing the expression of bygone emotions, but at other times a dance of old Java may be an unforgettable experience, as much of the moment as the flight of a bird. Indeed, most moving of all the dances I saw was one performed by the sisters of the Sultan of Djogja. It was a religious experience.

President Soekarno is a great patron of the dance and is said to be an excellent critic as well as a faithful promoter of good dance groups. Each year on the evening of Independence Day, August 17, he and Mrs. Soekarno present a variety of the national dances to their guests who sit in the garden under the stars with great old trees standing guard. On one such night Indonesian friends around us buzzed with comment that the President had paid $37,000 for the costumes; some thought the amount preposterous when the poor needed et cetera, but others thought he was supporting a high tradition in keeping alive this essence of Indonesian culture—and I thought the amount of money probably handsomely exaggerated. The saucer dance from Sumatra was a frolicsome affair in which each dancer was a little juggler with two lighted candles and a saucer, all of them in rapid motion—saucers, candles and dancers. While *legongs* from Bali held us rapt, refreshments were served, each guest receiving a cardboard box containing sandwiches and cakes, a delectable sweetmeat of rice and fruits wrapped in a piece of banana leaf, along with a good fruit drink.

Bali is the home of the living dance. While traditional dances still persist, passed down from teacher to pupil, there are also improvisations for new moods and occasions, and the dance moves from temple to stage with no self-conscious delineation between religious and secular. However, there are ritual-magic dances performed by the priests, sometimes with incense pots in their hands; sometimes indeed in a trance during which they may dance on live coals. But for the most part religious festivals such as temple birthdays are held for the entertainment of the people quite as much as for the gods. And many an evening's dance and music are contrived for pleasure only.

Some of the grace which characterizes the people is certainly the result of children's imitation of the village dancers most acclaimed by their elders; but dancing is also taught and not only girls but boys learn the classical movements, just as American children used to learn the piano before the advent of television. Thus the dance influences the people as a whole and they in turn afford a wide base of skill from which more great dancers are developed.

Indonesians delight in going to the theater in the sense of gathering in the village square or at a wide place in the road or in a temple courtyard to see a play enacted. They also delight in having the theater come to them. Whenever there is a celebration of some distinction there is almost sure to be a shadow play or puppetry, and aristocratic families who own their own full cast of *wayang* figures may designate a night for entertainment without any special reason.

Wayang kulit—*wayang* meaning *shadow* and *kulit* meaning *leather*—is universal in Indonesia but in derivation is essentially Javanese and behind that Hindu, drawing on the Hindu epics for story material but often augmented by Javanese or even Chinese folklore. The leather puppets are made from buffalo hide dried over a bamboo frame in the sun, the hair scraped off, then smoked, after which the wayang maker polishes the figure, dips it into a mixture of

bone ash and glue, dries it, passes it on to the decorator—
who may be himself—to paint, gild and ornament. Finally
the wayang is flattened between two padded boards, fitted
with a handle of horn, and ready for use by the *dalang*, or
puppeteer.

The dalang is a man of extraordinary memory, sometimes
with a fine voice, and blessed with an audience sense. For
his play a screen of white cloth is set up. If the play is to be
presented in the open the men of the audience usually sit
on the shadow side of the screen and the women and children
on the puppet side, but in a more sophisticated setting—
perhaps a pavilion or a drawing room—the guests all sit on
the shadow side. The puppets are arranged in rows with their
handles stuck into two short lengths of banana-tree trunk,
good puppets in one row, bad ones in another. The story is
told in a high-pitched monotonous voice to the accompani-
ment of a small orchestra which takes its direction from a
little metal instrument the dalang beats with his right foot.
Since the language of the poetic recitation is nearly always
archaic it needs interpreting, although the audience seems
to enjoy the words for their sound and cadence. Frequently
the interpreter sits beside the dalang paraphrasing the recita-
tive, but sometimes the dalang is his own interpreter, singing the classical story and then telling the audience what he
has just sung. A small lamp, ordinarily a wick in coconut oil,
hangs above his head to intensify the shadows, but more
modernly a shaded electric light is used.

Ordinarily a good wayang lasts from midnight until dawn,
but some begin much earlier and also last till dawn. The
audience never seems to lose interest, although children fall
asleep snuggled against their mothers, later to waken and
enjoy themselves again. Adults may wander in and out for

refreshment but no one goes home until the show is finished —except the foreign guests, who usually fade from the scene around two A.M. unless held by scholarly interest, a wager, or extraordinary politeness. For the true audience the wayang experience takes the place of lecture and sermon, for the stories besides being interesting have ethical connotations. I admit to being one who could sit indefinitely, but sometimes I wondered if I were in a trance.

Another form of wayang uses puppets of wood with arms joined at shoulder, elbow and wrist, head able to turn and nod so that extraordinarily lifelike movements are possible, or at least movements with gleeful caricature. The puppets, elaborately painted and often beautifully dressed, are introduced at the beginning of the play, after which the nobility—a dull lot, high-minded but easily tricked—carry the thread of the story while their attendants furnish the ingenuity of plot and the witty, even ribald, dialogue. These subservients are the characters loved by the people, who unconsciously equate themselves with the fast-thinking, day-saving attendants, loyal to their princes through all tribulation.

There are also varieties of classic drama in which people do the acting, often with masks so cleverly contrived to represent individual foibles and temperament that it comes as a surprise to have the actor behind the mask reveal himself. Sometimes one man takes all the parts, changing masks, voice and characterization with almost incredible skill. Whatever its form, theater is nearer the life of the people than is the case in Western cultures. For Westerners going to a show is merely an afterthought tacked onto a full life a good deal as candy may or may not be passed at the end of a meal; but in Indonesia theater is part of the staple diet if not, indeed, the salt which savors the everyday food.

Painting is also a part of daily fare. That is, many people paint, young and old, whose lives are not dedicated to art. Painting is a traditional pastime, an old art, predating in primitive form the Hindu era and then later turning to Indian forms and Hindu subjects for its materials. With the advent of Mohammedanism, however, it fell by the way because Islam forbade religious art and discouraged secular art, but under the Dutch some Javanese studied Western technique and subject matter, as many of the best of the young painters still do. There is no real school of painting, although there are certainly marked tendencies apparent in a kind of unity of background and subject, in a somberness of tone, a freedom to subordinate proportion to emotional effect, a vehemence which suggests the sufferings of a people rather than of an individual. Some of the best painters are self-taught and I often wondered whether they would be better under the discipline of demanding teachers or whether their new-found spontaneity might wither.

In Bali works are not signed and are often the combined effort of master and pupils. The old paintings show skill and taste and some modern painters are still painting with fine regard for old-time compositional style, with events in series crowding the scene, divided only by semi-stylized mountains or flames. For a human figure the three-quarter face is considered correct and a very Javanese face it is, with prescribed features denoting whether the character is "good" or "bad." The old paintings are limited in their color combinations but often lovely in tone. Present-day painters buy cheap paints and usually process their canvases by starching cotton cloth, but for all the adverse influence of the tourist trade some excellent work is produced.

One expression of the current acute nationalism is the pride of the people in their ancient arts and a widespread determination not to let them die out. Although teachers are everywhere in short supply, place is made in the grade school curriculum for drawing, for which the children seem to have more than ordinary aptitude, and young painters give their time free to hold art classes. President Soekarno is also a patron of art, a warm personal friend of many painters, and his palace is almost an art gallery. If wide interest in the arts is guarantee of spiritual vitality, then beneath the workaday life of the people there are living roots in the ancient soil. To the people their art matters and this is an important thing for the government to realize, for every government has to operate within the framework of the people's interests. The way the majority work and the kind of work done make a difference in political aptitude. Also the way in which people spend their leisure time conditions their work habits. The things they set store by are their values and must either be conserved to their satisfaction or replaced by substitutes which will not leave them emotionally bereft.

. 3 .

Family to Nation

WE HAD NOT BEEN LONG IN INDONESIA before I realized that individuals can scarcely be known in any real sense apart from their families. Of course that fact is true to a degree in any culture and we had surely experienced it in China. Indeed almost anywhere in Asia one comes to expect the financial success of one member of a family to be shared by as many relatives as can get a thumb into the pie. One expects to see impecunious and fairly distant in-laws move in on the prosperous one, and conversely if an individual becomes jobless, maimed, in need, one expects other members of the family to rise up with succor. Maybe I imagined that in Indonesia the coherence of family members was almost organic, but it certainly seemed difficult for even a sophisticated individual to extricate himself completely. Not that he should slough off his family, but perhaps he should be able to peel himself away when necessary.

Because of this close-knittedness, the disruption of the war and postwar years was particularly disastrous. Not only were people uprooted geographically, often for the first time in hundreds of years of family history, but they were torn apart. It was like a willow tree's being pulled out by the roots, stripped of limbs, then transplanted to alien soil (even the distance of Djogja to Djakarta is alien soil) where trunk and limbs are replanted and told to grow. They do grow after a fashion. But they aren't the old tree and they seem always aware of their brokenness. I often noted that brilliant young men of the capital city spoke only half their mind when they expressed an individual conviction about politics, social problems and economic trends, because in the next sentence they would go on to say how their father felt back in the home village, or to illustrate their country's lag by explaining their mother's addiction to certain religious customs which they felt to be largely superstitious, but still. . . .

Nepotism in high places is the accepted order. A cultural officer runs into constant difficulty because names for travel or study grants presented to him by responsible individuals highly placed often prove to be relatives of the nominator. The same custom prevails in naming appointees to Indonesian government positions. Then there is the swapping of recommendations: you propose my wife's first cousin's brother-in-law and I'll recommend your uncle's son-in-law by his third wife; everywhere a kind of political inbreeding difficult to keep free from duplicity. A few educated Indonesians sense the dilemma and wish to make no family appointments, but often the pressure is too much for them.

The whole problem of extricating the individual and making him important and independent because he is an individual is a major task for a country to whom democratic ideals are new and democratic practices still newer. Indonesia has neither the tradition nor the generations of experience which supports Western democracies; she starts cold with a fine set of abstractions about individual responsibility but a deep-grained habit of effecting changes by family units and village groups.

The most extreme example of family solidarity we came across is the setup of one branch of the well-known Djajadiningrat family. This family, which has furnished many distinguished leaders in Java, is an offshoot of a Hindu colony known as Badoej, made up of forty families who walled themselves inside three remote villages around the year 1400 when the Moslems took over Java. Although they own only fourteen square miles of countryside they are completely self-sustaining, growing or making everything they use except salt, which must be bought outside, and in exchange for which they always give double value. Buying and selling leads to cupidity, they feel, which in turn dulls the spiritual sensibilities. They speak an old form of Sundanese, have no written language, count by means of bundles of five sticks, weave their own cloth. There is no polygamy, no remarriage after death of a partner, and no marriage outside the forty families—each of which is really a small clan. Instead of producing a decadent stock, just the reverse is true and the members of the clan who have left the walls have proved particularly brilliant.

Some 300 years ago the great-great-grandfather of our special Djajadiningrat friend refused to accept the headship of the clan because acceptance required his remaining all his life within the confines of his own house and garden—restraint within restraint. So he had to leave, as was customary. He entered service in the household of Java's most influential rajah, became a stable boy, proved his exceptional worth, married the rajah's daughter and established a distinguished line.

The home village keeps track of the absent members and

their progeny by watching forty stone jars of water and forty trees. They know from the jars and trees when an absent member is ill or in trouble. This is simply a statement of fact. Whenever there is illness in one of the out-families, someone from the village will appear with assistance, sometimes bringing a beneficial herb, not exceptionally a specific for the disease; sometimes the messenger has "power in his hands" and effects magnetic or spiritual healing; sometimes he brings advice about a political move or a financial undertaking—about which there has been no communication.

For generations scientists and government officials have wanted to make a study of this walled-off group but have largely respected their wish for privacy. However, a generation ago a Dutch commissioner insisted upon going into the segregated district. He was warned that things would not go well with him, but he laughed off the advice and went in. He was not molested; he gathered such statistics as he could get unaided and prepared a draft of his report, later published. Then two weeks after his visit he died in his bath, very peacefully. Some Javanese have also insisted upon going into the group for purposes of checking taxable property or some such errand. Each has died a short while after, always peacefully. I wanted to go to the village—but I wanted to be invited. Not merely because I would rather die outside my bath but because surely much can be learned there.

Sharing family life in Indonesia is a heart-warming experience—with exceptions. Everywhere we went there seemed to be consideration between parents and children. Children are treated as little people with judgment and rights. Especially in Bali children have an amazing independence. Babies are not allowed to crawl, for going about on all fours like animals is beneath their dignity and some fond relative is always willing to carry them until they walk. With children so well considered it seems odd that there are no children's holidays and that children's games are comparatively few. Indonesian children have overmuch capacity for just sitting in their doorways, more especially in Java than in Bali and more commonly in the country than in the city, where an Indonesian version of the movies' "cops and robbers" sets many a neighborhood in an uproar.

Family life is best observed as a part of desa life but in order to see inside a village one must be a part of it, a difficult thing for a foreigner. While there is a general pattern, the customs of one locality may be foreign to a nearby locality, especially if a mountain or natural barrier intervenes. If a desa is of any size, it is divided into kampongs or neighborhoods. Chief magistrate of the desa is the *lurah*, elected by the people who own houses in the desa, unless otherwise specified.

A few miles outside Bandung is the representative village of Sukarasa. I went with a friend to spend a day there. We stopped first at the lurah's office, a sizable open pavilion with a screened-in corner which was the secretary's office and contained the records. We chatted with the lurah, a big man who beamed and gleamed his well-being. He was dressed European style except for his black velvet Moslem hat, wore a large wrist watch and three rings, one with a wonderful big ruby; in his breast pocket two fountain pens. He is a *hadji*, a title of respect denoting that he has made the haj, or pilgrimage, to Mecca. I felt him to be a man of affairs, intelligent and capable. He is paid by the people, receiving a small share of the village taxes plus the use of twenty acres of land. He appoints his own assistants—scribes for keeping records, ward heads, local officials to look after education, the division of water for irrigation, land boundaries, deaths and marriages. Money to run his office is derived from various sources, including registration fees for any transaction which needs an official stamp and 8 per cent of the local taxes. People with an income over R. 2,400 a year pay their taxes to the central government. Tax rates are not high. If a man makes only R. 600 per year, he pays R. 5 per year. But alas, everything except taxes is high and in these modern days the people do not want to pay the lurah. This resentment toward the expenses of the local government is a new attitude. One phase of *merdeka*—the passion for freedom from restraint which marks the new day—is that the people want the national government to furnish unprecedented services and charge nothing. What else is the meaning of democracy? Thus, as the lurah pointed out, his position has become difficult; he cannot resign but neither can he get the cooperation and respect which have traditionally been his. This lurah said that he felt as if he were the filling of a sandwich being pressed from both sides.

Out of a population of 9,000 in Sukarasa, 1,800 owned land, although 270 of that number lived outside the desa. The largest holding was sixteen acres, but fifteen persons owned more than ten acres. Only fifty acres were owned by foreigners, meaning Chinese and Dutch, absentee. In total, around 100 acres for 9,388 persons, close to 2,500 houses, and about five children per family.

A few men had more than one wife. We met one dapper chap with painted red fingernails, riding a bicycle, who had three wives. When I asked the marriage age for girls, the secretaries thought for a while, and said nine to sixteen, depending on size. I said they probably meant depending upon development but they said no, they meant, depending on how big a girl was. They thought the age was slowly being raised and that probably most girls were now married at twelve. Some claim the average marriage age for girls is higher, perhaps as high as fifteen years. Many of these villagers go into Bandung to earn wages; probably 400 of them are merchants' coolies, carriers, servants, laborers, part of the long line of men and women which starts pouring into the city long before daylight, usually on foot.

The two government schools had 680 children enrolled in the six grades, but the average school day was one hour for each child because of the shortage of teachers. Schooling was free except for slates and chalk. Courses were the traditional reading, writing and arithmetic plus a small amount of geography and drawing. The children's drawings, which they were proudly carrying home, seemed to me clever indeed. The Moslem religion was taught in the schools.

We walked through the village, one crooked path to another, not missing a house. Hidden under the trees as the houses are, one is surprised at the size of the village and also at the trees. There were many *kenari* trees with their large, notched leaves and a fruit which is used as a vegetable when young. Orange trees covered with tiny oranges; coconuts on their palms, some of the palms having several kinds of fern growing up their trunks, as well as lovely mosses and lichens; clumps of bamboo with six-inch trunks seventy-five feet high. In moister sections, they told me, bamboo may grow 125 feet tall with trunks measuring a foot in diameter. Near the houses were the special bamboo trees used for making rope. It is now forbidden to use bamboo for house construction because rats hide inside the bamboo and may carry plague. However, bamboo still has plenty of uses in the village. Planting and harvesting tools are made of it; cooking utensils, musical instruments, bellows, bridges, rafts, furniture, baskets, suitcases, umbrellas, hats, bows and arrows; also the famous blowpipe, a deadly weapon varying from two to nine feet in length and carrying a dart touched with a poison which kills in a few moments. Thus are birds shot for food; monkeys, large game, and on occasion the enemy. One tree especially cherished was the *tereng*, or eggplant tree, whose fruit is not edible but whose wood makes quick fires. The *galingum* tree furnishes fine dyes for coloring sarongs. Coffee trees aplenty bearing their green berries; avocados, bananas, betel palms, a jumbo tree with fruit. A specially lovely tree called *luchina glauca* makes the best charcoal and its lacy leaves have a high vitamin content; the Dutch tried feeding them to people but the people's hair fell out; fed to pigs the leaves caused the sows to abort. Guava trees, *menteng* with a good edible fruit, huge banyans with their small figs; all sorts of shrubs, medicinal and otherwise. It was easy to see how a village can be self-sustaining.

Water buffalo at work or in their pens; sheep and goats in their pens raised three feet off the ground; wooden plows with spike teeth; wells with their old oaken buckets; ponds of gorgeous pink and white lotus; rice drying in dooryards; enormous long-legged roosters; Muscovy ducks which lay huge white eggs; big baskets hung under the eaves, against which leans a long bamboo pole with protrusions used as steps *by the hens* who march up to their basket nests to lay their eggs where they will be safe. A wooden drum used to call the faithful to prayer on Fridays hung outside the prayer house. There was a small cemetery. Dozens of children sat quietly in their doorways or on the stone-hard earth of the dooryard. We were not interrupting their play; they weren't doing anything. Many of the houses were so enclosed by trees that sunshine could not possibly enter, and the small children looked pale and sickly. Every dooryard was swept clean by its own toothless grandmother. Some of the very small children used the dooryard for a toilet, but the grandmother quickly swept up the deposits with a short broom made of reeds and threw them into a nearby ditch. No running water except in the irrigation ditches outside the village. No trained midwife or doctor. The general pattern of Sukarasa fits thousands of other villages.

Homes mean houses. The style of housing varies in different parts of the archipelago. I did not get to visit the nomadic tribes who live to hunt, to eat, to mate, to dance, to propitiate their gods, perhaps to go to war, without need of permanent structures. I heard tales of tribes who live in trees and of tribes whose huts are built on rafts which can be poled through the marshes so that the whole village is mobile and I saw fisherfolk who live out their entire lives in boats except for occasional forays ashore to get coconuts and vegetables. The famous long houses of Borneo last for generations but not in one place, for when the village wears out its land and moves on, the great house is taken apart and the main timbers and long hand-hewn boards are towed behind canoes to a new site where new walls and partitions of grass matting or split bamboo are added.

In Java houses are usually built directly on the earth, but in Sumatra, Celebes, and some other sections we found the houses raised on pillars, usually of wood, with ladders used for access. The raised house is dryer, cooler and more free of snakes. The big Batak and Minangkabau houses of Sumatra, designed for several families of relatives, have high sharply slanting roofs, ridge poles curved upward, gabled ends elaborately painted. Stone is used chiefly in building temples and mosques. In Bali temples are built of a soft stone called *paras* which lends itself to intricate carving but hardens after exposure.

Not only are Indonesians strongly identified with their homes, but they have a warm feeling of identity for their particular locality. Regional rivalry is marked. In Djakarta "we Bataks" is often spoken with proud disdain, for the Bataks in the capital city tend to feel they are a shade smarter than the rest of their countrymen, an opinion with which some outsiders agree. "We Menadonese are having a party at the Des Indes," whereupon hundreds of highly placed officials and their consorts turn out en masse. But in scorn of lesser breeds no one out-hauteurs the aristocratic Javanese.

Although families of all sectional backgrounds flock to Djakarta for government positions, each group is suspicious of encroachment on its home territory. Whenever I was in Macassar I was impressed by the way people expressed approval and appreciation of their governor and his administration and yet all were working to have him recalled. Why? He was a Javanese. It was as if the Georgians of 1870 had found themselves with a governor sent down from Massachusetts. In Menado when I presented my letters of introduction to an official, he at once poured over me his grievances against Djakarta for draining off the best school teachers, officials, administrators from this highly literate area, impoverishing the district. "Better we should belong to the Philippines; scores of students smuggle themselves by small fishing smacks into the Philippines every year in order to get a chance at higher education. What does Djakarta care about us?"

Thus the stresses and strains of a transitional period: on the one hand the need for a sharpened sense of individuality with its responsibilities, and on the other a broader loyalty to the whole of Indonesia. But millions cannot think in terms of all Indonesia because they know almost nothing about other parts of the country, and of course even less about their own history. They are only vaguely aware that there was ever a time when the Indies were not ruled by the Dutch. To be sure, the country's leadership is exceedingly well versed and the younger generation is beginning to connect present events with past experience because literacy is spreading and the young are studying history. National solidarity will take on meaning when the people know their own inheritance and see the current scene in historical perspective.

.4.

From Early Days

ANCIENT INDONESIAN HISTORY BEGINS WHERE
you will. Pithecanthropus erectus, famous Java man
and nearest thing to a missing link yet discovered, was a
humanoid somebody in Java some 500,000 years ago. After
him waves of migrants poured down from Asia, channeled
through the present states of Siam, Burma and narrow Malaya,
to fan out over the islands of the South Pacific. There were
the Negritos, a dwarf Negro stock, traces of which can
occasionally be seen; a frailer light brown, long-headed Ved-
doid strain which still marks the more remote areas; the
Australoids who journeyed through the Indies on their way
to become the ancestors of the Australian aborigines, their
bearded faces and beetling brows still marking the Flores-
Timor region; the frizzy-haired and dark-skinned Melanesians
who fathered the modern inhabitants of Fiji and the Solomon
Islands; and the tall, long-legged, curly-haired, sharper-nosed
Papuans in New Guinea and parts of Celebes. The earlier
Malay strain approaches the Caucasian, or white, type and
is the dominant strain in the Greater Sundas, of which Java
is a part. The later Malayans are more strongly Mongoloid,
often with the typical eye fold which marks the Japanese and
Chinese. The total impression of the present Indonesian

people is of small sun-tanned Europeans and the sum of the ancestries is a varying and pleasing aggregate.

Among the nobility in Java and Sumatra the mixture of Hindu blood is apparent in taller stature, longer limbs, finely poised heads and clear-cut features. Around the fifth century Hindu traders brought their culture, including the art of writing, into the Indies. The best data on that era was contributed by a Chinese Buddhist traveler who went on tour about the time Alaric was sacking Rome. In Central Java the great pyramidal monument, Borobudur, raised in tiers from ground to peak with relief carvings depicting the life of Buddha on every wall, was erected in Central Java around the time Charlemagne was persuading the Pope to crown him Emperor of the West. By the time William of Normandy had conquered England and the Holy Roman Empire was at its height, the rulers of Java had scribes recording their achievements. And there were always achievements to record. In 1294, not so long after the Greeks had recaptured Constantinople and England had assembled her first Parliament, the armies of the Singosari Empire drove back the force which Kubla Khan had sent to the north coast of Java. During these troubled centuries the Javanese and Sumatrans struggled for control of the whole archipelago, with the Javanese winning out, after which for almost two centuries, roughly from the beginning of the Hundred Years' War to Columbus, the empire of Majapahit with its capital in eastern Java included most of the present Indies, the southeastern portion of Asia, and all the Philippines.

One figure, Gajah Mada, stands out in the period of the later Majapahit kingdom which flourished in the fourteenth century about the time gunpowder was first used in Europe. He was a prime minister of parts who knew how to deploy his king's armies, raise his taxes and keep the gears of government meshing. It was he who first united the islands of the Indies under one ruler, bringing Bali and Sumatra back into the fold. He was also a businessman and set up a first-rate cartel of spices, using his navy as revenue cutters for protection of the king's interests.

Then came Mohammedanism. Late in the fifteenth century, after the conquest of Granada, the reunion of the Netherlands, the revolt of Martin Luther, and the defeat of the Moslems by Baber the Turk, Moslem fortunes picked up in Southeast Asia. The new religion came in along the shipping routes and thrived in the coastal areas. Moslem traders became kings in all but name; they had their slaves, their harems, and certainly their tribute. The princes and princesses of the once great Javanese houses married into the new merchant kingdoms. Thus the Javanese aristocracy gradually took on the religion of the foreign merchants and the missionaries of Allah slowly built up an understanding of Moslem tenets, sometimes speeding their work by use of the sword. Piety and piracy made a profitable marriage, as has likewise been the case with Christianity at various times in history.

In the early sixteenth century, not long after Vasco Da Gama's visit to the coast of India, a Portuguese named Albuquerque brought the fire of the Crusades to the Far East along with a yen to command the spice trade. Pepper, cloves, nutmeg and Christianity struggled against pepper, cloves, nutmeg and Mohammedanism, with the latter winning out. Then the French and Spanish horned in on the trade and the Spanish finally pre-empted the Philippine end of the business.

Enter the Dutch. In 1595, after the defeat of the Spanish

Armada, the first Dutch expedition came into the port of Bantam. Over in Europe the struggle was on to free the northern Low Countries from Spanish rule. After brisk fighting with the Portuguese and later with the English, the Dutch built up lively trading bases in the Moluccas, those valuable Spice Islands between Celebes and New Guinea. In 1602 the Netherlands East India Company was formed, sponsored by the Dutch government, which furnished both financial and military aid. The company had to deal both with European rivals and with the native princes, each of whom dominated a section of the shattered Majapahit empire. If the native states had ever stood together and offered united resistance, their domination at that time probably would have been impossible because the Netherlands East India Company never had at its disposal more than a few thousand Dutch troops and a small number of ships. But the princes distrusted each other and in an effort to maneuver Dutch support to themselves found themselves maneuvered out of their own power. Not out of their jobs, however, for the Dutch always ruled through native potentates whenever possible. While the company was involved in subjugating princes the spice trade lost ground, largely because once the Dutch were in complete control of the Moluccas they insisted on reducing production in order to keep European imports small and prices high, while the natives discovered profit in smuggling spices to English, Portuguese and Danish traders. In 1780 Holland went to war with England, further draining Dutch resources. In 1795 England blockaded the Java coast and three years later the company went bankrupt. From that time the Indies were put under direct administration of the Netherlands government, and there they remained until

World War II except for the brief interlude of Napoleon's grandeur when Holland itself became a tributary state.

By terms of the treaty of 1824 the Dutch left British India and the Malay Peninsula, while the British gave up their claims to Sumatra. In 1859 a treaty between Holland and Portugal gave the Dutch the western half of Timor and the surrounding islands. Division of Borneo was not made until 1891, and in 1895 boundaries were set in New Guinea between the British, Dutch and Germans. So year by year and acre by acre Indonesia was divided among its conquerors and no one thought the matter of thus carving up a country at all peculiar—not even the Indonesians—for the doctrine of self-determination was scarcely in gestation.

British return of the East Indies to the Netherlands did not mean that the Dutch could move in and expect to find welcome mats spread out. In 1825 Central Java, centering around Djogjakarta, drummed up a stiff rebellion known as the Java War, which lasted five years. After 1830 most of the East Indies were operated on feudal principles with every Javanese family compelled to devote a percentage of land and labor to raising crops for the government. When the crops included coffee, spices, quinine and rubber the system became exceedingly profitable—for the Dutch. Naturally some officials, both Dutch and Indonesian, pirated more than the legal amount from the people—a custom still prevailing in remote sections of North America. By 1890 land and income taxes had replaced crop division and forced labor excepting the twenty days work per year required of all able-bodied men under fifty for construction of roads and public works. To be sure, a man was allowed to furnish a substitute or pay a head tax if he wished but no more than one-fifth the population could pay in this fashion. The rest grumbled, sabotaged, threatened, capitulated.

All of the islands were not so compact and homogeneous, and hence amenable to occupation, as Java. In some islands the coastal areas were occupied by native states governed by sultans or the equivalent who were open to negotiation-with-pressure or to direct combat, but the interior was filled with loosely organized tribes whose chiefs must be bribed or subdued. The problems of administration were varied, human nature being varied, and often taxed the ingenuity of the patient Dutch. Coastal Sumatra was costly but not difficult in subjugation, as those piratical days went, but in Menangkabau, west Sumatra, the fanatical Moslems occupied the Dutch forces for fifteen fierce years, 1820-1835. Among the last Sumatrans to give way were the pagan Bataks, now largely Christian, and the fierce Cayos, Moslems. Not until 1904 was the domination of the Cayos assured when a Dutch force of 240 men fought their way straight through the mountains, conquering village by village and literally house by house, even the women and children resisting with *krisses* until killed. The Moslem Achinese of north Sumatra held out from 1873 until 1908 and cost the Dutch thousands of soldiers and hundreds of thousands of guilders. Borneo, still largely unexplored, offered its greatest resistance along the coast where Chinese pirates had the upper hand until the advent of steam-driven gunboats. Minahassa in northern Celebes was easy to persuade toward cooperation because the people were grateful to have been freed from Spanish rule and were soon Christianized. The Moslem sultanates of South Macassar fought until 1910.

Most tragic of all was the conquest of the Balinese. They seem a peaceful people on Bali, skilled in the fine arts, good farmers, loyal to their Hindu gods and customs, courteous, serene, proud. Perhaps their pride was their undoing. They would not be conquered nor submit to an injustice. The last serious revolt of 1908 grew out of a minor incident in which the Balinese felt they were required to pay inordinate indemnity for the supposed looting of a wrecked Dutch merchant ship. The Rajah of Klungkung made his stand. All of his household, male relatives, wives, little princes and princesses, accompanied by the nobility, the common people down to the least, dressed themselves in their best and went forth to meet the enemy, krisses in their hands. When the Dutch soldiers hesitated to fire into these helpless gala people, the populace rushed at them until the Dutch had to fire to protect themselves. Nor would the frenzied ecstatic Balinese retreat one step. Man by man, even child by child, they were slaughtered. Dutch garrisons remained in Bali until 1914, after which the hereditary rulers were restored to as much of their power as the Dutch felt practical. And so these rich and fertile islands which lie so tranquilly and fight so fanatically under the tropic sun were brought to heel. Hundreds, thousands of Indonesians were killed while fighting the European conquerors or battling each other.

Military exploitation of the Indies was only one facet of Dutch domination. Although the first duty of colonial governors was to see that the Dutch flag flew unchallenged, still the flag was chiefly a symbol of Dutch determination to make the economic best of a good thing. They were in the Indies to make money. They had long-range determination and were willing to match their vision with the work of their hands and heads. As the inter-Asia trade, at first the backbone of their enterprises, began to slacken and the markets of Europe developed new demands, they became planters.

Governmentally theirs was a philosophy of gradualism, making changes so slowly that the ship of state and all the little *prahus* and canoes of state would not rock. Dutch colonial administrators were no doubt the world's foremost scholars of primitive law, so thoroughly trained that they could preside over native courts, needing only the assistance of a specialist in Moslem canon law. They knew also the special laws of the Chinese, Hindu and Arab blocs and administered even more complicated cases involving a European and a Chinese, say, or a Hindu and a Moslem. On the whole the record of Dutch jurisprudence and the generous Dutch attitude toward native religious preferences is enviable.

Moreover, the Dutch maintained a farsighted land policy which prevented the outright sale of his holdings on the part of a harassed peasant, thus saving the land for the people and the people for the land. They built roads and canals, elaborated native irrigation systems, modernized cities. In this expansion the Indonesians themselves were allowed a part at the lower levels and under proper restrictions. Schools were built for the natives, not too many but enough so that some Indonesians prepared for university training and were encouraged, even aided, to go to Holland for higher study. They came back as doctors and lawyers, the equal of their Dutch colleagues. Alongside their other pursuits the Dutch were scientists of the first water. At Bogor, formerly Buitenzorg, they developed a botanical garden second to none, with smaller botanical gardens on other islands. They constantly explored the problems of nutrition, studied tropical diseases, made their findings known, never flagged in their zeal for making the Indies a more healthful place in which to live. In their homes they treated the natives like children; often there was great warmth of affection between master and servant. They understood the Indonesian nature probably as well as a colonial power has ever understood the personality of a conquered people.

The lot of the Indonesian people was better under the Dutch than it had ever been under dominance of their own kings and rulers; they had more rights conducive to life, liberty and the pursuit of happiness. Left to themselves it is exceedingly doubtful if the Indonesians could have come so far along the path of civilization, however defined, as they did under Dutch supervision. In many ways they have been given a head start over much of Southeast Asia. If these things alone could be remembered Indonesian-Dutch friendship might be highly advantageous to both nations.

But in the other column of the ledger the figures add up differently. The Indies were despoiled of their resources and the people permitted scant share in the profits. At the outbreak of World War II they were around 7 per cent literate. Such educated men as there were, were kept in subordinate positions. As technological experts they were scarcely allowed to exist. There were no Indonesian statisticians, few engineers, fewer scientists. Politically they were allowed their own ancient democratic form of government in the village, subject of course to Dutch control, but above that level their rights were dealt out sparingly and without consultation.

It was inevitable that the Indonesian people, living so closely with the Dutch, sensitive to their excellencies, resentful of their domination, should grow restive. The passion for freedom began to stir in their breasts. Modern Indonesian history might be dated by the organization in 1908 of Boedi Odomo, Pure Endeavor Society, led by aristocrats who had become disgruntled or aspiring and dedicated to the development of "the life of a dignified people." Within a year there were 10,000 members, mostly civil servants and students. It was then an easy step into politically oriented organizations. And soon there were plenty of political orientors, for Dutch Social Democrats arrived from Holland, Marxism on their tongues, ready to pass on the great word. To depressed peoples it seemed indeed a great word, an articulate word, a rally call. However the going was not easy for propagandizers: colonial rule was efficient and the islands too spread out to be organized blithely; the tightly knit Islamic faith even then looked askance at communism; stubborn regionalism and high illiteracy were barriers. Moreover Islamic leaders of modern mien countered the radicals with the organization of Sarekat Islam, devoted to promotion of religious unity as well as to national unity and the elimination of foreign control, beginning with the Chinese in business.

In 1913 Sarekat Islam held its first congress. The Dutch took note of this fast-growing people's organization and tried to disrupt it, but opposition only wakened more of the people. Suddenly the National Indies Party bloomed forth, emphasizing racial equality, social justice, ultimate independence. At this point Handrik Sneevliet arrived from Holland with money and men to launch the insurgent Marxist Social Democratic Association. The Dutch looked at him askance and the Moslems looked at him with steely eye because both groups knew that he and his kind were seeking to accomplish just one thing—domination of the common people.

The Netherlands government answered the unrest, whether caused by radical socialists or by persistent Moslem nationalists, by calling together appointed representatives from all the Indies to form the Volksraad, or People's Council, which became the official advisory council of the land, its purpose being to interpret the government to the people and the people to the government. Throughout the ensuing decades its powers were considerably increased but the Dutch Governor General always held the right of veto. Thereafter some of the most intelligent of the nationalist leaders worked in and with the Volksraad, holding it to be the logical instrument of progressive democracy. Actually its uses were more imagined than real, a fact the Dutch knew all along.

At its third national congress Sarekat Islam represented nearly half a million members; at its fourth, two and one-half million. In 1919 more than a score of trade unions, many of them organized by Sneevliet, united in a Trade Union Council. When he was forced to leave the country the more radical of his cohorts formed the Partai Kommunist di India (Communist Party of the Indies), known ever since as the PKI. Later the party joined the Comintern, but this outside domination complicated the local program because Russian directives ordered communists everywhere to support parliamentary and nationalist independence movements, which meant cooperation with Sarakat Islam, the one organization able to trim the communist sails. At the same time the Comintern ordered all communists to combat all reactionary and fuedal elements in colonial countries, which meant conflict with Islamic conservativism and canceled out whatever advantage might have accrued from jogging along with Sarekat Islam. From that day, PKI has had to jump a lot of fences, swallow its previous commitments, reverse its decisions, but it seems able to perform such acrobatics without embarrassment. By 1921 PKI had representation in Moscow, whereupon the Netherlands Indies government refused communist representation in the Volksraad, holding that a good representative of the people of one country could not pay allegiance to directives from a foreign government. Tan Malaka, one of the party's all-time most successful leaders, was exiled. Communists and Sarekat Islam struggled for domination of the new organization of port workers, army and police force. Communist doctrines, trimmed to fit the locale, were bound to appeal to the oppressed. But Hadji Agus Salim, now the Grand Old Man of Indonesia, then one of the ablest of modern Islam's young leaders, was always ready and able to argue down communist promotion of class struggle, for in his eyes—and thousands saw with his eyes—Mohammed had preached a sufficient doctrine of social economics twelve centuries before Marx was born. He and his fellow leaders kept the going rough for PKI.

Over in Holland, Indonesian university students organized a liberal and dynamic student union known as Perhimpunan Indonesia, through whose activities many of their country's more influential leaders were trained. They knew their Marx as did most young intellectuals of the twenties, but they were nationalists first, socialists second, and seldom followers of Russian leadership.

After the government discovered plans for an out-and-out communist revolution to be precipitated by a strike of railway workers, communist organizations were refused the right of assembly, which short-circuited the revolution so that it broke out prematurely in Batavia instead of in Sumatra as planned. Some 13,000 arrests were made, resulting in 4,500 prison sentences and around 1,300 internments. Under Dutch rule the communists never made a comeback. But the nationalist movement in general gathered momentum, fed in part by the development of some 200 Tamen Siswa schools whose aim was a synthesis of Western and Indonesian cultures without political bias. Soekarno, then a brilliantly minded young engineer, formed the Indonesian Nationalist Party, known as PNI, which lent its weight to promoting cooperatives, labor unions and education. By 1929, PNI had 10,000 members whose general anti-government tactics were effective enough so that Soekarno and a few other leaders were sentenced to imprisonment for attempting "the overthrow of the Netherlands Indies authority."

In the early thirties, with Soekarno exiled and PNI outlawed, new organizations sprang up and two of the country's most exceptional leaders came to the fore—Mohammed Hatta and Soetan Sjahrir—both intent upon developing a small, compact, intelligent, politically conscious organization whose leadership would be more difficult to remove. Although they worked quietly, they were spotted, removed and exiled without trial to Tanah Merah where they remained until released in 1942 by the Japanese. Soekarno, released briefly, had resumed political activity for a short time, but was again exiled and also waited out his time until liberated by the Japanese. New parties came into being. Nationalist hopes rose only to meet a sharp setback in the rejection of a petition passed by a majority of the Volksraad asking for discussion of plans for developing Indonesia toward self-government over a period of ten years within the limit of the Dutch constitution.

Toward the end of the decade a Japanese invasion loomed as a possibility and prompted some of the more influential leaders to stress the need for closer cooperation with the Dutch but only on a basis of equality. However, by 1940 the Germans had occupied Holland and the Netherlands government made it plain that the mother country had more important things to think about than the political future of the Indies. In that case, the Indonesians asked, what did the Netherlands signature mean on the Atlantic Charter if not

Dutch underwriting of the principle of self-determination for all people? From London Queen Wilhelmina answered vaguely that after the war there might be conversations. But many Indonesians were not too much interested in Holland's surviving the war; except for a few of the farsighted, most of the people felt that the Dutch were getting their just dues. Pro-Axis feeling grew. In February, 1942, the Japanese "liberators" arrived in Sumatra, a fortnight later in Java. The Dutch Commander in Chief of the Allied forces quickly surrendered. Not a few Indonesians felt the surrender premature, but most were glad for the liberators.

. 5 .

War and the Republic

ONCE THE JAPANESE WERE INSTALLED THE
problem of collaboration faced the Indonesian leaders.
In Java, Sjahrir and Sjarifoeddin took to the mountains and
quietly built up a resistance organization. Soekarno, on the
other hand, had no reason to distrust the promises of the
Japanese and so he took the practical course of as much
collaboration as was necessary while he and Hatta built a
stronger nationalist movement.

At first most Indonesians went to work with a will on the
Japanese co-prosperity program. With the internment of the
Dutch, Indonesian personnel in administrative positions were
automatically advanced; the future looked good. But not
for long. Soon prosperity was all flowing toward the Japanese
homeland. Moreover, the Japanese language was required in
schools and government administrations, not a popular requirement of a people who were just beginning to use their
own national language. And finally, Japanese rudeness, often
cruelty, shocked the common people. The Dutch had seldom
been cruel. Cooperation lagged.

Nevertheless the Japanese taught the Indonesians one
significant lesson, namely, that the Dutch, who stood for the

white race, colonial masters and Western domination, were not invulnerable. The Japanese forced the Dutch from their homes and business, from plantations and factories, from command of harbors, railways and communications, herded them into freight cars and trucks and took them off to internment camps where they called on all bystanders to note that the new masters were strictly Asian and the new slaves strictly white. The Indonesians noted. They also noted that they themselves could often perform the administrative jobs of the Japanese as well and sometimes better than the new masters.

The life of the Dutch during the occupation was extremely rugged. They were first confined to their homes except during business hours while the Japanese learned the ropes in business and officialdom from them. The meticulous Dutch bureaucracy with its neat eye for detail was no doubt congenial to the Japanese mind. After Dutch internment in Surabaya, Java's second largest city, the problem of food distribution became acute so that hundreds of Dutch officials were released from prison for more than a year; then, when the Japanese had the matter in hand, they were returned to camp.

Near Djakarta is an old camp, bamboo barracks with corrugated roofs, formerly used by hundreds of Dutch women. Driving by the prison one day I asked a Dutch friend how she stood the heat in so swampy a locality with the humidity so high. She said that while in prison she seldom suffered from the heat; indeed, many felt that the climate had taken a change for the better. Actually they were so undernourished that there was relatively little oxidation going on in their bodies. After the first month or so none of the women menstruated; their bodies conserved such energy as they had.

Medical supplies were hard to come by. Hundreds died of malaria, even more of dysentery, and most of malnutrition. Daily rations were held at 900 calories for many months. There was an incredible amount of talk about food and many women began compiling cookbooks! Most families lost one or more members from sheer starvation. I met a score or more of large women, normally weighing 160 to 185 pounds, who came out of camp weighing 80 pounds or even less.

Work was hard and unremitting; also whenever possible it was degrading. Cultured women were required to empty officers' toilet pails, carry the contents to the field and work the refuse into the soil with their bare hands. Water for bathing and washing was usually at a premium, sometimes one cupful per person per day for all washing purposes. Toilet facilities were inadequate, scores having to use one latrine which, in a dysentery epidemic, was an impossibility.

With the Dutch in prison production fell sharply, except for quinine and a flaxlike plant called ramie which the Japanese introduced. Tea went down by 95 per cent, coffee nearly 70 per cent and rubber by some 80 per cent. These figures are important because they indicate something of the disruption of industry and production which faced the new Indonesian government at the end of the war.

All during the war Soekarno was constantly pushed into prominence. First he was made president of an appointed representative council for Indonesia; then a communication system was set up with radios in practically every town square and a public address system in the cities, and he was frequently called upon to exhort the people to cooperation. Although he spoke with fiery eloquence he was such a master of double talk that his listeners understood him to mean that their actual cooperation should consist of getting rid of the

Japanese. In building solidarity he was able to accomplish more under ostensible Japanese supervision than he could probably have done in two decades under the Dutch.

In the spring of 1944 the Japanese wooed cooperation more assiduously by honoring local Islamic leaders, but the fact that the people were forced to bow toward Tokyo canceled out the good will. Politically speaking, on the right a council of Moslem organizations called the Masjumi came into being, forerunner of the Masjumi party. On the left, Sjarifuddin and certain leaders of the underground PKI were sentenced to life imprisonment, later commuted. However, Sjahrir's underground continued strong, widening its base among peasants and students. The Japanese trained a volunteer army of 20,000 men, highly useful when the postwar revolution got underway. Finally a commission on preparation for independence was set up, followed by an announcement from Tokyo that Japan would give Indonesia independence "in the near future." The red-and-white flag of the new republic and the stirring national anthem "Indonesia Raja" came into the open.

In the early summer of 1945 committees on preparation for independence went into action, sponsored by the Japanese in spite of—or because of—growing anti-Japanese feeling. In early June Soekarno outlined the Pantja-Sila, the five basic principles of Indonesian social philosophy and democratic government which both reflected and fired the minds of Indonesian leaders. On August 8 Soekarno and Hatta were flown to Indo-China by special Japanese plane to perfect plans for the Emperor's declaration of independence on the day Russia should enter the war. But the Indonesian people were in no mood to accept independence from anybody, especially from their conquerors. They decided to declare their own independence. Students were mobilized and workers prepared for insurrection. Then on August 15, earlier than anyone expected, the Japanese surrendered to the Allies. But the great moment was less significant in Java than elsewhere because the Japanese immediately became agents of the Allies to keep the peace until the victors could get around to occupying Indonesia and prepare for the return of the Dutch.

On August 17 Soekarno read the Indonesian Declaration of Independence to a determined group waiting outside his residence, then broadcast it over the nationwide radio and telegraph network. The popular response was tremendous. Flags went up on public buildings. The republic had come to pass.

During these exciting events the Dutch in prison camps knew little about the new republic. Nor did the Dutch in Holland realize what was happening, nor the Netherlands Indies government-in-exile in Australia. Sturdy man-child Indonesia was born into the family of nations without so much as a groan from unconscious Mother Holland or a sign of blessing from any godparent. The reasons, however, were adequate. After the Japanese first occupied the islands there was practically no Allied intelligence concerning Indonesia. Such reports as began to reach the Dutch did not seem reasonable and so they were not true. When last seen the Indonesians had been docile enough subjects. Now that the status quo was about to be restored, why should they be otherwise? Q. E. D.—they weren't!

It was a full six weeks after the Japanese forces capitulated before representatives of the victors arrived to accept their surrender. After five years of German occupation the Dutch were in no shape to take on so large an immediate responsibility. Originally it had been planned that the United States would take the surrender in Java, and experts had already been trained in the Malay and Dutch languages. But it was the British who arrived. Although it may have been strictly military strategy which effected the change in plans, nevertheless the British were strategically advantaged to have oversight of political and economic affairs so near to their own important holdings in Malaya. But they found the task tougher than they had anticipated.

Chinese friends who had shared their spacious home with some of the incoming British officials told us many amusing tales about the bewilderment of the British when they first arrived in Djakarta, October, 1945, and saw the Red-and-White flying from government buildings, Indonesian signs on the ministries, merdeka (freedom) on every tongue. Indonesian police with Japanese equipment patrolled a peaceful city. Since the only government at hand was the Indonesian government the British worked with the men in control. But as soon as word of their cooperation with the Republic reached Holland an explosion occurred—and the British could not afford tension with the Dutch because they needed Dutch support in the Security Council. However, with their limited troops in Indonesia they knew they could not maintain peace and public utilities without the cooperation of the new government.

The situation of the defeated Japanese was also difficult. At times the British had to call on them to help restore order among Indonesian extremists. Moreover, the Japanese had to continue to police some of the Dutch prison camps because the highways were suddenly unsafe for Dutchmen. And as Dutch women and girls emerged insecurity increased. Girls particularly were lured from camp by telephone or written messages purporting to come from friends who were waiting to restore them to fathers or brothers, but when they went to the appointed place they were murdered by young Indonesians whose twisted minds remembered the days of their own social segregation and found a kind of vindication of self-esteem in killing young women.

All in all, the hard days of the war were easier for both the Indonesians and the Dutch, and also for the Japanese, than the first days of peace. For there was no peace. The immovable Dutch were confronted by the irresistible force of the Indonesians and the result was bound to be cataclysm.

As soon as the Declaration of Independence had been issued on August 17, 1945, the Preparatory Commission, previously set up, swiftly elected Soekarno president and Hatta vice-president. They were destined choices. Both are dynamic men, given to action, known to the common people, and both have a contagious faith in Indonesia's destiny. Sjahrir, third in the trio of leaders, was made chairman of the Working Committee of the temporary governing body known as KNIP, a group consisting of 120 national leaders of a wide variety of opinion, chosen to oversee the whole administrative setup of the country. For a time enthusiasm for the new government outweighed private differences of opinion. Aristocracy and peasant alike, except the minority who stood to profit by the return of the Dutch, threw the weight of their support behind the new venture.

Immediately Republican leaders requested clarification of the Republic's status before the Dutch civil administration and armed forces should return; but the British ignored the request and began releasing the imprisoned Dutch, who naturally tried to take over their old government positions, business, and homes. They met massed Indonesian protest.

Often there was shooting. No Dutchman felt his life was safe and for the best of reasons; it was not safe. But neither did the Indonesians feel safe from the returning Dutch. And the new government felt least safe of all. When the British had first arrived, Soekarno and Hatta had issued orders that British troops were not to be interfered with in their task of implementing the Japanese surrender. However, the British were doing more than effect the surrender; they were preparing for the return of the Netherlands authority and troops. Also they began to utilize Japanese troops to force the strategic cities of Bandung and Surabaya to make way for Dutch control. The Indonesians looked to their rights. They had a functioning government, an Indonesian government; and they had no intention of having any other government, not even temporarily. They took up arms, largely equipment sold or given them by the Japanese. The chief struggle centered in the port city of Surabaya where house-to-house fighting caused heavy losses on both sides. After some days the British ostensibly won out but, oddly, the Indonesians still think of that particularly violent clash as the turning of the tide in their favor because it was there made plain to the British that the Indonesian people as a whole, not merely a minority group of nationalists, were behind the determination to be free of colonial rule. Unless the British wished to implement their forces largely and to sustain heavy casualties and to occupy the country section by section in the same bloody manner, they would have to negotiate with the leaders of the Republic. A madness of pent-up injustice and frustration had seized the normally mild and reasonable Indonesians and the force of their will to independence was not to be stemmed by any ordinary military restraint.

The returning Dutch also had a lot of resentment. There

were Indonesians living in their homes, refusing to move
back into the kampong huts! Some Dutch tried the per-
emptory commands which had worked well in the old days,
only to have their teeth knocked out with the butt of a gun
in the hand of a teen-aged patriot. When the regular Dutch
troops arrived from Holland under orders to re-establish the
status quo, they fought in more orderly fashion than the
Indonesians but without anything resembling success.

Early in 1946 the turmoil began to lessen. High level
British administrators saw for themselves that the good old
days were not going to blow in with the next monsoon. However, they had no thought that the new Indonesian government would be permanent. For them it was merely temporary
strategy to allow Sjahrir, then Prime Minister, to come to
Djakarta to open formal negotiations with Lord Inverchapel.
That conference eventuated in a temporary agreement in
which the returning Dutch government was to recognize
the limited authority of the Republic over the islands of
Java, Sumatra and Madura. The end of November, 1946,
the last British troops left Java bequeathing their bases of
operation, eight strategic bridgeheads in Java and Sumatra,
to the 92,000 newly arrived Dutch troops, largely British
trained and equipped.

The ensuing months were given to conferences, sporadic
violence and mutual recrimination. Sjahrir for the Indonesians and Van Mook, former lieutenant governor general
for the Indies, headed the rival camps. The Dutch granted
that a bit of overhauling of the Netherlands East Indies governmental architecture was contemplated for the future but
that first the Netherlands would tutor the Indies, speeding
their education to the extent of expanding the school system,
recognizing the new Indonesian language as co-official with

the Dutch, abolishing racial discrimination and permitting the formation of a representative Indonesian parliament composed largely of Indonesians. From the Dutch point of view these were radical commitments. But to all offers of loosened apron strings the Indonesians answered with raucous adolescent laughter: they would now take care of their own government and school system and make their own blueprint of national life. Back and forth the Joint Committee traveled, Java to Holland, Holland to Java. In Holland Dutch economic interests gradually began to outweigh political interests; better to compromise with these recalcitrant Indonesians and reap the rubber *et al.* Arguments among Dutch factions were heated and in their midst the Dutch cabinet fell. Time was then needed to shake down the shake-up.

Back in Indonesia the Dutch Commissioner General agreed to meet the president of Indonesia for conference at Lingajati. After having long been the man who wasn't there so far as the Dutch were concerned, Soekarno materialized, adequately equipped with his own ideas. The Dutch took a firm Dutch stance and offered to compromise: henceforth the Republic would be recognized as the current authority in Java and Sumatra; then the governments of the Netherlands Indies and of the Republic would cooperate in forming a federal state, the United States of Indonesia, consisting of the Republic of Indonesia, just recognized as in existence, the State of Borneo, and the Great Eastern State, meaning all the eastern islands. The Republican government surveyed the proposal from all angles. It was plain that the new organization was a lopsided affair for the two other sections, Borneo and East Indonesia, had only 15 per cent of the population with about the same proportion of the import-export trade while each of them would have as much voice in political decisions as Java-

Sumatra, but the Republican government accepted the proposal so that their country could proceed to develop peacefully. Immediately some radical Indonesians took advantage of the general resentment against the inequalities of this proposed Linggajati Agreement to discredit the new government, and as a result the Sjahrir cabinet fell. Nevertheless, on March 25, 1947, the Linggajati Agreement was officially signed by the proper dignitaries at the Dutch Palace in Batavia and thereafter the Republican government acted with the increasing independence which it felt to be its right, while the Netherlands government also acted with increasing independence. Van Mook also acted independently, forgetting to consult the Republican government in setting up the administration of East Indonesia directly from Batavia. When it came to practical deployment of their troops in Java, both sides were jumpy, both Dutch and Indonesian patrols keeping their guns cocked. Practically, there was neither peace nor progress.

Inevitably a time came when the Dutch decided things could not go on in so indeterminate a fashion. Their trade had not picked up. Moreover, the maintenance of Dutch troops in Indonesia cost the equivalent of a million gold dollars a day, which had practically exhausted the Dutch gold reserves. The Dutch were all the more irritated because on the Republican side economic conditions were not worsening. Definitely rehabilitation was proceeding. The Dutch decided that on all important administrative matters theirs must be the decisive word until the federal union was effected. On May 27, 1947, the Commissioner General representing the Netherlands government sent an ultimatum to Sjahrir that if the Republican government did not submit to an interim government in which the Dutch Crown was to have the power of decision until the United States of Indonesia became an actuality, then the alternative would be war. Thus high-handedly was the Linggajati Agreement abrogated.

In order to prevent war, Sjahrir, after days of deliberation with the advisory council, KNIP, agreed to the special position of the Crown's representatives. In late June, he went to Djogja to address the coalition of parties most securely behind him, but even his own Socialist party was not single-minded in approval of his compromise. Feeling his leadership in question, he handed in his resignation. Immediately the opposition reversed their position, urging him to reconsider. At the same time a note from the government of the United States urged cooperation between the Republic and the Dutch without delay and promised financial aid to assist the economic development and rehabilitation of Indonesia, a promise interpreted as support for Sjahrir. However, Sjahrir felt it best that he remain free to serve as an international ambassador when his services might be needed.

Sjarifoeddin, communist-minded socialist and former Minister of Defense, formed a new cabinet which made several further concessions to the Dutch, but when the Dutch demanded joint control of Indonesian troops Republican leaders drew the line. Sensing that they could get no further except by military coercion, the Netherlands command ordered the Dutch army to open an all-out attack whose purpose was to crush the Republic for good and all, a military move since referred to euphemistically as the First Police Action. On July 20, 1947, Dutch troops launched operations from seven main bridgeheads. They felt that their course was justified by their intent to keep the peace and effect long-time liberalization of the Indonesian government. The Indonesians claimed that the Dutch could have called into consultation "a chairman of another nationality with a deciding vote" as provided by the Linggajati Agreement.

The Republic was not well armed against the 109,000 seasoned Dutch troops with their mechanized forces, their highly adequate air and naval support, their excellent morale, their eagerness to fight to the finish so they could go home. To be sure, the Republic had some 200,000 troops, 50,000 of them in Sumatra, but their troops were far less well trained and they had only 150,000 rifles, a limited supply of small arms and machine guns, homemade land mines and hand grenades, plus forty ex-Japanese planes and bombers with half as many pilots. Hence the army of the Republic had to avoid open conflict where possible, decentralize its command and return to guerrilla warfare. But it augmented military strength with a scorched-earth policy—much of it carried out by a growing communist-dominated labor organization— and destroyed huge stockpiles of estate crops valuable to the Dutch. The Republic also had an imponderable asset perhaps greater than all else: in the eyes of the world as in their own eyes they were the set-upon. They were the ostensible victims of an effort to restore colonialism.

The Republic's best hope seemed to be to get their case before the United Nations. By way of Australia and India their plight was placed on the Security Council's immediate agenda and Nehru issued an Indian Monroe Doctrine, at the same time threatening to ban Dutch air traffic which depended upon Indian bases. On the Netherlands side, the Dutch held the trouble in Indonesia to be strictly an internal problem of the Netherlands and hence no concern of the Security Council. Nevertheless on August 12, over Dutch protests, Sjahrir was seated and made a stirring statement of his cause. So then the powers lined up. At first the four colonial powers stood together—England, Holland, France, and Belgium—with Australia, Syria, Russia and Poland against them and the United States, China, Colombia and Brazil trying to remain neutral.

Indonesian leaders hoped for out-and-out support from the United States. They were well aware that the credit which America was giving Holland for reconstruction of the Netherlands home economy could provide pressure on the Dutch to suspend military operations in Indonesia, and that time consumed in argument worked in favor of the Dutch because the Java territory under Republican control was a deficit food area and the Dutch blockade cut off supplies. The United States, however, was in something of a predicament. First, it did not seem likely that the Indonesian government would be able to hold its ground, and second, it seemed completely necessary to maintain Holland's unstinted cooperation in the European Defense Pact.

Eventually the Security Council appointed a Committee of Good Offices and in October, 1947, the Committee arrived in Djakarta where negotiations were opened on the U. S. Navy Transport *Renville* anchored in the harbor. It was the middle of January, 1948, before both sides were ready to sign a compact incorporating agreement on a military line (staked out by Van Mook); on free elections within a year for self-determination by the people of their political relationship to the United States of Indonesia; on Netherlands sovereignty over Indonesia, to be transferred after an interval to an independent United States of Indonesia of which the Republic was a member state. Republican leaders felt the Dutch advantage basically unfair and that in a prolonged showdown of force they would win out; but in order to save large numbers of lives and hasten the peace, the Indonesian representatives signed the Renville Agreement.

No sooner was it signed, however, than Masjumi, largest of the political parties, withdrew from the cabinet in disapproval of the terms, Sjarifoeddin resigned, and a presidential cabinet was formed. The Republic's troops withdrew from territory now declared to be Dutch, but the Dutch delayed in appointing representatives for the UN-sponsored political discussions; freedom of speech and assembly was suppressed in Dutch-dominated areas and Dutch infringements of the agreement brought no protest from the Security Council. Then came a fiasco plebiscite staged by the Dutch in Madura with Republican representation finagled off the boards, after which the resulting new State of Madura was officially recognized by the Dutch as separate from the Republic of which it had been a part. Then the Dutch also set up a new and separate state of West Java. The struggle was on again, with the Dutch constantly overstepping their bonds and the Indonesians calling for enforcement of the terms of the treaty. Members of the Good Offices Committee tried to break the deadlock by submitting compromise proposals to which the Republic agreed but which the Dutch rejected in toto. The Good Offices Committee stated frankly that the Indonesian delegates evidenced greater willingness to cooperate and compromise than the Dutch. "Incidents" multiplied. Tension climbed.

In the Security Council the Dutch took heart at all delays and in Indonesia tightened their import-export controls into a highly effective blockade which cut Republican food and textiles to the point where inflation developed, wages dropped, illness rose sharply. No magazines, books or newspapers got through and the paucity of outside news provided a field day for the heavily subsidized local news organs of the communists. By the fall of 1948 Republicans were thoroughly disillusioned. It was well known in Indonesia that the Marshall Plan aid of $506,000,000 given to Holland in the spring of 1948 provided that $84,000,000 could be used in administration of Indonesian affairs, which looked to the Indonesians like a United States subsidy for Dutch perfidy. Indeed, many officials of the Netherlands administration in Indonesia interpreted the subsidy in the same way, feeling that Dutch military action might soon be unnecessary for the Republic would simply collapse from within. Communist leaders made much the same evaluation and laid their plans to seize power.

However, in September, 1948, the Committee of Good Offices was reconstituted. A new plan emerged incorporating a few more concessions to the Dutch but both sides refused to discuss the plan. Days were tense. Two months passed. Then the Netherlands foreign minister arrived to open direct talks with Republican leaders, ignoring the committee. The talks broke down over the question of the Dutch right to send troops into whatever area they felt to be disturbed, the Indonesians insisting that they could maintain order in their own territory or in an extremity ask for help. In December the Netherlands authorities informed the Committee of Good Offices that they were tired of finagling with the Republic and would go ahead on their own to set up an interim government. Republican leaders made further concessions, asking only for definite standards of action. The answer was a Dutch ultimatum that the Republic had eighteen hours to sign an agreement under whose terms the Republic would enter into a federal organization of Indonesia on the same footing as the Dutch-controlled areas, now grown to fifteen.

Republican leaders in Batavia felt that since the Republic

represented a majority of the entire Indonesian population the compact was suicide. Moreover, eighteen hours was too short a time to allow them to return to Djogja for discussion with the advisory council. But the Dutch would not extend the time and on December eighteenth declared the Renville Agreement terminated, refusing permission for their note of abrogation to be telegraphed to the government in Djogja.

And so the Republican government received its notification of the abrogation of the truce in the form of a handsome attack of Dutch bombers on the Djogja airport. The Second Police Action was on. Dutch plans were well laid; their troops, including paratroopers, moved rapidly and effectively. When Soekarno refused to order complete surrender he and Hatta, along with Sjahrir, Hadji Agus Salim and a few others, were taken prisoner by the Dutch and flown to Sumatra.

I once asked Hadji Agus Salim about those final days of exile when they had no way of making contact with their people, when it must have seemed as if the entire Indonesian struggle had been in vain. The old philosopher's eyes twinkled and he said that at the time he was ill and in desperate need of rest, so he said to himself, "Here it is! Lake Toba is one of the most beautiful spots in all Indonesia; the Dutch have to furnish me good medical care and I had best recover my energy." Which he did. Here in exile plans were laid to cover various eventualities, personalities were reappraised and spiritual resources were definitely strengthened. Back in Java the removal of the top leadership threw a burden of responsibility upon other leaders who had been schooled against just such a day, and the fact that the President and his associates were held prisoner fired the people as even their presence might not have done. Their exile, which seemed at the time a trump card for the Dutch, may have given the Indonesians the final trick.

In Java the ensuing weeks did indeed appear the last days of the Republic. Disintegrated Republican forces fought on, supported by the people, but the report the Dutch gave to the outside world was that people were welcoming their deliverers. Even some of the Dutch troops believed they were helping to free oppressed people. It is altogether probable that the Republic would have folded up permanently in these bitter and desolate weeks had the government not had excellent representation in its observation mission in the United States. The Indonesian representatives saw to it that some accurate reporting got into the American press, while Dr. Philip Jessup, American representative on the Security Council, worked to get a cease-fire measure through an emergency meeting of the Security Council. A curtailed measure to cease hostilities and release the political prisoners was passed, but the Netherlands government ignored the order. Violent fighting continued.

On January 10, 1949, the Republican leaders-in-exile were told that the Dutch no longer recognized the Republic and hence they no longer had any political position. The price of their restricted freedom would be their promise to refrain thereafter from all political activity. They did not promise. These dark days still rankle in Indonesian hearts. Republican leaders saw the predicament of America and West European economic and military security. They also saw that the Dutch were determined, for both economic and political reasons, to defeat the Republic militarily, to divide-and-rule through a score of states which should make up the United States of Indonesia, and to obtain international approval of their program. Today in Djakarta it is not difficult to get the play-by-play account of those weeks, told by Republican leaders and their wives who lived under almost constant attack in Djogja but who managed to keep the rice-line open from the country people to the city population; told also by ordinary citizens whose homes were burned and whose sons were killed; by reporters, even by former Dutch soldiers.

Gradually American public opinion became vocal in behalf of Indonesia. American speeches in the UN had all along been more favorable than the American voting record. Indonesians still point out that from April, 1948, to April, 1949, American aid voted to the Netherlands was somewhat more than $402,000,000, while the estimated cost of maintaining the Dutch forces in Indonesia was almost the same figure. But eventually the U.S. Senate became incensed over the Dutch refusal to honor the Security Council's cease-fire resolution and a strong faction threatened to delay, if not defeat, the military equipment program for Western Europe so long as the Dutch portion of the arms went to fighting the Republicans in Indonesia. Debate became heated.

Nevertheless in Indonesia it was late March before the UN Commission for Indonesia got the idea over that long-suspended negotiations had better be resumed immediately, and it was April 12 before the leader of the Dutch delegation arrived in Djakarta thoroughly aware that Congress was ready to suspend American help to the Netherlands until some settlement was reached in Indonesia. The weight of the United States Department of State had swung behind the Indonesian demands, partly as a matter of justice, partly because of the fact that leadership in Java and Sumatra was rapidly shifting to the communists in the absence of the Republican leaders, and partly because the prestige of the UN was suffering through continued Dutch defiance. When to agitation in the U.S. Senate and sympathy for the Indonesian people in the American press there was added a vote of the General Assembly to open debate on the Dutch-Indonesian question before the middle of May, the time seemed ripe to the Dutch actually to negotiate.

Discussions opened in Djakarta but ran into constant snags. Mr. Cochran, the American delegate, continually pressed Mr. Roem, the Indonesian delegate, to give in to Dutch demands in order to reach a solution. In general the American position was that Indonesia could afford to grant a lot more than strict justice demanded, for the sake of complete and immediate independence and to save Indonesian lives. Once again Indonesian leaders felt they need not overcompromise because they could ultimately win their independence without undue concessions, but on the whole they shared the American point of view and coveted American support. On May 7 the Roem-Van Royen Agreement, ordering restoration of the peace and participation in a Round Table Conference at the Hague, was adopted by both the Netherlands and the Republic, the latter making most of the concessions. Dutch constituents were not satisfied but they realized that if economic investments were not to be wiped out and communism entrenched, then drastic changes would have to be made. They also realized that American opinion had finally crystallized into definite pressure in behalf of the Republic and could not be ignored.

It was August before a cease-fire became effective. Then at the Hague for more than two months argument continued between delegates of the Republic, of the Netherlands, and of the Federal Consultive Assembly, a name given by the Dutch to the group of representatives they had chosen from all the federal units of Indonesia recently set up by them. These territorial representatives had equal vote even though the small island of Billiton, for instance, had a relatively small population while East Java alone had a population of 10,000,000. Assistance in drawing up the final agreement was lent by the United Nations Commission for Indonesia. One of the most pressing questions was the amount of debt to be assumed by the Republic of the United States of Indonesia. The Dutch held that the Republic must take over all the debts of the Netherlands Indies government as of the time of transfer of sovereignty, both the external and internal debt. The Indonesians agreed to take over such debts as were owned by the Netherlands Indies government at the time of Japanese occupation, but refused to shoulder a debt which consisted largely of millions of guilders spent in fighting Indonesia. Indeed, the Indonesian delegation figured that the Dutch actually owed the Republic something over 500,000,000 guilders. Debate was warm and involved, the logic of the figures depending upon the premise accepted. Finally, Indonesia accepted a debt of almost $1,130,000,000, which in effect forced upon them payment for the cost of the military action against them.

The second big dispute at the Hague centered around the transfer to Indonesia of the western half of New Guinea, known as Irian. In area Irian is about three and a half times the size of Java but completely undeveloped, with a population approaching a million, largely illiterate. Why Irian was chosen for retention is difficult for an outsider to figure except that it was furthest from Djakarta and the Indonesians might therefore be persuaded that it was less important to their well-being. The Dutch argument was, and is, that ethnically the people of Irian are not Indonesians, that the Indonesian government cannot properly administer the island, that the people do not care for Moslem domination, that the Netherlands has a right to this territory which it has long fostered. At the time of the Round Table talks there was an additional psychological factor: by holding Irian the Netherlands would not seem to be conceding Indonesia all its territorial demands nor going out of business as a colonial power in Southeast Asia. The Indonesian answer is that Irian always was considered a part of the East Indies and there is no logic for disengaging it, that the people are definitely a part of other racial stocks incorporated in Indonesia, that Indonesian control is necessary to prevent Irian's being used as a haven for rebels (in support of which they point out that the rebellion in the Moluccas could not have occurred without Irian's use as a base), and that the Indonesian constitution guarantees religious freedom.

At the time of the Round Table Agreement public opinion in Holland favored transfer of Irian to Indonesia primarily because administrative costs were high. Likewise at that time many Indonesians agreed that Indonesia had no spare civil servants, technicians or teachers to send to Irian, and hence there was no great point in demanding its return. But now both sides have their dander up and neither has the slightest notion of giving in. The Dutch would be glad to have the issue fade from the international scene; the Indonesians intend to keep it alive and vocal. In mid-1953 Holland was reported to be spending 25,000,000 guilders annually in development of Irian while the country is yielding 95,000,000 guilders worth of oil and other products. In Indonesia the return of Irian is a rallying cry for all sorts and shades of political gatherings. Even people who scarcely know where Irian is, and certainly have no notion whether its return to the fold will work ill or good, can be counted on to fume and probably to fight for Irian.

As a matter of record, the draft transfer of authority provided that New Guinea should remain in Dutch control until a future date to be set by negotiation between the two governments within a year of the signing of the transfer—four years ago. Currently the Indonesian government holds that since the Draft Union Status says that either contracting party may abrogate the Round Table Agreement at will, now is the time to abrogate both for advantage in the Irian decision and to disown the preposterous amount of the debt to the Netherlands. Abrogation of the remainder of the debt now seems a certainty of the near future.

If the Irian dispute is not amenable to satisfactory adjustment now, much less was it open to settlement at the Round Table Conference. Nevertheless, with sufficient problems compromised, transfer of authority finally took place on December 27, 1949, and was ratified by the Netherlands Parliament, the provisional government of the Republic of Indonesia, and the fifteen other states of the projected United States of the Republic of Indonesia, known as R.U.S.I. However, the Republic of Indonesia resented the form of the over-all federation of the Republic of the United States of Indonesia, composed as it was of sixteen constituent states varying greatly in size, the largest being the Republic of Indonesia, made up of Western and Central Java and the larger part of Sumatra—some 35,000,000 people—and the fact that the officials of the other states had been placed in power by the Dutch. Popular support was definitely not behind R.U.S.I. and a move for centralization was immediately afoot. A unitary government, as it was called, could administer all the constituent states rather than sixteen separate governments, one of the practical arguments being lack of trained personnel to staff sixteen governments.

Arguments against a unitary government came largely from Dutch-appointed officials, particularly and most vociferously from former members of the Dutch Colonial Army, KNIL, some 26,000 of whom had been absorbed into the armed forces of R.U.S.I. Under the Dutch most of the crack troops had been drawn from Ambon and Minahassa, both Christian areas, and received higher pay than soldiers from Java and the western areas; consequently they feared for their preferred position under a strictly Indonesian government.

Some of the member states of R.U.S.I. immediately requested incorporation into the Republic of Indonesia, but concurrently intransigent groups of KNIL began fomenting armed disturbance. A certain Captain Westerling, demobilized from KNIL with a previous record of cruelty against civilians in Celebes, organized ex-KNIL Indonesian soldiers along with some Dutch soldiers in an attempt to take over the city of Bandung, supposedly to be followed by descent upon Djakarta and the murder of outstanding national leaders. The *coup d'état* was a failure but it put a serious strain on Indonesian-Dutch relations because of the part played by Dutch officers and the desertion of Dutch police to Westerling. Sporadic armed resistance continued for many months. As late as April 1950 ex-KNIL companies seized control of Macassar, capital of Celebes, for a time. Later a larger insurrection on the island of Ambon took the form of a demand for recognition as an independent state. Here the armed forces of the Republic fought against the revolutionists for months before order was restored and the national government recognized as authority.

In spite of recalcitrance in certain areas, however, the move toward a unitary government was strong and persistent. Indeed, the inability of constituent states to deal with trouble

did much to discredit the federation. By April, twelve of the
sixteen states had merged with the Republic. Since there was
no longer profit in recalcitrance, an acceptable draft of a new
constitution was agreed upon and on August 17, 1950, anni-
versary of the Declaration of Independence, the new fully
constituted Republic of Indonesia, made up of all the islands
of the former Netherlands East Indies except Irian, became
official. Except for the large contingent of Dutch advisers,
civil servants and specialists, Indonesia was entirely Indonesian. Not long after, the Republic of Indonesia took its
place as the sixtieth member of the United Nations.

. 6 .

Democracy in the Making

THE NEW GOVERNMENT HAD TWO IMMEDIATE responsibilities. First, to set up a functioning structure and man the posts; second, to persuade divergent elements of the population that the government intended to govern. In form the government was, and is, a democracy with President, cabinet and unicameral legislature commonly called Parliament. Popularly the term "the government" means the President and his cabinet and yet the cabinet is not his in the sense of being responsible to him. He picks the *formateur*, who presents for his approval a slate of ministers, but parliament can dismiss any one or all of the cabinet members.

Parliament is made up of one representative for every 300,000 of the population. Legislation is directed by a steering committee supposedly representing all political trends. Theoretically parliament is divided into sixteen sections corresponding with the fifteen ministries plus a section to scrutinize the problems of internal security, but actually since 1952 the sixteen sections have been combined into ten. Cabinet policies are defined by the two score or more parties which support or obstruct its program, so that no understanding of the government's record is possible without knowledge of the dominant traits and record of the parties.

Masjumi is oldest and largest of the parties, dedicated to

78

promotion of a Moslem state but lacking unanimity as to exactly what constitutes a Moslem state and how it shall be achieved; supported by many of the well-to-do but also by the majority of village leaders; conservative in point of view and evidencing responsibility in office; always well represented in parliament but currently not represented in the cabinet, which makes it the leader of the opposition and a salutary influence against extreme left-wing policies. One of its off-shoots, Nahdatul Ulama, more orthodox in composition, often votes against the parent party and hence in effect throws weight to the present communist leanings of certain elements in the government.

Parti Nasional Indonesia, known as PNI, started by President Soekarno in his young days, comes second in size. It is always well represented in parliament and currently in the cabinet; supported by local administrative government officials, the small industrialist middle class and a wide range of middle-of-the-road clerks and businessmen, less stable than formerly and given to compromise with communist elements. Persatuan Indonesia Raja, called PIR, an off-shoot of PNI, wields a fair-sized influence, has a sizable number of seats in parliament, and furnished the *formateur* of the current Ali Sastroamidjojo cabinet.

Partai Socialis Indonesia, PSI, is the Socialist party founded and dominated by Soetan Sjahrir; not large in number but with an educated, trained membership; at the median line in parliamentary representation but with considerable influence on other parties, currently not represented in the cabinet, always anti-communist but not overtly pro-West.

Partai Komunis Indonesia, the communist party, known as PKI, has known periods of eclipse, as when outlawed by the Dutch shortly before the war, and periods of strength, as when in 1946 it attempted a *coup d'état* against the government at Maduin, and currently when it is reported to be a dominant influence in the army and in SOBSI, largest of the trade union federations. It is particularly adept at bargaining with leftists and opportunists in other parties, effecting a major crisis over a minor matter, as in the fall of the Wilopo cabinet in 1953.

Fraksi Demokrat represents a rather loosely knit group composed primarily of civil and administrative officers from the Lesser Sundas, Celebes and north Moluccas. National People's party, PRN, emphasizes planned economy and state control of natural resources and basic production. The Catholic party, "based upon belief in the Divine Omnipotence in general and the Pantjasila in particular," has a middle-of-the-road voting record. Other small parties, five-seaters or less, include Partai Buruh, the labor party, which is non-communist in outlook and record; PSII, which votes with the conservative wing of Masjumi; the Christian party, which emphasizes health, social welfare and democratic representation; Parinda, conservative and dedicated to the perpetuation of Indonesian culture; Partai Murba, originally a coalition of pro-Tan Malaka groups, strongly anti-imperialist, anti-capitalist, aiming at the country's membership in a proletarian world government. Other parties come and go, some of them combining forces around specific issues, and no doubt more parties will be born tomorrow. The establishment of a new party is one of Indonesia's most facile gymnastics. The big question is whether the parties can so combine as to effect a stable government.

The volatile relationship of political parties to cabinet and hence to government is best seen in the cabinets. Primarily Indonesian cabinets fall because of the need for a scapegoat.

Complicated problems not amenable to rapid solution call forth divergent opinions on procedure; restive members of parliament then blame the cabinet for some decision; the cabinet replies that it did the best it could under the circumstances. But some party is sure to have its feelings hurt. "I'll take my ministers and go home," and with ministers withdrawn and dissatisfaction rampant a vote of confidence fails.

The Wilopo cabinet, which took office on April 3, 1952, and resigned on June 3, 1953, offers a good illustration. That cabinet had rough going over several issues, the final one being the land distribution program in north Sumatra. Contention centered around Home Affairs Minister, Mr. Mohamad Roem, popularly credited with being Indonesia's most astute statesman in regard to foreign affairs. The facts behind the contention over land distribution were that sizable tracts of land in North Sumatra had been leased by the former Netherlands East Indies government to foreign estate planters, but during World War II, when the estates could not be operated as such, squatters had moved in, possibly 70,000 families. Dr. Roem's policy, inherited in the main from the former cabinet and implemented by the governor of North Sumatra, was to return to the concession owners as much of the land as they needed to operate and to redistribute the squatters on the remaining land, where each peasant family would be given 7½ acres of fertile land, two-thirds the amount in dry land and one-third paddy field, plus R. 300 for moving expenses, with the promise that if the land were successfully cultivated for three years the peasant would be given ownership title. Some 9,000 families were moved. Some peasants found their new land more fertile and some less fertile, but in the overall shift the peasants stood to profit.

Enter communist dissenters, calling on the peasants to refuse to move and propagandizing that they were being dispossessed in favor of foreign capitalists. The Masjumi party supported the Roem program as a sound long-range method of reconstruction furthering peasant responsibility and foreign investment. On the other hand, communist-dominated interests in parliament promoted a motion for change in the government land policy. Enough opposition from left-wing PNI members and others was mustered to cause the resignation of the cabinet. Most of the Indonesian press saw the fall of this cabinet as a needless sacrifice of governmental stability in the interest of individual politicians.

The latest cabinet, headed by Dr. Ali Sastroamidjojo, formerly ambassador to the United States, came into office in August, 1953, after the government had been without a cabinet for fifty-eight days. In order to form a cabinet at all Mr. Wongsonegoro of PNI, the *formateur*, had to eliminate Masjumi, the Socialists, the Christian and Catholic parties, thus presenting the cabinet with strong opposition in parliament. Indeed, the cabinet represents only about 50 per cent of parliament. The communist element seems bent upon widening the breach between Masjumi and PNI, splitting both major parties. The Minister of Defense, appointed under pressure from strong elements within the army, was once jailed as a leader of the Tan Malaka communist rebellion and pro-communists also hold the ministries of justice, finance and education. The Indonesian press almost unanimously expresses lack of confidence in the cabinet, but the prime minister still assures the people that he can effect security, raise the standard of living, guarantee general elections, chart an independent foreign policy, while maintaining the present enthusiastic communist support without losing American cooperation. Whether there is enough party and personal discipline among the top leadership to weather the increasingly stormy seas is now an open question.

If the cabinet could meet its problems seriatim it might have a chance to effect stabilization but unfortunately the problems are interlocking. Nevertheless some are more immediately important than others; for instance, both foreign policy and internal policy wait upon survival policy. If the government is to continue to exist, then political democracy has to be activated and security effected.

Although political democracy is one of the chief ends for which the people have struggled, to date they have had no voice in selecting a parliament, so the members of parliament feel small responsibility to the people but large responsibility to the political parties which put them in office. This situation is cumbersome, ineffectual and subject to periods of partial disintegration when cabinets fall. Much of the uncertainty in the matter stems from the need for a permanent constitution which has now been drafted and will no doubt soon be adopted. In principle it embodies the Pantjasila (meaning five pillars) which came into being as a five-point speech made by Mr. Soekarno in 1945, a speech which may well go down in history as one of the great pronouncements of democratic principle. The people took it to be their declaration of independence, their charter of rights, their "so be it known to all the world."

Nationalism, defined as "the unity between men and place," the unity of the whole people; *humanitarianism*, "one family of all nations"; *democracy*, or government by consent, providing that "within the people's representative body Moslems and Christians should work as if inspired"; *social justice*, a climate in which "every man has enough to eat, enough to wear, lives in prosperity"; *belief in God,* incorporating the conviction that "every Indonesian should believe in his own particular God"—these are the five pillars. But in conclusion Soekarno epitomized the Pantjasila in the Indonesian term *gotong rojong,* mutual cooperation. "Mutual cooperation is a dynamic conviction" meaning "one endeavor, one charity, one task . . . toiling together, sweating together, a struggle of help-me-to-help-you together." The Pantjasila has become a national document in the sense that it is quoted as authority for principle behind action and pictorialized in the Indonesian coat of arms. Indonesians understand their coat of arms; it came into being out of the experience of living men; it links their past with their present, and to hear any schoolboy describe it is to realize that it also speaks out their hope for the future. The bearer of the coat of arms is a mythological eagle, the garuda; its flight feathers are seventeen and its tail feathers eight, signifying the date of Indonesian independence, the seventeenth of the eighth month. The shield portrays the five principles of the Pantjasila: the central field with the star stands for faith in God, the head of the native bull for the principle of sovereignty, the banyan tree for nationalism, the sprays of rice and cotton for social justice, the linked chain for humanitarianism, while the black line across the center represents the equator and the device bears the old Javanese words meaning unity in diversity. It now remains for these principles to be codified in a permanent constitution and demonstrated through national elections.

The first election above the level of the desa was held in the regency of Minahassa in north Celebes, but because this area has been Christian for some time the people are 95 per cent literate and hence not typical of the country as a whole.

The first large scale elections in a typical area were the elections for parliament of the province of Djogja—population around 2,000,000—held in August, 1951. However before that election could be held a popular census had to be administered, carried out by village officials, after which 59.1 per cent of all citizens over eighteen reported for registration. According to proportionate representation, around 7,500 electors were required to declare themselves but almost 19,000 actually declared, each sponsored by ten men who appeared together before their village committee. On the day of the election of electors hundreds and sometimes thousands of eligible citizens assembled in their villages to hear the reading of instructions, after which they waited their turn to exchange their registration card for a voting card. At the voting place candidates sat all day for inspection by the voters, behind each candidate his symbol. Of the 1,200,000 citizens eligible to vote, 51.6 per cent cast ballots.

Next came the actual election of members of the provincial parliament. These candidates declared themselves on the bases of party membership and elections were conducted under sponsorship of general all-party officials. None of the parties presented clear-cut issues, since lines of division lie as often within the parties as between them and the chief issues of the day were scarcely discussed except by the communist front. It was noteworthy that the strongly Moslem Ministry of Religion, which helped with the publicity program behind the elections, did not throw its weight behind the most ardently Moslem candidates. The total of corrupt practices appears to have been small while the main objective of arousing wide and critical interest in representative government was handsomely achieved.

The cost of the Djogja elections was one of its significant

aspects. The central government appropriated R. 918,000 for the election of the electors, and R. 800,000 was spent on the election of parliament members. Another R. 800,000 was spent by the Ministry of Information in general promotion. Amounts spent by the parties and by the candidates themselves were not recorded.

The estimated cost of a general election is R. 350,000,000 and an estimated 50,000,000 persons are eligible to vote. The voting age is set at eighteen but all married persons of any age are permitted to vote. Since many Moslem girls marry at twelve and a majority are married at fifteen, there may be thousands of child voters.

General elections will be a magnification of the Djogja experiment. Registration of voters is to be carried out within the smallest administrative unit, but in many parts of the country these units have not been specified. The number of such units is estimated at 40,000, which means that 120,000 persons have to be appointed for registration committees alone. Each appointment is subject to political argument.

Some parties feel that all major issues should be frozen where possible until a representative parliament has been elected. Left-wing parties fear a landslide on the part of ignorant voters toward the strictly Moslem parties, while many right-wing adherents fear a landslide toward communism in the cities where the labor movement is strongest. But most informed persons feel that such risks will have to be taken in the interests of ultimate democracy.

One of the big risks of which the coming general elections seem free is pure demagoguery. Although President Soekarno stands for the Republic in the minds of the masses, there seems no disposition to idolize him. His picture adorns all government offices, railway stations, restaurants, schoolrooms and public places in general to an extent which amazes an American, but the universal display is not out of line with the Dutch proclivity for exhibiting the picture of the Queen. There seems no tendency on the part of any political group to set up holy personalities and freedom to criticize the President is as much of an actuality as in the United States.

Conditioning the success of national elections is Indonesia's foremost internal problem—security. Unless this problem is treated promptly and sternly, the end of the noble experiment —democratic Indonesia—seems in sight. Business and government operate all the time with insecurity as much a part of the context of daily life as the heat. It is the accepted climate, which does not mean that no attempt has been made to rectify the matter but that the attempt has not been wholehearted. The abnormal has in a sense become normal and people adjust to the status quo.

First of all, there is the constant thievery so that open windows have to be watched or books, knickknacks, dishes, furniture, disappear while the owner has gone into another room. In the preferred area of Bandung where we lived, one of our neighbors had a jeep and window drapes stolen, another his typewriter and radio, a third the family clothes, a fourth cooking utensils, a fifth the clothes off the line, all within one city block and in the same week. Notwithstanding the fact that we lived in the kind of house difficult to lock securely, we never had but two things stolen: an orchid off the outside wall of our house and a silk dressing gown from an outside pocket of a traveling bag.

After we moved from Bandung we sometimes returned for week ends in the lovely home of a friend. One night an acquaintance newly arrived from America stayed in the room we usually occupied and while he slept thieves entered through a window, took his watch, wallet, wedding ring, fountain pen, then proceeded to his hostess' room, took her wardrobe newly assembled for a trip to Europe, knocked her in the head and left her lying in a pool of blood. The American returned to Djakarta, bought a new pen, watch and wallet, cashed a sizable check and that afternoon was held up in his hotel room. He ran to the street for a betja and headed for his office, but the betja was run down by a car and thoroughly demolished. He was uninjured but decided his first twenty-four hours in Indonesia were rugged.

Large-scale robbery, arson and murder are more serious matters. Daily, villages are reduced to ashes by armed bands, animals carried off, rice stolen, estate crops spirited away, people killed. After a bandit raid a village builds up its defenses, doubles its guard, tries to secure its granaries; trouble dies down; a degree of prosperity returns—and so does the bandit gang. Fires followed by robbery are epidemic in Djakarta and other cities. Trains are held up, passengers forced to lie down in the aisles while stripped of their belongings. On main highways cars and trucks try to travel in transports because of sudden forays by armed bands. When a foreigner arrives in Djakarta and sees business apparently going on as usual, the stories of insecurity appear exaggerated. Things *look* normal, but one soon experiences the actualities of insecurity.

Why? In this garden spot of the world where people are amiable and the necessities of life not too difficult to procure, why is insecurity so prevalent? Recent history provides the answer: during the war thousands of young men and schoolboys trained as guerrillas and during the struggle for independence they were encouraged in the ways of plunder for the sake of the lives of their families. When hostilities ceased they had to choose between returning to the too-small family farm to grub out a substandard living in the dull routine of peace or continuing to live by their wits and arms. Often some trumped-up cause was offered them and they did not see that they were being driven to a false "patriotism" which might cancel out Indonesia's future as a democracy.

Theoretically the armed forces might be expected to settle affairs for they are well organized and experienced. During the days of their struggle for independence the army made an astounding record of tactical defense and guerrilla offense in the face of an enemy immeasurably better armed. When independence was achieved the army was oversized, still poorly equipped, underpaid and technically understaffed. Until early 1953 it was Dutch-tutored under the Round Table Agreement both for purposes of training and in order to keep check on Indonesian activities. But to date no one has been able to persuade unneeded privates to lay down arms and go back to gainful pursuits. A few hundred have accepted land and returned to the soil; some have gone into trade schools; but the majority prefer army life to anything presently offered in civilian life.

Under the Sukiman cabinet, last before the present one, Sultan Hamengku Buwono IX became Minister of Defense with the understanding that he should have a free hand, within the law, in effecting security. Public opinion, peasant to highest official, seemed unanimous that he *could* achieve his end and at the same time build a better army, although opinion was divided as to whether he *should* make security the primary consideration. As soon as it became apparent that the Sultan was tightening control and intending to cut the 200,000-man army in half, powerful former guerrilla groups opposed the cut, fearing they might be weeded out in favor of Dutch-trained regulars. There appears no doubt but that anti-Sultan opposition crystallized under communist direction. On October 16, 1952, a majority of parliament passed a motion which in effect registered them as against reduction of the oversized army. From the record it appears that many parliamentary votes were traded, non-communists promising support of the anti-Sultan measure in exchange for communist support on other matters. The next day a group of high pro-Sultan army officers petitioned the President to dissolve the unrepresentative parliament, while at the same time mass demonstrations in behalf of dissolving parliament broke out in Djakarta. The demonstrators were dispersed and martial law and a curfew operated for some days. Some of the blame for the demonstration was laid at the door of pro-Sultan army officers who felt that it was time for a showdown as to whether the Minister of Defense and loyal Republican generals or the forces of insurrection ran the army.

The next day a subordinate officer ousted the commander of his division and sent President Soekarno an ultimatum that the army officers and civilian leaders who staged the demonstration in the capital must be prosecuted. In all, three of the army's seven divisions were seized by subordinate officers opposed to their chiefs and to the Sultan. For a time the cabinet and President stood their ground behind the Minister of Defense, but ultimately the desire to be approved by the *in* commanders of the army, however they got there, proved stronger than loyalty to the Sultan. Then the Sultan resigned his cabinet post. Since that time security has worsened rapidly, while popular conviction has increased that the government is not strong enough to do anything effective in behalf of security. "If the Sultan couldn't bring order, nobody can," is the general kismet attitude.

This widespread respect for the Sultan—almost any sultan

but particularly this sultan—is only understood in relation to Indonesia's traditional class structure: sultans and rajahs at the top, peasants and manual laborers at the bottom. One of the great responsibilities of the new government is the task of leading a class-conscious society in the paths of democracy. It is one thing for all people to be equal before the law but another to make them appear equal in their own eyes.

I asked many government officials about the present position of the sultans but the answer was always that nobody knows exactly. There are some 300 of them and currently grants in money are continued, direct or indirect, until some over-all plan is worked out. Probably no one in Java, excepting the President and vice-president, is more influential than Hamengku Buwono IX, Sultan of Djogjakarta. (The name of this important old city is written indiscriminately on various official signs as Jogka, Jokja, Jocja, Djogja, Djok-jakarta—*karta* meaning city—indicating Javanese, Hindu, Arabic and modern Indonesian influence.) It lies on the south-central coast some twenty miles inland and has a population approximating half a million persons. During the Hindu era, Djogja was the capital of the dominating kingdom and has always been the cultural center of Java. It is a conservative city: most men wear sarongs with the striped cotton coats of an earlier day; high-sided carts with brightly stenciled patterns are pulled by oxen; small phaetons with side seats jostle in and out among the bicycles. A newcomer feels that he has stepped into a previous century. From Djogja the influence of tradition travels out on invisible waves to the farthest corner of Java, all the more powerful because the new university, Gadja Mada, stands as proof that the spirit of progress runs hand in hand with precedent. Another reason for Djogja's influence is the presence of the Sultan.

The Sultan of Djogja is a quiet personable man in his early forties, medium in height, square of shoulder, with a direct gaze, a slow smile and an air of authority. But he wears his authority lightly, which is a significant factor where the common people respond with profound respect to authority which they feel to be intrinsic and historic. He is democratic, both by training and conviction. His father decided that his sons must have a thorough Western education, and so at the age of five they were sent to live with Dutch families, which they did not care for, coming back to the Kraton—the walled palace—for vacations, which they loved. One day I asked the Sultan's brother, Mr. Bintoro, now ambassador to Siam, how many brothers he had; he thought for some moments and then answered that there were thirty-one boys, explaining that his father died young, at thirty-nine, so their family was small.

The present Sultan spent ten years in Holland studying political science, in which he has his B.A. degree, living simply, having no great amount of money to spend, learning a lot more about government and democracy than came in texts. When the war broke he returned to Java and upon his father's death took up his responsibilities as best he could under Japanese occupation. The Japanese treated him with respect, allowing him to keep his own soldiers, who were merely a bodyguard armed with guns used in the French and German war, able to shoot four shots without reloading. Even without armed authority, however, he was the only man in Java who seemed able to protest effectively against forced labor and atrocities. At the close of the war the Japanese of that area insisted upon surrendering to him personally, handing over the entire garrison minus two officers who committed hara-kiri as their military car drew up to the Kraton gate.

One of the Sultan's friends told me that during the Second Police Action when the Dutch were desperate for the cooperation of Indonesian civil servants, the Netherlands Commander in Chief, General Spoor, requested an interview with the Sultan, ostensibly to protest the participation of the Sultan's guard in "protection" of the city. The Sultan returned word that it was not customary for his soldiers to act without his orders and he had given no such order—which was no doubt true but he could scarcely have been unaware of their participation in the fighting. The press, and therefore presumably the Sultan since most of the press were sympathetic to the Indonesian cause, also knew that General Spoor was prepared to offer the Sultan the position of head of a new state to consist of his entire section of Java and to be incorporated into the federation they were then forming. The Sultan refused an interview. So the General sent word that he would enter the Kraton in a tank, a thing he must have been too intelligent actually to attempt if he ever hoped to make peace with the people. Rather than add to the bloodshed the Sultan sent word he would grant a ten-minute interview. This friend who was present on that memorable occasion told me that the Sultan kept the General waiting, then appeared in casual dress without a coat, and instead of debating cooperation stated that there was only one topic open for discussion, namely, the time of the departure of the Dutch troops from Djogjakarta. At the end of the ten minutes, with no further amenities, he turned and left the room. Even in their extremity, the Dutch never attempted imprisoning him. The President and his ministers, yes, but the Sultan, hardly!

The Sultan has only one wife, a quiet charming woman. She is not the Sultana and the marriage is not official in the sense of being the partnership of "royalty" of equal rank, for while she is a granddaughter of the Sultan's own grand-father, her maternal grandmother was not equal in rank to his grandmother. There are not many available choices of his rank. The Sultan's children go to public school. When President Soekarno lived in Djogja, his children went to a private school. Significant is the often-heard comment, "If the Sultan's children could go to public school, why not the President's?" The Sultan drives his own car and makes no fuss about changing a tire. Neither does he demand a low license number, as people also point out. The neighborhood abounds in stories of his democratic dealings with his fellow citizens. For instance, a friend of his told me that one afternoon when the Sultan was driving in the country he met an old woman staggering under a heavy load of grass; he stopped, lifted the grass into the back of his car, offering to take her to her village. Not knowing who he was she flew at him for a robber of the common people but finally got into the car in order to keep her eyes on her grass. When he deposited both woman and grass at her village all the neighbors fell on their faces before him while she, overwhelmed by the honor done her, almost dashed out her brains against the stones at his feet.

Happily, we were invited to the Kraton. Inside the main gate guards wearing the traditional Javanese dress walk in bare feet or sit immovable on the ground with tall wooden spears beside them; the spears are good for exactly nothing, of course, but guards have sat in that position holding spears for generations. Covered passageways lead from courtyard to courtyard. Life-size statuary, Chinese blue tables, enormous vases of fine old porcelain, brass braziers, French mirrors and clocks, gorgeous chandeliers, caribou tusks, the instruments of the gamelan, pictures of past sultans and their consorts—

a priceless array of presents to and from past potentates ornament the halls and courtyards. In an open alcove can be seen the bed of Devi Sri, a goddess, with incense and a little coconut oil lamp always burning before it as these lamps have burned for more than 200 years without being extinguished. The present sultan, ninth in his family line, is a Moslem but his earlier ancestors were Hindus and the customs of the ancestors prevail.

Beyond the dining pavilion with its floor of patterned tile and its stained-glass frieze are the women's quarters where the female relatives and dancers—some 300 in number— are quartered. The Sultan is the only male privileged to enter. Wild cocks, deep gray, with damascene wings, vermilion cheeks and egrets for topknots, are kept in lantern cages to waken the household with their musical crowing. Elaborately carved dragons with intertwined tails guard the spirit walls; enormous doors with huge padlocks of brass close off the courtyards at night. Menservants approach the Sultan in the half-crouching position required by custom. His cigarettes and tea are carried to his office on a silver tray held head-high, a great yellow umbrella of state over all. Under a giant *waringen* tree guards are changed on the hour. A measure of the Sultan's prestige stems from the fact that he makes no unnecessary changes in the amenities, a conservatism which has enabled him to carry with him into the new day the cooperation of large numbers of the old aristocracy who might otherwise have proved recalcitrant.

But the pattern of aristocracy is definitely changing, partially from legal curtailment with loss of taxes and prerogatives and partially from the encroachment of modern education into the ranks of the young princes and princesses themselves. The Rajah of Karangasem in Bali, for instance, a young man scarcely thirty, educated in Java, is an ardent nationalist, interested in economic reform. His father, a personable and active gentlemen in his mid-sixties, wearing an emerald as large as a dime on his first finger, has stepped aside for his son and the new ways. The father explained to me gravely that he preferred his summer palace, his quiet wives, and his interest in the land, all of which escape the turmoil of the new day.

In Bali sons and daughters of the rajahs are among the more vocal and volatile political leftists even though it is their own privilege they are abolishing. However, in them one sees the battle of their proud inheritance against their new convictions, for at one moment they may be addressing their inferiors in the common tongue of the Republic, *bahasa Indonesia,* to prove the political equality of all people; but in the next moment their eyes may flash when an acquaintance of lesser rank, falling into Balinese speech, presumes to forget the special form of address due the highest caste. These days the aristocracy may not be consistent, but to minimize their influence just because they have lost their authority to tax and decree is entirely to miss the tenacity of custom and its saving cohesive power in a society precipitated into independence.

At the other end of the social scale are the vast majority of the people, the unskilled workers. Among them servants are not a class in themselves, since they are recruited from farm and village life, but are an important occupational group, third in number after farm and factory workers. It is among them that one finds the greatest class consciousness. One day I asked our pretty maid, Eda, who liked to dress up and go out with her husband, why she did not pleat the front of her new batik *kain.* She gave me a worried look. "Only *njonjas* [ladies] do that."

So many foreigners owe so much to Indonesian servants. Westerners seldom understand them and their gentle sunny ways; their penchant for sudden taking off without warning or good-by after years of generous treatment (more, perhaps, to save argument and emotion than with any intent to deceive); their proud adolescent insistence on all the privileges of the new day plus all the security of the old; their longing to improve their status alongside their acceptance of inferiority; their dependence upon routine and their casually diverted attenion, their easily hurt feelings and at the same time their almost grateful appreciation for a good round scolding. No more do the Indonesian servants understand Westerners and their persnickety notions about germs and food, their big faces betraying every emotion, their public caresses, their predilection for alcohol, their rushing off in all directions, their shouting for emphasis, their condescending kindness. The wonder is that the impact of our cultures upon each other all within the intimacy of a household produces a fairly satisfactory life for all concerned.

For the white-collar group the standards in dress and social life remain inordinately high in relation to the salary scale. That is, teachers, government workers, office staff and the like are expected to live in real houses along the good streets rather than in kampongs; to dress well, including shoes, which even well-to-do farmers need not bother about; to observe the social amenities of semi-Westernized life. The common people look up to men and women of education especially if they have government positions, a respect which is part of the feudal heritage. And in order to maintain their position, white-collar groups effect their economies behind scenes, which often includes cutting the food budget below any standard of nutritional health. There is a kind of valiancy in the expanding middle class which merits more than psychological respect. If the government put the same energy into raising teachers' salaries which is put into political rivalry, the middle class could provide the stability without which no democracy can long endure.

If making and administering laws conducive to the liberty and well-being of the Indonesian people were all the new government had to do, the task would have been—and would be—much simpler than it is. But there are also millions of non-Indonesians who make Indonesia their home. Before World War II there were nearly a quarter of a million Dutch in Indonesia. At present there are around 45,000 in Djakarta and another 80,000 in the rest of the country, roughly 16 per cent of whom have become Indonesian citizens. They own the department stores, the best jewelry stores, the best hotels, manage all sorts of import-export business, and still man many of the important government posts.

Almost apologetically they say to a newcomer, "Before the war Java was like heaven," but Java is not like heaven for them now. To live continually on guard is a psychological strain on the stoutest natures. They also live at a lower economic standard than formerly; they dress simply; their food is prosaic and meager; few outside of government positions can afford cars. During the war their record players, records, books, fine furniture and objets d'art, often a lifetime's collection, disappeared. All over the country Dutch families are living gallantly on almost nothing. All in all, it is no wonder that the Dutch migration to Australia and New Zealand has taken on proportions.

The problem of the Dutch is exemplified in the case of neighbors of ours in Bandung, particularly valiant and generous people, who had lived in Java for 25 years, had been interned during the war, and after their release had started a furniture business which soon boomed. But security constantly lessened and when a truckload of furniture started for Djakarta there was never any knowing whether it would get there. At the factory workers turned out less work, demanded higher pay plus the innumerable Indonesian holidays, quit without notice. Then electricity was turned off during the dry season so that the factory periodically had to close. In their own home they were robbed three times in a month, the last time by robbers using a Stamm gun to back them against the wall. Shortly afterward a brother-in-law was killed for no ostensible reason other than that he was Dutch. They decided to sell the business and follow thousands of other Dutch families—where? In Holland the winters are too harsh after the tropics and work too scarce. No place in Europe would there be any certainty of a job; in the United States living costs are out of reach even if the quota permitted entrance. They decided on Australia. Money was transferred, housing found in Perth, but they were refused entrance on the practical grounds that they had no children and did not wish to do manual labor. For similar reasons New Zealand was out. After a year's persistent effort they returned to Holland where they have built a houseboat. Their difficulties are representative of thousands of Dutch forced by events and public opinion out of Indonesia. So the trek of the Dutch continues, some of them so glad to get away that they scarcely care where they go but most of them sad to leave, for the warmth of life in Indonesia and friendship for Indonesian people are in their blood.

In all colonial dependencies, and of course in some democracies, "half-caste" is a term synonymous with "problem." The Dutch were much more open-minded than some colonial powers toward their dark-skinned wards, but equality would be too strong a word. The present predicament of the Indo-Dutch is only one aspect of the whole outmoded business of racial superiority, a kind of nightmare game in which everyone must play but only those with feathers sprouting from their elbows—or maybe the accident of white skin—can sit at the table.

Indo-Dutch in Indonesia are estimated to exceed 100,000. Some authorities hold that 65 per cent of the prewar European population of 250,000 was Indo-Dutch. Before Dutch law, a half-caste child takes the citizenship of the father, unless he prefers otherwise, so that thousands of Indos consider themselves Dutch and by inheritance, custom, home training, education, language, and service in the Netherlands Army, they are Dutch. As Dutch citizens a limited number of them are moving permanently to Holland but the Netherlands government discourages anything approaching mass migration because of job shortages. Therefore most of them have taken Indonesian citizenship and are settling into the economy of the new Republic.

The origin of the half-castes in Indonesia is a facet of colonial history. In the early days, few white women came out from Europe; living conditions were far more hazardous in the tropics then; travel was difficult and costly. Most of the women who came were the wives of government officials. Traders, soldiers and lesser officials had no white womenfolk and so they married native women with varying time-clause reservations. The liaison often became a permanent marriage, or when a man moved to another post he might pay his mistress amply so that she could make a very good marriage among her own people. Her social standing was seldom affected adversely; indeed there was a glamour about her for having been chosen by a white man. Children of such unions grew up in the desa but as adults frequently had prestige as partial members of the dominant culture group.

Prewar the situation had already changed greatly. Dutch officials and businessmen either brought their own wives or came ahead to establish themselves and then sent home for their glove-brides. However, the countryside still bristles with romantic tales of Indonesian girls who grew to love their Dutch husbands and to understand and enjoy the Dutch way of living, only to find themselves suddenly cast off. Tales, too, of Dutch brides coming from Holland to find that the persistent "cook" who came each day demanding her job back was in reality her husband's concubine. A few sensitive Dutch women adopted a half-caste son or daughter into their own homes.

Generally speaking, Dutch-Indonesian half-castes are fine-looking, tending to be tall and broad-shouldered like the Dutch but having the slender limbs and waists of the Indonesians; most have dark brown hair and brown eyes but occasionally one meets a very blond sister or brother among siblings of darker shade. Half-castes are said to be less strong physically than "pure" Europeans, more liable to succumb to epidemics.

In the old days many went to Holland for their education, an estimated 5 per cent rose to high postions, some 25 to 30 per cent became minor officials and the rest held menial jobs. Nowadays the picture has changed and the relationship between the Indo-Dutch and the Holland-Dutch is less strained, for in business and government positions the former often outrank the latter. However the Indo-Dutch are often by-passed in business and government by less well-trained Indonesians, although they are usually accepted as equals socially, especially in the capital city, and are often looked up to because of their superior training and indeed often *because* of their despised Dutch blood. A great many Indonesians still operate under this schizophrenic attitude; when they learn to relax and accept the fact that neither mastering nor being mastered denotes superiority or inferiority, they will have a smoother time. Social anthropology would be a wonderful study for the Indonesian school system, beginning in the grades.

The Chinese in Indonesia have a long history. From the earliest days of Dutch domination they were encouraged to settle in the country. The first governor of the Indies, J. P. Coen, wrote, "There is no people in the world which serves us better than the Chinese; too many of them cannot be brought to Batavia." Indeed, he urged his successor to send a fleet to China to capture as many Chinese as possible for export to the Indies. They became intermediaries for the company, gathering native produce, often squeezing the farmers in the country while practicing usury in the towns. The natives looked on them as part of officialdom, for in the early day various monopolies were delegated to them, such as the right to levy bazaar fees, to collect road tolls and customs, and to sell salt. It was through these monopolies, particularly the right to tax bazaars, that their long-time control of the rice trade took shape. Whole villages were leased to them. In the eighteenth century on the north coast of Java, 1,134 villages out of a total of 16,000 in all Java were leased to Chinese who became overlords with approximately the same position as regents. In 1860 there were 221,-000 Chinese; now there are about 3,000,000. Primarily they live in the large coastal cities, well entrenched, still acting as middlemen for rice and home-woven textiles. Roughly one-third are in commerce, largely traders and shopkeepers; one-third farmers and fishermen; one-third in industry, particularly in woodworking and preparation of foodstuffs, primarily rice milling.

The Chinese prosper because they work. Family ties are very strong. Corollary to being bound to common ancestors they are bound to common achievements. Besides outworking most of their contemporaries they can outbargain them all. An explanation for their drive may lie in the fact that the Chinese in Indonesia are descendants of those hardy pioneers who had the gumption to leave home in search of better livelihood. They maintain their customary respect for education. Prewar at least a quarter of them were literate and the proportion is growing rapidly as schools become more numerous. There is no Chinese college and European and American education is extremely expensive, but in communist China college education is cheap. A deposit with the Chinese Peoples' Government of R. 5,000 (around $450) entitles a student to four years in college and the number of Chinese boys yearly going to China for higher education now runs into the hundreds.

It is noteworthy that the Chinese give money in support of their schools, churches and hospitals. The idea of private giving for the endowment of private institutions is not widespread in Indonesia. Practically all schools and hospitals, except those supported by the Dutch, the Chinese or under Christian auspices, are subsidized by the government. Except for some of the larger Dutch and European business organizations, the Chinese are the largest source of income for welfare drives and popular institutions. Indonesians tend to be a bit scornful of Chinese donations, saying that after all the Chinese have the money and why shouldn't they give it, or accusing the Chinese of buying good will. No doubt these factors operate but they do not entirely explain away Chinese participation in public enterprises.

In the matter of citizenship, most Chinese think of themselves first as Chinese, strong in their traditional loyalty toward their homeland. But his homeland to a Chinese is more a matter of his home village, the locality of his ancestors, than of his whole country. Moreover, he thinks in terms of generations. Where an American speaks glibly of moving his home, a Chinese moves only his family. Wherever he lives he has as little to do with "the government" as possible, for in his traditional philosophy a good government is an inconspicuous government; Confucius said it. His village to a Chinese is more or less a family affair, self-sustaining and democratic, so that dependence upon a regional or national government is nominal. All of this tradition is in the back of the Chinese mind as he orients himself in Indonesia. He or his forebears came to Indonesia for one reason—to better the family fortunes. As his economic position improves he sends more money, *sub rosa* if necessary, back to his clan or sends for more members of the clan to come to him. Being a very practical creature he is a master at accepting the status quo, enjoying himself where he is, accepting his share of responsibility for community well-being. Often he marries an Indonesian wife and his children seem to adapt easily to two sets of traditions. In a peculiar way he is a citizen of two cultures.

Nowadays, however, a third element complicates his dual loyalty. Which Chinese government represents his homeland? Should he give his allegiance to the Chinese People's Republic because it is the functioning government in his home-land, or should he remain loyal to China's leaders in exile on Formosa? Thousands of Chinese in Indonesia never had experience with either political democracy or with communism. It is doubtful if a dozen Chinese in all Indonesia have ever voted in a national election anywhere. So their loyalties are determined either on the basis of their knowledge about democracy and communism in other countries or by emotional loyalty to the position of their clan back in China. Thus most Chinese acquire a point of view but few have anything so strong as a conviction, except among the newly indoctrinated communists, who are indeed vehement in their new loyalty, or among the well educated, who understand the philosophy of democracy and take a stand in its behalf. Because the mill-run Chinese are *pro* whatever stands as a national symbol, it is important to the democracies that a non-communist symbol, such as the government in Formosa, be maintained if the 20,000,000 overseas Chinese in Southeast Asia are to remain non-communist. It is just as important that they experience democracy in the country to which they have migrated, as, for example, Indonesia. When the Indonesian government recently demanded that foreigners register their foreign citizenship or automatically become Indonesian citizens, most Chinese became Indonesian citizens. To be sure, they had something to gain in so doing, for as citizens they can own property and develop businesses without making a place for other Indonesian capital, and besides they no doubt realize that they can reclaim their Chinese citizenship any time they wish to relinquish their Indonesian investments and go home. But most became citizens, as they frankly say, because they *are* citizens. Indonesia *is* their home.

Politically the strength of the Chinese in Indonesia is growing. There are several Chinese delegates in parliament, not as representatives of the Chinese bloc but scattered throughout the various political parties; one Chinese is in the cabinet. In the government in general, however, there are few Chinese in posts of distinction. Repeatedly, well-trained Chinese are demoted in favor of much less efficient Indonesians although both are citizens. This sort of discrimination breeds bitterness, for the Chinese feel that they are as "Indonesian" as the Polynesians, Melanesians, or any other of the racial strains which make up the country. Moreover, they have a contribution to make for they are given to hospitality, quick and keen in business transactions, and have a gusty sense of humor. Their loyalty is proverbial. If their assimilation into Indonesia's national life can be speeded, everybody concerned stands to profit.

The Indonesian government estimates about 80,000 Arabs in the country, most of them now Indonesian citizens, living largely in Java and Madura. A high percentage are traders, dealing principally in textiles and a mixed retail business. Some are in agriculture, some in food preparation, in tailoring, in road traffic. As fellow Moslems they are pro-Indonesian in foreign relations and hence inclined to be anti-Dutch, or at least anti-colonial powers and the British-Arabian tension carries over into their political attitude. Because of their ardent Moslem affiliation they are also anti-communist, but that fact does not make them pro-Western democracy.

There are no current figures on the number of Indians in Indonesia but they probably approximate 30,000. Although India exerts a great influence on Indonesia, the Indians within Indonesia have no particular influence on public affairs. The more affluent among them are in the textile business, as is true all over Southeast Asia, importing the fine silks and prints of Europe and the Near East for the wealthier strata, and at the same time offering cheaper cottons, rayons and silk substitutes to the less well-to-do. They tend to remain self-contained and are certainly oriented toward their homeland no matter how long they may have lived abroad. On the whole they are a literate group, often well educated. Being ardent nationalists, all, they tend to follow Pandit Nehru's rather mercurial lead; hence it is hard to say whether they are pro-democratic or pro-communist. They are law-abiding, do not fraternize overmuch, and although they make as much money as the Chinese in their particular businesses, still the Indonesians do not seem to resent their encroachment. They are in Indonesia but not of Indonesia.

The Japanese have been slow in returning. A handful never left. Usually acting as chauffeurs for Chinese families, their identity is lost in the Oriental shuffle. They are of course known to the people of their own locality who take them as individuals rather than as representatives of yesterday's enemy. Although the Japanese are still unpopular, nevertheless everyone appears to take it for granted that they will return and that no country is more important to Indonesia's future than Japan.

Europeans include a varied group. In Djakarta there are somewhere around 700 Britishers; in the whole country an estimated 2,000. They are not a dominant influence in Indonesian life although they have figured at important points in history. Economically their interests have suffered in recent years. There are some Hungarians in Java's larger cities and they furnish some of the best Western music for many excellent musicians, caught in Java when the war broke, were unable to return home afterward. These days they carry their trouble double because living is so much more expensive and because of constant worry about their families in Hungary. A few Germans remain and more are likely to come since diplomatic relations and trade pacts with West Germany point the way to freer exchanges. In Djakarta there are also small groups of almost every other nationality, a total of almost 50,000 foreign residents. No breakdown is available for the rest of the country.

There are also around 1100 Americans in Indonesia. Some 800 are businessmen and their families, a few are missionaries and their families, and embassy personnel and workers for foreign aid programs account for the remainder. The American foreign aid program, currently known as Foreign Operations Administration, is concerned largely with giving American technical and medical aid, including provision for training leaders in the United States. Around 150 Indonesians are now coming annually for study and travel in the United States. Fields of interest are a commentary upon Indonesia's needs and American-Indonesian relations: animal feeding and breeding, cooperatives, horticulture, land tenure, agricultural statistics, farm machinery use and operation and maintenance, rural credit, medicine, industrial vocations, chemistry, audio-visual aids, highway transportation, credit unions, trade union operation, labor-management relations, labor administration, public services administration, plus several branches of education. The yeasty relationship between Indonesia and the United States is part of the overall spread of training in democracy.

But the development of democracy cannot go much further until the people learn communication of ideas through the written word. A modern government is an impossibility for an illiterate nation. It may be a bit tough to learn to read on the run, but that is Indonesia's predicament and task.

.7.

A Nation at School

THE DRIVE FOR EDUCATION MARKS NOT only Indonesia's leaders but most of the rank and file. The young are caught in a contagion of wanting to learn and the middle-aged feel they have been cheated of their birthright. On the latter point someone was always offering us statistics. In the last year of Dutch domination, 1941, only one child in ten had a chance to go to school and most of them did not get to attend long enough to learn to read a newspaper; a few thousand reached the junior middle schools and vocational schools and a much smaller number the senior middle schools and universities. But after five years of independence, some 6,000,000 of the 32,000,000 children under fifteen were in elementary schools, close to 200,000 in the middle schools, around 10,000 in the universities, and some 25,000 in various teacher training courses. The pivotal problem is of course the training of teachers. A considerable number of those now teaching have only an elementary school background augmented by short normal school courses.

Not many countries have to inaugurate their educational system by first inventing a language for instruction, but under the Dutch regime the Indies lacked a national language. Regional languages were used in the village primary schools and above that the teaching was in Dutch, logical enough since most of the pupils allowed to go on were Dutch. Indonesian pupils were naturally expected to learn the language in which European culture was available, and so today practically all educated Indonesians past thirty think in Dutch. Even in official gatherings where proceedings are conducted in Indonesian, a speaker who wants to drive home his point will turn to Dutch unless there is a ruling against its use. Only children who have started school since the Republic came into being are able to speak the same language at home, in their schools, and in general community life.

In the old days, although none of the regional languages, such as Javanese, Sundanese, Balinese and the like, had wide use geographically, there was one lingual common denominator by means of which people of different areas could exchange ideas of a limited and concrete nature—an abbreviated form of Malay known as *pasar* or market Malay. Originally brought in from the Malay peninsula in the days of the old Malay conquerors, the Malay language was for some time the speech of the court and of trade, an adequate vehicle of culture and the *lingua franca* of most of the Indies. Long before the war it had dropped out of official usage, but the common people continued to use it in a vastly simplified form because it was the only means of inter-regional communication for those who knew no Dutch. In the early thirties, as the movement for independence gathered momentum and youth groups, patriotic organizations, poets, writers, teachers all demanded one flag and one language, the most feasible foundation for a common language seemed to be the ubiquitous Malay. In 1933 an Indonesian Language Congress declared Indonesian Malay to be the basis of a new national language, *bahasa Indonesia*. Scores of people, and after them hundreds, began to learn and use the new language, augmenting it at will. Soon magazines were published in it and ardent nationalists attempted to use it in public meetings. In spite of its difficulties it was spreading steadily when the war came.

Immediately the Japanese prohibited the speaking of Dutch, intending to enforce the use of Japanese throughout Southeast Asia as rapidly as was feasible, but in the interim promoting bahasa Indonesia as part of their drive for national unity. They made the new language compulsory in all schools and government offices; everybody in public life had to learn Indonesian; all directives of the conqueror were published in it. And since the Japanese penetrated even the remote villages, using Indonesian as they went, the language took swift hold. At the close of the war the Indonesian government made its use official for the entire Republic. A language commission began to shepherd the new language into form, realizing that too rigid a Malay pattern was not practical because Arabic, Dutch and regional words had already become coin of the realm; on the other hand, following the vernacular of the press and daily speech would foist an illogical hodgepodge upon the people. One of the immediate problems was the need to fix scientific terms, then specialized terms in other fields, then compilation of a grammar and a dictionary, both still in process of completion. Without intention the Dutch had previously made a great contribution in the common use of the Roman alphabet for teaching the regional languages. If they had remained in Arabic script progress would have been much slower.

Following independence, the first Ministry of Education had to decide whether to commence the use of the new national language in the first grade or to teach beginners in the regional languages. In spite of the passion for Indonesian, the decision went to the regional languages for the first three grades because primary school teachers were trained in these languages and many were still inept in bahasa Indonesia. By grade four, however, both teachers and students were expected to know enough Indonesian to effect a transfer. But at middle school level the problem was further complicated by lack of textbooks in Indonesian, so the government was in the predicament of trying to stamp out the use of Dutch while forced to use it in middle schools and universities. However, as fast as possible courses have been shifted into Indonesian, although teachers still tend to interject important explanations in the regional language or in Dutch. Textbooks in Indonesian are not yet adequate for the universities. Not too long ago, when patriotic college students in Bandung urged the teaching of certain courses in Indonesian, only two professors were able to comply; then at the end of a fortnight the students had to reverse their petition because they could not understand the lectures.

Everywhere we went, we found all schools crowded and all communities underschooled. In Djakarta we lived almost next door to an elementary school which could accommodate 200 students, sardine-fashion, and we watched that school fill and empty three times a day. There in the capital city the 150 elementary buildings operate twice as many "schools" and teachers average around 450 students a day. In the country, where buildings are smaller and teachers even fewer, I often found six "schools" a day; but everywhere enthusiasm and no discipline problems because the honor of being allowed to learn is still a distinction. There must be stupid children, but in the many classes I visited the youngsters seemed exceedingly quick on the pick-up; maybe the less bright are eliminated by the pressure of the scores waiting to take their places. I've never forgotten a button-bright

A terraced rice field in Java

Lake Toba, central Sumatra.
Terraced field to the left

Section of wall of the Borobudur, ancient
temple of Java, showing scenes from the
life of Buddha

Carved temple gateway, Bali

(Above left) President Soekarno (in dark suit) with Dr. Roem, statesman and minister in various cabinets. (Above right) Vice-president Hatta. (Left) Hadji Agus Salim, Grand Old Man of Indonesia, and Nonja Salim, en route to England to represent Indonesia at the Coronation of Queen Elizabeth II. (Below left) Soetan Sjahrir, head of the Socialist party, *formateur* of several cabinets. (Below right) Sultan Hamenku Buwono IX, Sultan of Djogja, several times member of cabinet

Wide World ↓ ↑ *Maurey Garber*

(Above left) Tapping the rubber tree. (Above right) Bringing the latex to the factory. (Right) A family of rubber tappers. (Below left) Rubber sheets before smoking. (Below right) Smoking sheets of rubber in drying house

(Above left) Picking young tea leaves. (Above right) Bringing tea leaves into the factory. (Left) Spreading tea leaves on racks to dry. (Below left) Sorting tea before packaging. (Below right) A tea worker's home

(Above) Fishermen of West Java. (Above right) Sorting peppers. (Right) Salt from the sea. (Below left) Palm oil tanks, North Sumatra; note men on scaffolding. (Below right) Salt worker, Madura

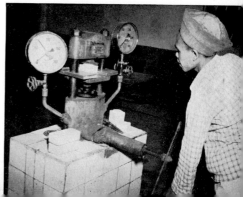

Mary Effendi Saleh, founder of the Mothers Schools, and her family

One of the Mothers Schools

Factory workers learning to read and write in their off hours

Home economics class

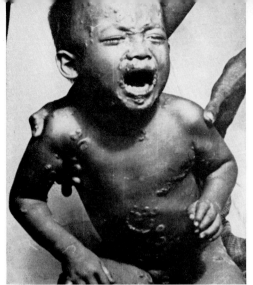
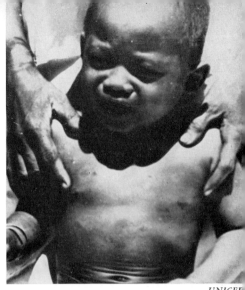

(Above left) A small boy with yaws, one of the million persons—most of them mothers and children—who have had penicillin through the United Nations International Children's Emergency Fund. (Above right) The same child two weeks later after one shot of penicillin. A fifteen-cent investment for health

(Right) Day nursery at a hygiene center. (Below left) A traveling clinic. (Below right) A modern children's ward in Central Hospital, Djakarta

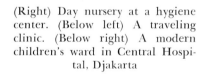

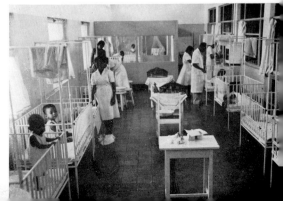

Legong dancers and attendant, Bali

Dahlia and Polak, dancers of Denpasar, Bali

Garuda dancer, Bali

Nontji dancer, from Menado,
Celebes

youngster of eight in Bali whose father came to see if I could use official American pressure to get the boy in school because he had already been on the waiting list for three years and was told it would be three more years before his turn came up.

Middle schools, corresponding to the American junior and senior high schools, usually offer three years each of standard work more or less after the Dutch pattern. Traditionally middle school students have been expected to learn French, German and English, as well as Dutch, to be able to read the literature, use the textbooks, and converse easily. Visiting schools in the outlying islands where middle school opportunities are at a premium, it seems little less than tragic to see so much time devoted to European languages when the average student will never travel abroad. However, since English has been made the second language of Indonesia in line with its currency in the rest of Southeast Asia, it is bound to receive increasing emphasis.

It seemed to me that the major problem of the middle schools—next to teacher shortage—was their need to turn out practical technicians and scientists in spite of having practically no equipment for teaching science. Maintenance of a 250 per cent import tax on laboratory equipment is only one of the instances in which ministries block each other's welfare, not so much intentionally as for lack of system and clearance. The first science classes we visited were in Singaraja, capital of Bali, where an excellent teacher, educated in Holland, was instructing his physics class in the use of quicksilver. But he had no quicksilver; he had no retorts, no crucibles, no metals, no acids. Fortunately he could draw very well and made blackboard sketches of his supposed experiments. He had one copy of a Dutch or English text which he had to translate day by day so that his students could learn their physics and chemistry by rote. We thought the situation peculiar to Bali and began writing home for aid, but it is the same everywhere except for an occasional school such as the Methodist English High School in Medan where there is one set of physics equipment which the professor uses at the one demonstration sink in the middle of a large amphitheater classroom. In time teachers will no doubt be able to improvise considerable equipment, as has been done in medical and pharmacy schools.

Recently the ministries of finance, public works, and education got their heads and budgets together and decided to set aside R. 25,000,000 to build additional schools, half the amount to be repaid to the Ministry of Education from funds raised locally after each building was completed. However, with local communities unaccustomed to financing education and with the general feeling of "let the government do it," the outlook for local support is not bright.

Compared with opportunities for higher education in neighboring countries, such as the Philippines, Indonesia makes a poor showing. Under the Dutch regime a technical college was established in Bandung in 1920, followed by faculties of medicine, dentistry and pharmacy, law, literature, philosophy and agriculture in Djakarta, Surabaja, and Bogor, all of the faculties together constituting the University of Indonesia. Practically all the professors were Dutch and they maintained high standards, so that courses were interchangeable with their counterparts in the Netherlands. Professor Supomo, president of the University, is one of the only two Indonesians appointed to a full university professorship under the Dutch. After the war the new government promptly reconstituted the universities, the faculties remaining predominantly Dutch but with Indonesian replacements effected as rapidly as possible. The student enrollment now runs around 6,500, most of the students older than their counterparts in Western countries because of the disrupted decade.

The technical branch of the University at Bandung has a 70-member faculty for 1,500 students, 10 per cent of whom are women. Dormitories under direction of an excellent Dutch dean are an innovation. Approximately two-thirds of the lower classmen never graduate, partly because of financial pressure but partly because the faculty is not free under *merdeka* to keep the entrance requirements as stiff as formerly and instead must weed out the weak students throughout the class year. The government absorbs practically all the graduates, many of whom go to Europe and America for graduate work.

There is also Gadja Mada University at Djogjakarta, named for the famed prime minister of the Majapahit empire—and rightly named I thought because it got under way during the worst of the Republic's struggle against the Dutch and obstacles have been its meat and drink. Currently some 3,500 students are still housed in a section of the Kraton, or Sultan's palace, but a modern complex of considerable proportion on a campus of 250 acres is under construction and a faculty of distinction and gumption maintains high standards against odds. I mean odds. Educated Indonesians seem determined that no one shall say they dropped their standards when they dropped the Dutch. The Academi Nasional in Djakarta also offers a variety of late afternoon and evening courses with university credit to some 700 students, many of them young government officials. Half our friends seemed to be teaching there, practically all on a part-time basis, for which they received only transport allowance. The medical school at Surabaya is again operating at full capacity and plans are laid for two additional medical schools. Colleges of law have opened at Macassar and Padang and announcement has been made of a projected cultural university which sounds like the extension division of an American state university.

Having an eye trained to the needs of educational institutions, I made notes on a few of the university problems which would ordinarily require a trained staff: standardizing the courses, assembling a qualified Indonesian faculty, finding foreign professors who speak Indonesian and training advanced students to understand lecture-English, importing laboratory equipment including biologicals, producing library facilities, procuring or composing textbooks, stemming the constant drain-off of professors to positions in the ministries, effecting prompt communication between administrators and the ministries upon whom they are dependent, providing student housing and health facilities. And the personnel for handling these matters has to be trained while the problems are being met. Foreign educators, who come gladly to lend a hand, almost lose their minds because basic decisions are delayed for months on protocol, because certain officials are jealous of their prerogatives, because red tape is deviously devised, Dutch fashion, and then circuitously snarled, Indonesian fashion. But through it all higher education mounts higher, spreads wider, and yearly caps its own goals.

Oddly there are no junior colleges. Some educators feel that the junior college might be a practical answer for certain sections of the country now clamoring for a university, since two-year courses in general education or two years of pre-professional work could be much more easily administered in the outlying areas than in crowded Djakarta, Surabaya and Bandung. At present there are several natural openings for junior colleges. For instance, in Padang, Sumatra, a fine beginning has been made on a school of law known as Pantjasila University—the university being a blueprint in the minds of hopeful sponsors. In all Indonesia there are only about 300 lawyers, five of whom decided to form a law faculty at Padang, giving their time without pay and dividing executive responsibilities, each quarter a different man acting as president and secretary. An excellent building was subscribed by private funds and immediately students enrolled for classes, which were offered in late afternoon and evening, the lectures in Dutch and German. At present students number around 150, about one-tenth of them girls. Some of Pantjasila's supporters feel it would be advantageous and not too difficult to augment this law faculty with professors in the social sciences and humanities, perhaps also in medicine, and from a secure beginning, a university might grow, especially if other sections of Sumatra also instituted junior colleges.

Foundations for junior colleges are also laid in the Methodist English schools at Medan and Palembang, each of which now enrolls more than 2,000 students and has a faculty approximating fifty teachers, with courses offered in English and bahasa Indonesia. In both schools classrooms are crowded and equipment limited but impressive by Indonesian standards, and the initiative of the students is apparent in their school magazine, public debates, assembly programs, choral societies, dramatic offerings, literacy campaigns and public services. Moreover there are other excellent middle schools in the same general areas which could contribute students, as for instance an Indian English middle school administered by Sikhs, and several government schools. To its distinction as the home of Indonesia's most famous mosque Medan might add the honor of sponsoring the first city-wide junior college.

In Bali there are now two senior middle schools, several junior middle schools and a normal school, but rarely can a student afford to go to Java for higher education. In 1951 a group including the wife of the resident general, Mrs. Bagus Oka, conceived the idea that senior middle school students and young teachers who knew theoretical English but never had opportunity for practice would profit from a week's seminar conducted entirely in English. So a government rest house was found on Lake Bedugul where some forty students and eight faculty members could be housed, the faculty consisting of two Indonesians, one Britisher, one Chinese, one Hindu, one Pakistani and two Americans—a Catholic priest and my husband from the American embassy—under the directorship of a distinguished Dutch educator, Mr. Jeff Last, and the sponsorship of Mrs. Oka. Several local organizations worked together to effect transportation, provide food, look after necessities, and a curriculum of lectures, discussion, recreation and music was set up, emphasizing the theme of international understanding. This seminar was also Bali's first experiment in recreation shared by boys and girls of marriageable age. Before the end of the week the students were full of plans to enlarge the group, lengthen the time, make the camp a permanent institution. At the second camp both President Soekarno and Dr. Mohamed Roem, one of Indonesia's most distinguished and exhilarating statesmen, were visitors, and now the Ministry of Education is patterning other camps after this venture in Bali.

But Mrs. Oka has set her sights higher. She was born a pioneer. In the Bali of the old day, meaning back in the early twenties, few girls went to school but this particular little girl, member of a high caste family, insisted upon going to school even though she had to learn Dutch. When she completed elementary school there was no higher school to attend, but her insistence on more education elicited the interest of a Dutch official who persuaded her father to let the child go "abroad" to Java to live with a Dutch family. There she remained until she completed her studies, after which she married a brilliant young Balinese who has since become governor of the Lesser Sundas, including Bali. Now at thirty-one Mrs. Oka is the mother of six sons. She has a great deal of official entertaining to do but she also teaches English in the Singaraja middle school, sponsors a woman's and children's clinic, and fosters the English camps. In 1953 she came to America on a leader's grant to observe rural education and to investigate the work-study plan of Berea College with an eye to adapting the plan to Bali's future junior college. Knowing little Mrs. Oka's spirit I figure the Ministry of Education had just as well start budgeting.

Nobody seems to know the number of schools supported by private funds and administered independent of government control because many are not registered; but among them are some thirty-odd Dutch schools known as Concordant schools, signifying that their courses are synchronized with schools of corresponding grade in Holland, and around a thousand Chinese schools, most of them elementary schools. Among their 250,000 students 75 per cent are Chinese. Recently a Chinese educational foundation in Malang, central Java, announced the immediate construction of a 25-classroom middle school for 1,500 students, to cost R. 1,000,000.

Throughout the villages there are unnumbered private Moslem schools, taught by the *kiajis,* where children learn the Koran by rote and are indoctrinated with Moslem law and moral and social principles. Most educators seem to feel that in the hands of an enlightened kiaji such a school is a community asset, but the majority of kiajis are not well educated. We heard some ardent arguments between modern and conservative Moslems over the compulsory use of mosques for schools, utilizing the time between prayer periods when the buildings stand empty, and over the policy of compelling kiajis to teach modern subjects in a modern manner, as has been done in Turkey. There are some modern religious schools called Madrasah (Arabic for school), organized by Moslem associations, teaching modern subject matter firmly rooted in Moslem religious principles.

The famous Taman Siswa schools are less religious than nationalistic. Begun in 1921 by Ki Hadjar Dewantara, formerly known as Soewardi, shortly after he returned from political exile, they have consistently sought to further a curriculum which combines the best of Eastern and Western cultures in a practical manner. Prewar there were some 200 of these schools, not overtly promoting revolution but certainly instilling the principles of nationalism. In Djakarta alone there are now at least half a dozen Siswa schools with close to 4,000 students. Although they have government subsidy, they are privately directed and their aim of giving freedom content is emphasized in terms of self-help, self-determination, self-confidence and self-reliance.

Perhaps the most famous of Indonesia's private schools is Mohammad Sjafei's school near Bukittinggi in the mountains above Pandang. Mr. Sjafei had a distinguished part in the national struggle for independence and after the war was Minister of Education in Sjahrir's second cabinet; later he was elected to parliament but has not served because of his responsibility for his 350 students. On his own initiative he arrived at the modern conception of general education, grounding the students in the four basic fields of the physical and biological sciences, social science and the humanities, with special emphasis on the fine arts and with ardent student participation in an orchestra, dramatics, sculpture, painting and some of the crafts. Dr. Sjafei knows his students individually and helps to plan their advanced study, often abroad. The problem of government subsidy for such private schools is complicated in Indonesia, as everywhere. All schools need encouragement, but where public funds are invested the government has a natural desire and some responsibility to dictate procedures.

One great advantage Indonesia has over most of Asia is coeducation. Before the beginning of the twentieth century a few country girls had entered village primary schools, but if daughters of the aristocracy received any education they got it within the walls of their own homes. Credit for opening the way for the modern education of women goes to Raden Adjeng Kartini, a little princess with a lively and curious mind, born in 1879 into the family of the Regent of Djepara in Central Java. When *adat* (custom) decreed that she give up her schooling at the age of eleven and remain within the "box," as the walls of the palace are called, she set herself to learn Dutch adequate to acquiring her own education. The help and understanding of influential Dutch friends and an unusual *approchement* with her father cushioned the hard years of her "imprisonment" in spite of her father's being custom-bound and philosophically perturbed. Her voluminous correspondence with friends in Holland depicts the circumscribed life of a girl of her day. Handed from father to husband, hedged by a thousand polite restrictions, as ignorant of physiology as of foreign affairs but expected to function as family nurse as well as hostess to diplomats, the aristocratic daughter of a high-born house led a curtailed life.

Finally Kartini and her two sisters opened a school for upper class girls in their own home. In 1903 she was married to the Regent of Rembang, who assisted her in opening another school in her new home, but a year later she died at the birth of her son. When her letters were published her spirit and ideas began to spread and in 1912 a school for girls was subscribed in her memory. Now at the mid-century mark her birthday, April 21, is celebrated all over the archipelago, and most educational institutions are open to women. Throughout the countryside as well as along the city streets, little girls traipse off to school with their brothers and the middle schools are available to girls and boys alike, although boys predominate. This freedom between the boys and girls is a heartening sight in Asia. I certainly thought of Kartini when I visited the excellent normal school for domestic science teachers in Macassar and again in the same city when visiting a school where ever-so-young married women learn the three R's they never had a chance to learn earlier.

Impetus has been given to the development of vocational schools by the need for demobilizing large numbers of soldiers, including some 15,000 in the former student army. For most vocational schools six years of elementary schooling are prerequisite. Advanced government vocational schools in operation or prospect admit students after ten years of schooling to a two-year technical college course in commerce, business administration, home economics, laboratory techniques, meteorology, geophysics, instrument making, glass blowing, inspection of weights and measures, tailoring, book-keeping, radio mechanics, sheet metal work, navigation, aviation. Every one of these fields needs a sizable group of trained men and women. For instance, the geological service alone could use 100 experts who would need 25 years to make a complete survey of the country's mineral resources.

Some foreign enterprises, such as the Dutch-owned Borneo-Sumatra Trading Company and BPM, largest of the Dutch oil companies, offer training facilities. When I was in Balik-papan, Borneo, the BPM grade school was housed in a fine new building with 700 children of BPM employees enrolled in the first four grades and two grades to be added; ten teachers had been brought from Java and were paid almost double the government rate; in the classrooms there were actually maps on the walls. This school fed a technical school, which consisted of one year of class work followed by two years of supervised shopwork, after which the student was given a three-month general tryout and then assigned to a department. Procter & Gamble and some other firms send promising employees to America. Caltex and Stanvac have excellent training programs.

In all some 200 Indonesians are brought to America each year, more than to any other country except Holland; what they take back in the way of special training in education and technical subjects is important but their general impressions are perhaps even more significant. Almost all of them mention first how hard the American people work; having thought of Americans as rich they also thought of them as taking life easy. Most of them return home weighing more than when they left, in excellent health, and overwhelmed by the excellence of the food—even though they are often hungry for rice and their good Indonesian dishes. They are unfailingly impressed by the responsibilities carried by women in business and family life, in politics and social welfare. They are struck by the extent of welfare and medical services. Even more impressive than the number and quality of the schools is the unpaid unstinted work of the Parent-Teacher Association. The wide use of radio and television is a new experience. No matter how much they may have heard about the high standard of living, they are amazed by the number of cars and even more amazed to see ordinary workmen, black and white, going to work in their own automobiles. The fact that white as well as black perform manual labor and that they work side by side is more notable than the fact that they frequently study in the same universities. Although some Indonesians have rather tough Jim Crow experiences one way and another, most of them are surprised —after the communist propaganda they have had—to find such good race relations and are heartened by the rapidity of improvement. Those who were in America during the last national election were flabbergasted to see pre-election animosities change into national good will and more or less friendly cooperation the day after election; some of them expected riots when the count came in. San Francisco gets the majority vote as the country's most interesting city.

On the adverse side they are surprised by the lack of leisure in the sense of time to sit in the garden and enjoy nature, to drink coffee with friends, to listen to music without talking, just to sit and think; also by the ignorance of the average American about world affairs. Where at home they expect only the educated "upper class" to be world-minded, here they expect world mindedness to be a by-product of a high level of education. They are amazed to find the average newspaper presenting little information about the work of the United Nations. Currently the loss of civil rights evidenced in Senate hearings and special committee investigations gives them grave concern and their reports back home are snapped up by the communists as proof of democracy's decadence.

Fortunately they usually add a strong word about the political and economic freedom of the American people, the way business leads the way in pioneering ventures, the way money can be moved freely from one enterprise to another, one state to another, and off to any part of the world where its owner wishes to put it to work—an impressive state of affairs after their own difficulty in getting a very small amount of money out of their country.

Back home again, the influence of the trainees is probably greatest on the young adults. Peasants and working people past forty who have never had an opportunity to go to school do not think in terms of political and economic trends and are not concerned with the state of literature, philosophy, psychology and the social studies. But the twenty- to thirty-five-year-old people are eager and determined. Among them the will to learn is strongest. They are the proponents and beneficiaries of the mass education movement.

When Dr. Frank Laubach, specialist in problems of illiteracy all around the world, was in Java he told us that Indonesia had the best paper plan for promoting mass education of any country he had seen. The program is applicable down to the last subdistrict, and the fact that there is a paper plan, soundly constructed, applicable to actual conditions, open for study by all concerned, is a distinct asset. Nobody can accuse Indonesia of muddling through educationally. Thanks to the paper plan it is possible to know where the education is going on and to keep planning the next step in development. Some work has been done in all of Java's 1,500 subdistricts. More work is being done this year than last. It seems a fair estimate that since 1951 a million adults each year are making a beginning at reading and writing.

To a person accustomed to a literate proletariat it comes

as a shock to plunge into a situation in which two-thirds of the persons with whom he comes in daily contact can neither read the street signs, the newspapers, their own mail, nor write a letter to absent members of their family. My first experience with illiteracy in Indonesia came through asking our cook why on earth he did not follow a recipe I had carefully written out for him. His face colored as he admitted that he could not read. Neither could he add except by drawing lines in groups of five and counting the lines; the neighbor's cook did the poor little scribbled accounts he daily showed me. So I taught him to write his name and the light on his face was not of this world—while the light on his wife's face was brighter. She now had a husband who belonged to the upper class. Incidentally she was much quicker than he but she never felt it expedient to go ahead of him.

Having experienced the intoxication of teaching, we then gave a dinner in Bandung's best hotel for a group of some twenty public-spirited citizens who were sponsoring Dr. Laubach's visit in the interest of mass education. By the time he reached Bandung the city was awake to his coming. His slogan, EACH ONE TEACH ONE, caught on. If each literate housewife taught her cook, each man his servant, each schoolboy his mother, each schoolgirl her grandmother, and so up the line, Indonesia's literacy problem would have a short time span. The first large meeting was attended by a sizable group of those willing to share their skills, by a crowd of men and women eager to acquire the new skills, and by the skeptical. Illiterate volunteers were requested for demonstration purposes. Shyly, hesitantly, two middle-aged women went to the platform, their reticence outweighed by their desire to learn. A teacher displayed posters bearing pictures of objects with their printed names broken down phonetically. For almost an hour the teaching went on—skillful, patient, sound, and also fascinating. At the end of the session the two women knew thirty-odd words. Many of the illiterate in the audience also knew many of the words. Amazement spread like a prairie-grass fire. Small each-one-teach-one groups sprang up across the city. The government program received exactly the impetus it needed.

There are other ways in which literacy spreads. People outside the school system decide to do something about the current needs. Mary Saleh is one such. She comes of one of Java's most distinguished families. Her father is a physician, Dutch-trained in Java. Long before the study of bahasa Indonesia was popular, he saw that, given the times and their temper, a national language was inevitable and that English would eventually become the second language of Indonesia, as of her neighbors. So he set his children to mastering both languages and took for granted their study of French and German along with their formal education in Dutch. During the war Mary married a young man devoted to Indonesia's new day. During the postwar struggle for independence while he was engaged in strategic work for his country, Mary had to flee to the mountains with her babies. They slept in every kind of makeshift hut; ate what they could get, which was very little; wore the clothes they had on their backs. With the cups, spoons and small kettle which were their household equipment and had to be carried on Mary's back, she also carried an English dictionary and kept studying. In due time she was able to come out of hiding, get the family together and assemble a home in Bandung. It was there that I first met her.

Mary was president of the Women's International Club, a group drawn from various nationalities which met to exchange understanding of each other's cultures and to promote educational interests in the city. I happened to attend the first meeting of the club and the first thing I noted was that Mary was beautiful; second, that she was thoroughly an Indonesian woman; third, that she didn't care in what language members addressed the chair. As the club progressed we were thrown together rather often. She became my teacher of Indonesian, although goodness knows where she ever found the time. In her concern for the millions of children who had no opportunity to go to school she was always wanting to do something to expedite teacher training and often came to look over the children's books, of which we had taken some five hundred to Java. We began to lend them to schools. Right away both children and teachers, who had never seen such books before, wanted to know why they could not have them translated. Whereupon Mary translated several, writing the Indonesian words interlinearly or pasting the translation in the back of the book. A forward-looking publisher became interested and put Mary on a committee to plan translation and publication of certain books and at the same time to commission or write Indonesian books for children. And so Mary wrote children's books, found an illustrator, and the first thing I knew her little books were in print. The second thing I knew they were in the schools.

By that time Mary knew how limited the materials for primary schools were. Teaching methods were also antiquated, meaning strictly Dutch and of the old line. Nevertheless, it was a Dutch woman, Rena Marsman, who helped her toward her next step. Together they invented a word-and-picture method of teaching small children. I say "invented" because they had never heard of the Laubach materials not yet introduced to Indonesia, nor had experience with any modern teaching materials. Fortunately they came upon the services of a tall, lank young Dutchman, Arie Schmit, who had become converted to Indonesia through having fought against Indonesians in their struggle for independence. He could draw; he could draw for children; he could work for little; his heart was in the enterprise. It still is.

So then Mary asked herself who would teach these new materials. Was there any untapped source for teachers? One day she thought of the literate mothers throughout the country, women who had had schooling at least through the elementary grades. Some of them were now middle-aged; their children were grown or at least had passed the stage of great demand. Some of those mothers could be taught to teach. They could teach the new materials and teach them to children who otherwise would have no chance to go to school. Looking about among her friends, Mary realized that the teaching mothers should come from middle-class homes, wives of teachers, government clerks, minor officials, post office employees and the like because wives of top officials and women of wealth and leisure are caught up in social affairs as well as being inclined toward dilettantism. Her mothers had to be dependable, regular, and dedicated to the idea.

She began with eight women in her home. They studied the word-and-picture teaching cards, child psychology, parent psychology, hygiene, foods, story telling, bahasa Indonesia and experimented with handwork materials. Mary drew in some help on the teaching but most of it she did herself and after four months the first mother-teachers were ready to begin to teach under her supervision. But they had no school. Moreover, there was no building to rent, nor even a good room. Bandung is just that crowded. But the Salehs had a garage!

Pupils were ready and waiting, twenty-two in all; children who could not get into any other school. They ranged in age from four through eight and their work covered preschool, kindergarten and primary grades. Children and teachers dug in. The atmosphere of freedom, diligence and self-expression proved exhilarating and also contagious. More children wished to attend school and more mothers to teach.

Because there was no money for expansion the Women's International Club and several other women's organizations lent a hand by giving the proceeds from an international fair. Then as the schools have grown the government has also provided limited funds, but not enough to keep the project from being strictly a private adventure in pioneer education. At the end of April, 1954, the schools celebrated their fourth birthday with fourteen schools in operation, thirty-two mothers teaching, more than five hundred children in attendance. The largest school is located in a suburb of Bandung and is a special cooperative venture of the Salehs. Mr. Saleh, an engineer, is chief director of the Indonesian railways, so when he began planning erection of a thousand homes for railway workers in this new suburb, his wife persuaded him to build a model school to her specifications, now the model for the whole project.

During the weeks when the schools are not in session Mary goes someplace where she can observe other working methods. One summer she went to Europe to study primary schools and what she learned she put right to work. In 1953 she came to America on a leader's grant and filled notebooks with observations, ironed out wrinkles in her procedures, gathered a small teaching library, studied toys with an eye toward having reasonably priced educational toys made in Indonesia. Then she went home to have her fifth baby. Kartini would no doubt beam on her, believing as she did that a woman's best contribution to education lies in being an excellent mother. Her own family is also Mary's best argument, which she does not need to put into words, to conservative gentlemen who consider the education of women very very risky business. As other communities hear of her schools they request help in setting up schools of their own, so that now there are teachers in residence from other islands. Mary needs trained helpers, and she needs to get some of her assistants abroad for further study. The *Jajasan Ibu*—Mothers' Schools—are on their way.

The training of Mrs. Saleh's mothers poses another pressing educational problem. Textbooks have to be written in Indonesian for Indonesians. Texts translated from other languages and other cultures take for granted concepts which are not current in Indonesia and omit other relevant matter which is necessary for thorough groundwork. The writing of some of these texts needs to be subsidized by private grants so that writers are free of government control, and enough texts are needed so that teachers have some choice.

Useful adjuncts of the mass education movement are the libraries, large and small. The largest library in the country is one inherited from the Royal Batavian Society for Arts and Sciences, containing about 400,000 publications chiefly on philology, ethnology and geography and a collection of periodicals and newspapers printed in Indonesia during the past century. There are also around 2,500 small lending or read-on-location government libraries with less than 500 books each. The department of education is aware that libraries should follow the demand of the community, but in Indonesia a community has first to be made aware of the usefulness of books before there can be a demand. A paper plan calls for a sizable library in each of Java's 79 regencies, each library servicing around 600,000 persons, with smaller libraries in the subdistricts. Three kinds of books are emphasized: large letter books for beginners; easy-reading books on hygiene, elementary economics, agricultural techniques and cultural interests for the newly literate; and books of general interest for more advanced readers. Most such books remain to be written, but if they were available they could not be put into circulation until more librarians are available. There is no professional course for librarians in the whole country except a limited course for assistant librarians in Djakarta. The first ten librarians with foreign training are beginning their work in 1954 and practical training is being provided for voluntary workers where they can be found.

The shortage of nontechnical books is scarcely less than tragic. When people learn to read they want to read something interesting. Under government classification books indispensable for schools get a foreign exchange allotment, but other books belong to an inferior category, along with canned milk, and the importer must put up 75 per cent of their cost before his order is approved, a procedure which ties up most of his capital and often sends the sale price up to five and one half times cost price. In 1953 the sale of imported books dropped 40 per cent off the 1952 import and many Indonesian importers of books closed down. Currently a restitution scheme may help book imports.

In order to augment the number of books available, publishers are now required to donate a certain number of each printing to the Mass Education Department. The All-Indonesian Private Schools Liaison Committee urges publishers "to print books of great value at lower prices," but the committee's advice sounds as if its members may not have studied the cost, with duty, of importing linotype machines, the difficulty of procuring paper, nor the predicament of private publishers in training printers only to have the government snap them up.

In addition to the Indonesian libraries there are modest libraries in Bandung and Djakarta directed by the British Council. And three libraries under direction of the United States Information Service, housing something over 30,000 books and serving some 90,000 users. A field service also offers packages of books to outlying areas and makes available a magazine called *American Miscellany*, published in English and Indonesian, as well as a wide variety of pamphlets published in Indonesian. Mobile unit films go out from all three centers and are constantly in use. The American library service is not publicized because of limited budget to increase its services but nevertheless demands far outrun resources.

The Department of Education put on a big exhibit in Djakarta's Municipal Hall with booths exhibiting textbooks, charts, maps, school supplies, library exhibits, students' handwork, films; in all an impressive display. More than 100,000 persons attended, asked questions and were so stirred by the possibilities of popular education that the Department felt its half million rupiahs well spent.

Probably the Ministry of Education best summarizes the future of education in the closing sentence of one of its own publications: "But if all these problems are real, so is the will with which they are being faced."

. 8 .

The Nation's Health

FOURTEEN HUNDRED DOCTORS FOR 80,000,000 people, some 300 of them in nonmedical government service. Twenty per cent of the 1,100 practice in Djakarta; another 10 per cent in Bandung; less than 800 doctors for the rest of the country.

One finds out the hard way how short the shortage is. On our first day in Bandung when the doctor from the small American hospital met us at the airport he sped us to his hospital because he had just admitted a boy with a broken femur who had been brought in by strangers who had seen him fall out of a coconut tree. The doctor had as yet no surgical nurse or anesthetist, and so our son held the boy's leg and my husband held his shoulders while the doctor set the bone. No one knew the boy's name or address; so many children fall out of coconut trees.

On the smaller islands the lack of doctors is more stark. A friend in Bali drove the length of the island to get a doctor for the young son of a colleague, but the doctor said the trip would mean leaving a hundred patients on his veranda untended. The child died. A second son contracted the same disease and our friend made the trip again, offering his own meager resources. The doctor said that from a money standpoint he could make more by staying in his office and from a humanitarian standpoint he dared not leave. The second child did not die. Later I saw this doctor's waiting room. He had children dying right there. He seldom finished with one day's patients; at midnight he simply had to close his office.

On the island of Lombok there are five doctors for 2,000,000 people. Dr. Lee, a German-trained Chinese, and his French wife opened their hospital against great odds in reconditioning a building, getting servants where no one wanted to work in a hospital, training their own nurses, buying equipment and medicine in the open market in Surabaya in order to make their meager resources meet their basic needs, being robbed by Indonesian stickup men of their personal effects and money. Sometimes they work twenty hours a day. Their X-ray and fluoroscope are housed in a windowless room where the temperature is frequently 100 and the humidity 90 per cent. They cannot afford a fan.

One morning in Djakarta a neighbor, a young Indo-Dutch widow, found her baby in convulsions and ran to a friend's home where she telephoned one doctor after another. All were too busy to come and her baby died. So then she had to get a doctor to certify death, for in that climate burial should be taken care of immediately. She called eight doctors; two offered to make the pronouncement if she would bring the baby to the office. Finally that night someone came from the Indonesian Red Cross and carried the baby in a betjak to a hospital where death could be certified.

Needless deaths run into the millions and each one is an individual tragedy—a situation which no one feels more acutely than some of the doctors. Human nature being the same the world over, there are many doctors in Indonesia who render service far beyond the line of duty, and there are others who are out for what they can get. Not infrequently a doctor working for the government sees a low-income patient in the clinic for the customary fee of one rupiah, but at the second visit suggests that he could give the patient better attention if he would come to the doctor's private office, fee R. 25. In many instances the patient has to borrow the money against a salary of perhaps R. 60 a month.

To meet the need for doctors the Ministry of Health is recruiting physicians from Europe—thirteen from Italy, Germany, Hungary went to north Sumatra in late 1953—and has asked for American doctors, but the effort is complicated by current insecurity in many localities where the doctors are most needed, by relatively low salary scale, by the housing shortage, and by the difficulty in taking more than a limited amount of money out of the country upon return to Europe. All doctors now coming to Indonesia or being graduated from medical schools are placed by the government where they are most needed. The three medical schools, soon to be augmented, are graduating around a hundred doctors a year, scarcely enough to replace the Dutch doctors returning to Holland and the normal losses of the profession.

The government reports 694 general hospitals, 19 mental hospitals, 9 eye hospitals, 20 maternity hospitals and so on, with a total of 50,000 beds, many of them bamboo cots without mattresses or sheets. The best of the hospitals are like good European hospitals except for crowding.

Among the best maternity hospitals is a training hospital for midwives in Macassar, Celebes. To be graduated nurses must have six years of elementary school, four years hospital training, two years practice in a government hospital, then back to the maternity hospital for two more years, after which they are licensed to deliver babies and to give medical care to children under one year. When I was there, the hospital was rounding out 10,000 births for the four years since its opening. Mothers were given excellent pregnancy care, although, to be sure, there were no sheets for the beds, no running water, although it was available in the city, no oxygen, no incubator, no isolation ward. A small space in the receiving room was curtained off for smallpox patients. The kitchen contained one very small refrigerator from UNICEF, had open wood fires for cooking, poor light, no screens. Apparently it had never occurred to any civic group to lend a hand with equipment. A great effort was made to instruct mothers in formula feeding when they had no breast milk, but the mothers quickly forgot the proper combination of ingredients and, not being able to read, had to return to the clinic for a reminder, often a long and difficult trip across the city. In Macassar no public health nursing is available, no check on homes even when a baby has a communicable disease.

Among the specialized hospitals one of the best is a hospital for the blind at Semarang, run by the Salvation Army. Everything the Salvation Army does is well done, whether running hospitals, orphanages, an old people's home, a home for unwed mothers, leprosaria, singing on the street, or prodding civic authorities for better jails. But perhaps their hospital for the blind is one of their most conspicuous services. Bandung Institute, originally started by the superintendent of the Amsterdam Institute for the Blind, also has 500 patients, but is short on staff and funds. There are an estimated 600,000 totally blind in Indonesia, 80 per cent of the blindness due to trachoma. "Trachoma still rages in the coastal areas," the Ministry of Health reports, "and is

found in those places where the standard of hygiene is low."
Since the standard of hygiene is low everywhere except in the
homes of the educated, there is a lot of room for trachoma
to rage in.

There are a few psychiatric hospitals or wards, but except
for the violently insane most patients have to wait for institu-
tional care until the chief physical diseases which sap the
nation's vitality are taken care of. When I was last in Macassar
the government hospital had two large psychiatric wards in a
fine new building, but the furniture consisted only of beds.
The physician, new to the staff, hoped for segregation of noisy
patients and introduction of handcrafts. Any country which
has known the hunger and violence of occupation years and
then the devastation of revolution with its grief and displace-
ment is bound to pay a price in mental upheaval. There is
also the widespread insecurity which makes thousands afraid
to go to bed at night, the adjustment of workers to factory
conditions, rising living costs, and among women in families
which can afford more than one wife, the constant tension of
rivalry and defeat, none the less mentally disastrous because
both the polygamy and the emotional reactions are taken
for granted.

Fortunately the services of physicians are augmented by the
work of *mantris* (male technicians and nurses), women nurses
and midwives. Nurses are estimated at 3,500 for the whole
country, mantris around 1,600, 46 of whom have a junior
high school background, as do the 1,400 midwives.

The government employs 30 dentists and around 100
dentists practice privately, not to count the unlicensed *tukan
gigi*, artisans of the teeth, mostly Chinese, who ply their
trade with all sorts of unhygienic implements but not a little
skill. For the whole of Indonesia there are nine pharmacists

with university degrees, and 141 assistant pharmacists, three-fourths of them Indonesians, who are high school graduates.

The pharmacist I got to know best is John Harry Dröse, a tall dark-haired Dutch-Swedish chap twenty-five years old. After high school in Holland he had a two-year pharmacy course and worked two years as an assistant pharmacist. When I met him he had been in Indonesia for three years and was located at Menado on the north tip of Celebes, where he acted as director of pharmaceutical services for the entire area. Actually he was the only trained pharmacist from Borneo to New Guinea, from the Philippines to the equator, probably one of the largest "parishes" in the world. When he arrived at his post in June, 1950, he found the drug stock of the newly opened government hospital composed of drugs left by the Japanese. Having no others, he tried to use what was there. A telegram from Djakarta ordered the decomposed sodium pentothal destroyed, but Dröse opened the capsules, added water, and concocted a good hypnotic which the chief surgeon told me proved invaluable to the hospital. Six months later some supplies arrived but they were wholly inadequate for one hospital, let alone all the hospitals and clinics of Minahassa.

Because of drug limitations Dröse was always inventing substitutes or concocting some brew of his own. Not infrequently explosive tetanus breaks out in a village and a score of patients may be rushed into the hospital. Dröse noticed that tetanus patients were likely to die of exhaustion after the disease was conquered, so he concocted a potent potion of raw egg, sugar, salt, vitamins C and B^1 and milk, and himself forced the mixture down the patients' throats several times a day. Thirty out of thirty-one of his recent cases had recovered. Lacking chloromycetin for typhoid, he hunted out an old supply of anesthesin and changed it into para-minobenzoic acid. The next two typhoids died but he kept trying and later results were excellent. Practically every doctor I met had a tale to tell, but many of the stories which were supposed to leave me goggling left me only gaping stupidly because I could not understand the substitutions involved in Dröse's inventions. But I could understand his concern for the outlying drug rooms which we jogged off to see—up into the hills and through the villages where most of the little hospitals and clinics are run by mantris. His salary was approximately $22.50 a month. I should add that Dröse was not popular with those doctors and mantris whose blackmarket sidelines he exposed nor with the administrators whom he prodded in Djakarta. One of the tragedies of neg-lected health service is indifference or resentment toward efficient organization.

Travel through Indonesia does not impress one as a tour among the ailing—indeed much less so than in many parts of Asia—but nevertheless one can scarcely walk a city block without becoming aware of the country's health problems. For instance, one day when I left the Health Ministry to return to my waiting betjak I found the driver sitting on the footrest shivering so hard his teeth chattered. I looked at him aghast for the day was particularly hot and humid. His trembling hand brushed his blue lips as he grinned and said, *"Deman kura."* Malaria.

World Health Organization estimates that an average of 30,000,000 Indonesians have active malaria, proportionately more than in any other nation, one-tenth the total malaria of the world. Around 10 per cent of all deaths are due to malaria besides its being a complicating factor in deaths from other diseases. Combined with malnutrition, it cuts the working hours of farmers and factory workers to a fraction of their potential. Any historian who holds that malaria was a primary factor in the collapse of Babylonia, and the underlying cause of the disintegration of the Greek and perhaps the Roman empires, can see his theory in operation in Indonesia. There are as yet no correlative statistics on the relation of malaria to agricultural production in Indonesia, but one sees the influence of malaria on agriculture on every hand. Next door to us in Bandung the owner of a small rice field and his entire family, except for one half-grown girl, came down with malaria the day before the rice should be harvested. Neighbors pitched in to help, but the family remained ill and were not able to return help to the neighbors who had counted on them. Nor were they able to get the next planting ready. Many times during the year they were down with malaria.

A World Health team working closely with the Pakistani government on malaria control in a remote and heavily infected corner of Bengal, population 250,000, states that at the end of one year: "the district Agricultural Officer reported an increase of 543 pounds of rice per acre for the year." When malaria vanished the people became stronger, worked harder, got better production. A perverse predicament for a country to have to deal with mosquitoes in order to increase production, but it looks as if Indonesia's fiscal experts had better join a malaria team.

Factory production is just as adversely affected. When I visited a batik factory in Padang the three dyers were home with aggravated cases of malaria. There were no substitute dyers available in the city. If such key persons are long absent, the weavers dependent upon them must be laid off; if the workers get no pay they have no food; if the labor unions force pay, then the factory owner is soon forced below the point where he can compete with imported Japanese cloth.

At the malaria headquarters in Djakarta some twenty students are taking their year of intensive training as expert malaria mantris. Djakarta is heavily infested with the anopheles mosquitoes which carry malaria, the average nightly production of the two most popular varieties being estimated at 3,000,000 mosquitoes per square mile of fishpond, stagnant canal, or buffalo-hoof puddles. Brackish water breeders are the strongest fliers, but once their range is spent then their victims form a human wall against further spread of malaria. Thus Glodok, Djakarta's terrifically congested Chinese section, has a high incidence of malaria but "protects" the regions beyond. When we lived near Tjikini market we felt relatively safe because of this human wall, but we slept in a tightly screened redoubt. I learned to recognize anopheles but my recognition remained so slow that by the time I made sure that a mosquito had assumed her characteristic posture of standing on her head to bite, the plasmodia were already injected. The deposit is made before any blood is drawn, a neat banking system which unfortunately breaks the bank. A little knowledge is an irritating thing for a wife to have and my husband would have preferred my smacking a mosquito on his neck without waiting to see which end it was standing on.

Experimentation with modifications of DDT is constantly under way. A good spray has a residual action up to one year and any anopheles which comes to rest on the impregnated wall will die before the end of the period necessary for the development of the malaria parasite. Villagers do not care a hoot about mosquito control but are interested in getting rid of bedbugs, hence if a sprayer misses a house he is promptly recalled by the entire family.

Some districts are undertaking their own spray campaigns and in no place is spraying more necessary than on estates newly opened in the jungles. Officials charged with moving some of Java's crowded population to other islands, as well as plantation owners on the underpopulated islands, sum up the possibilities of thousands of square miles of potentially productive hinterlands—"If we could only lick malaria." To underrate its importance in relation to the country's other problems is entirely to misconceive the burden of Indonesian life, to misappraise the temper and quality of the people, and to misjudge the performance of officials.

Tuberculosis is the second most destructive disease, also responsible for 10 per cent of the deaths, and the number of admissions to hospitals and proportion of sick leaves granted to government employees indicates its rapid acceleration. Continuing inadequacy of the national diet, crowded housing, general poverty, debilitation caused by other diseases, lack of public health facilities, and inadequate care for current tuberculosis patients are reasons enough for the increase. Practically all the tuberculosis hospitals lack equipment and each could be filled thirty times over.

Typical of a sanitarium without a full-time doctor is Rumah Sakit Noongan up in the hills above Menado. Formerly a private sanitarium run by a Dutch doctor for affluent patients, it is now partially restored and very much a going concern. And the reason for *that* is Sister Gerungan. All women nurses are called "sister" in Indonesia but the title especially fits Miss Gerungan, who has a sturdy sister-to-the-world look about her. As a graduate of an old-line Dutch hospital in Djakarta she has standing and directs this seventy-bed sanitarium on her own responsibility except for an occasional visit from a busy Chinese doctor, besides running a sizable children's clinic and a dispensary. Her chief assistant is a mantri trained in Surabaya, now hoping for postgraduate work in X-ray because new equipment has been sent out from Holland but no one knows how to install and run it. Nor is there anyone who can install the electric pump, also a gift. It was here that I decided to go into the electric fixture business but gave it up later in favor of a training school for electricians—some day.

Sister Gerungan seemed to have a green thumb for baby culture, as well as for the flowers which filled her gardens, for she had adopted a baby boy born in her hospital on Independence Day, 1950, to parents who had enough children and definitely not enough food. The whole community seemed immensely proud of plump little Augustus.

The shelves in Sister Gerungan's drug room contained mostly empty bottles and she was buying vitamins, cod-liver oil and codeine from her meager funds. When I asked what she needed most, she replied promptly, "A small operating room and someone to operate one day a month," and then added, "and a real chapel for daily services instead of using the narrow hall." We looked into each other's plain faces a few moments. What she was thinking I don't know, but I was thinking that few faces as radiant as hers and her nurses' emerged from the chapels I knew at home. When we parted we did not say good-by; we said we would see each other again and I, at least, was not thinking of heaven.

The big question about tuberculosis is how to attack the problem when its roots reach into so many aspects of daily life. Along with housing, the matter of birth control may have to be considered as is being done in India; also promotion of a more adequate diet, development of advanced chemotherapy, more thoracic surgery. The gardener of our neighbor, Dr. Sampemoen, exemplified the problem when he brought in his sister because she was coughing incessantly and could scarcely carry on her work as wash *babu* in a family with several children. Tuberculosis of the lungs. Problem: with hospital beds at a premium it would be difficult to get her in any place without a fee larger than her monthly wage; if bed rest were ordered then she would have no money to feed her family; if she were given medicine without bed rest then she might work a little longer but would continue to expose the family for whom she worked. Her brother the gardener could not take on another dependent, let alone a whole family of dependents. Help from public funds was largely theoretical besides being strangled in red tape. If the doctor assumed her support and her family's, then tomorrow the sisters and the cousins and the uncles and the aunts of the other servants, and then their sisters and cousins . . .

One specific and practical approach is the use of vaccine known as BGG, highly effective for babies at the age when tuberculosis has its highest mortality; 95 per cent of those infected in their first year will die. World Health Organization announces that under its program in 24 countries on five continents, 37,000,000 children have been tuberculin tested and 16,000,000 children vaccinated. Japan has vaccinated more than 31,000,000. Total vaccinations for the world exceed 100,000,000.

Indonesia's third major disease is yaws. Propagated by direct contact as well as spread by flies, it is easily passed around among members of a family. My introduction to yaws occurred at the U. S. Government rest house in Bandung when I stopped by one day to see how Ueng, the caretaker, and his wife were getting on. He had been especially good to me when I had bacillary dysentery. Ueng was in a great state of agitation; his sons were ill; he and his wife had not slept for nights. I went to his quarters. The four-year-old, usually as pert as a new penny, plainly had dysentery. The droll gingerbread-boy two-year-old was in an agony of pain with what appeared to be an open ulcer the size of a man's hand on his tailbone. He cried, then lapsed into a sort of momentary coma, then cried again. I piled the two children and Ueng into the car and took them to the small American hospital where I had to leave them—with money to get home by betjak. It was thirty-six hours before I saw them again. The four-year-old, still pale, was improving, thanks to sulfa. The two-year-old was *well*, running around the yard still shrieking, but this time with laughter. His ulcer appeared little more than a scar. One shot of penicillin had taken care of his yaws. It was American penicillin and this is my note of thanks to the taxpayers who gave one-half cent each to pay most of the bill for medicines in all Indonesia that year.

Around the beginning of 1950 the United Nations International Children's Emergency Fund moved in on yaws. Their staff was small, assistants and mantris few. There were administrative difficulties: reports had to be written in English, but competent assistants who knew English would not work for current government salaries; prompt reporting at the end of a long day was a new idea; often telegraphic connections were broken; roads through the jungles were poor and there were too few jeeps to feed the penicillin to the outstations; pilferage by stevedores on the ships and by carriers at the warehouses occurred at disastrous times and places. Moreover, for the mantris and drivers, personal discipline was a new idea. In time of war they are marvelous but peacetime is another story just as it is in other lands. Since the yaws program got under way in 1950, nearly 4,000,-000 individuals have been examined and around one-sixth of them treated. Close to 90 per cent of the population must be inspected or the untreated yaws will reinfect the area, but it is difficult to get so high a percentage out for inspection for the people are ignorant and do not understand its importance. Mr. S. M. Kenny, director of UNICEF in Southeast Asia, estimates that at the rate of 400,000 a year, a twenty-year job lies ahead. But Dr. Leimena, long-time Minister of Health, figures that by adding to the teams now at work, using trained lay injectors, enlisting the help of the many small polyclinics, laying responsibility upon all doctors in charge of government hospitals, the job can be done much faster.

Some of Indonesia's more miserable diseases are not serious, such as the "seven-year itch," or scabies, and Hongkong foot, the Oriental version of our old YMCA friend, athlete's foot. And prickly heat. I would like to know the number of work-hours of misery it causes. Eurasians are not free from it, but foreigners in the tropics are its special prey. It is a disease and not a state of mind, as proved by the fact that my husband, who never had a state of mind, looked as if he'd lain in a bed of cayenne pepper while I had scarcely a touch.

Then there is also leprosy. After a few weeks in Indonesia one tends to classify all beggars as lepers, but as weeks pass into months even a layman learns to recognize the obvious lepers by their distinctive nodules, their pink skin patches, or by their lionlike expressions. Central Leprosy Institute,

Djakarta, estimates 75,000 lepers but many old-time doctors think the figure should be much larger. With *merdeka* a man is free to keep his ills to himself and if he has leprosy he will surely try, for as in all the rest of the world the stigma of leprosy is overwhelming—a surprising fact in a sense because leprosy is only mildly infectious, not readily transmitted, less painful than many diseases, and not a rapid killer. But it is usually disfiguring, which probably accounts for the ostracism. His aloneness is a leper's heaviest burden. Although he knows he is taking on a life sentence when he goes to a colony he takes it on gladly, even begs for it, because in a colony he has at least a minimum of food and human companionship.

In all the leprosaria I visited there was excitement about the new drugs, all modifications of one discovery, which dramatically shorten the course of Hanson's disease—to use the modern term—if they do not indeed cure. However, it is necessary to administer liver extract and high vitamin B with them and most of the colonies could neither get nor afford the liver and B, so that often their supply of the wonder drugs was almost useless. Some colonies managed to treat the children only. Director for the whole leprosy project is Dr. Boenjamin, an Indonesian trained in Holland and distinguished in research. In his laboratories are collections of animals with leprosy—mice, rats, chickens, birds, dogs, cats, monkeys, and a water buffalo. So far no one has succeeded in inoculating an animal with the bacillus which appears to cause the disease in humans, nor in getting the bacillus to grow in artificial media. Still, Dr. Boenjamin pointed out, in villages in which animal leprosy is highest, human leprosy is also high. Assisting on the service was one other full-time physician who directs a public health program, trying to persuade sufferers to report themselves and educating families to take care of an afflicted member without fear.

The settlement outside Menado had a capable Indonesian physician in charge of the two hundred patients; the reception room was used also as a mortuary; long dormitories were filled with cots without bedding; rows of simple dwellings for families; small gardens of sweet potatoes and bananas. In having any sort of gardens they were ahead of the stark leprosarium near Samarinda, Borneo, in which patients longed for some of the bananas and coconuts growing abundantly outside the segregated area, but no one ever picked the fruit for them. At Menado government money often came late and rations were then reduced to bare subsistence. No electricity had been brought in from the nearby city, hence no refrigeration, radio or films. The lepers hustled me proudly into their church. Early Sunday mornings the chairs face toward a Catholic altar, later toward a Protestant pulpit, and on Fridays are turned in a third direction for Moslem instruction. At Macassar, where the colony is run by the Salvation Army, no doctor had stepped foot on the place for seven months, but the new doctor told me he expected to get around twice a month although there was then no medicine to administer.

At Belawan near Medan in north Sumatra the colony lies in low marshland, which means hosts of mosquitoes, and so Mr. and Mrs. Gues—a Salvation Army couple who have been in charge for twenty-five years—have put their patients to raising ducks in the narrow drainage ditches to eat the mosquitoes. Some of the patients lived in fairly good dormitories, meaning the roofs did not leak. The big need was for a generator to furnish electricity because lamps are difficult for many patients to handle and hence dangerous. There was a married people's row and the director said he had performed twenty-five marriages of lonely men and women who would never have had a chance for a home in the outer world. Several patients mentioned that their church had stained-glass windows and a sizable crowd escorted me to see them: two panes of red glass six by thirty inches. But they cast a lovely glow across the plain room and Mr. Gues pointed out the inscription over the pulpit: THE LORD HELPS US THIS DAY AND FOREVER. He believed in signs.

The leprosarium which out-problemed all the others I visited was Lenteng Agung, 28 kilometers outside Djakarta. A young California physician then on the public health staff of FOA, and Pearl Cheng, who has her Master's degree in hospital administration from Northwestern University, went with me. The day was drizzly, the road deeply rutted; finally our car couldn't made it and we walked the last three kilometers in mud to our shins. The place reminded me of a forsaken lumber camp, buildings huddled together, falling apart at their seams. I never saw a less inhabited piece of flat land in Java. The doctor who goes out there on occasion made rounds with us through the eight bunkhouses, many without windows, and the dark, crowded, cheerless children's ward. People trailed after us asking to have their roofs fixed for often there was no dry spot for a bed. In a segregated room at the back were a young couple with a new baby, all negative, who could have returned home but their village would not have them. In the community kitchen, which seemed the last word in desolation, food was being dished into big bowls on the floor, one set of bowls to each dormitory. As soon as I could see anything in the smoke and darkness, I gasped, "Why doesn't someone cut a window here?" The doctor

answered cheerfully, "No one takes an interest in this place."
So then we sputtered under our breath that an American
doctor would cut a window himself, and make a ladder to go
after leaves from the palms growing at hand and mend those
leaking roofs. Then it occurred to me that at least the Dutch
doctor was *there*, willing to work for an Indonesian salary. It
is noteworthy that it did not occur to any of us to ask why
some of the 53,000,000 Indonesians in Java did not lend a
hand.

Because of Mr. J. C. L. A. Van Hasselt, whose fingers were
stumps and whose legs were bandaged, 80 per cent of the
people in this settlement could read and write. In the plain
building used as a Protestant church, there were removable
walls which formed three schoolrooms on weekdays, and
adult patients were teaching all six grades of elementary
school, using the barest minimum of equipment. Several were
studying English, taught by Mr. Van Hasselt, who spoke
excellent English, for which he apologized, offering to speak
French, German or of course Dutch if we preferred, but we
did not prefer. The small Roman Catholic church had been
constructed entirely by the patients and it was beautiful. "We
lepers made the tile," Mr. Van Hasselt said. They were lovely
tile. "One of us carved the door and the heading above the
door." It was intricate, delicate carving. "We made the altar."
There it stood, a hymn of praise from grateful hands. "We
painted the Stations of the Cross." They were simple and
good and called to prayer. There was a small organ. Later I
wondered why the church builders could not also build a
kitchen. I'd wager the idea has never occurred to any Indonesian.

Oddly, there was an office for social affairs and at one time
there had been a store offering old clothes, toothbrushes,

thread, pencils, but now the shelves were empty. "If we could get materials to start up we could make it self-supporting and also provide work for people who could make their own clothes and do other handwork." When we went to leave the American doctor casually put out his hand to Mr. Van Hasselt, but Mr. Van Hasselt just looked at him, his face coloring. "Do you—do you mean to shake hands with me?" he asked as he slowly put out his stump. "It's been years and years since anyone has shaken hands with me."

That afternoon Pearl and I went to Tangerang, 22 kilometers outside the city in another direction, where a model leprosy hospital was being rushed to completion before the forthcoming regional meeting of World Health. The buildings were of brick, the floors tiled, the windows ample, the roofs tight. There were bathrooms. I wondered whether the inmates of Lenteng Agung, if transferred, could ever stand the shock. Marvel of all, there were two completed houses waiting for doctors, the only two empty dwellings I saw in all Indonesia. But there were no doctors in sight. No nurses, no occupational therapist, no social worker, no pharmacist, no bacteriologist.

The Ministry of Health is awake to the need for an adequate program to deal with venereal disease. Formerly the Dutch government provided compulsory treatment for members of the armed forces, but with merdeka compulsory treatment is not feasible. However, there are now VD clinics in several cities. In Surabaya four hospitals—one Chinese, one Salvation Army, two government—are working on special problems of maternal and congenital syphilis. Penicillin from UNICEF is now procurable free of charge but is not available in many hospitals. Sighed one physician after a trip through an institute for the blind, "If everyone in the whole world could be given a dose of penicillin on the same day, there'd me no more gonorrhea left." At least most of the blindness due to gonorrheal infection could be prevented.

The dysenteries are another of the government's major health worries. Since sulfaguanidine and some of its cousin sulfas have come into common use, bacillary dysentery is not the threat it once was, but most Indonesians could no more get than spell the new drugs. One Dutch physician who is also an inventor curtailed the dysenteries and other filth diseases in a big wholesale and retail meat business by installing a disinfecting contraption on the inside of all toilet doors; in order to leave the room the occupant had to put both hands into the receptacle and push two levers, and the disinfectant smelled so strong that he was glad to avail himself of the nearby washbowls afterward.

Thanks to Dutch surveillance the last cholera cases occurred in 1927, but bubonic plague is still endemic in Java, as much dreaded today as in the mid-1600's when it killed approximately one person in eight in London. Poverty and poor housing mean rats and rats mean plague. Typhoid along with the related enteric fevers is also prevalent in kampongs and desas but some of the larger cities have introduced inoculation of school children against typhoid and cholera. Probably few of the intestinal diseases cause more grief than roundworms. So many Indonesians are hosts to worms that it has been estimated that each year the worms inside of the people consume an amount of food equal to the food consumption of 100,000 people. At their worst worms crawl out of a child's mouth or nose or anus and engorge his jejunum like a stuffed sausage. At one of the largest government hospitals the first need mentioned was santonin "for the terrific number of cases of worms." There is also hookworm, which causes a severe anemia among plantation workers in some areas, a 50 per cent prevalence in much of Java and 80 per cent in the northern and southern peninsulas of Celebes.

Java was one of the first nations to practice inoculation against smallpox. An enterprising Dutch doctor sent a number of young boys to Mauritius, where one of their number was inoculated; then on the return trip the second boy was inoculated from the first, the third from the second, and so on until the last boy managed to have the pustule when the ship landed again in Java and country-wide inoculation was on its way. In 1884 another Dutch doctor in Java succeeded in preparing a very good vaccine from calves and before long the Dutch began to make vaccine on a large scale so that they were able to keep smallpox well in hand. The first postwar outbreak occurred in 1947 in Sumatra, imported from Malacca and carried by Madura fishermen who refused to be vaccinated in these days of merdeka. In 1951 Bali had the world's worst epidemic, estimated at 20,000 cases. On every hand I met with family tragedies from smallpox. In the general hospital at Balikpapan, North Borneo, I saw a mother and child, whose bodies were completely covered with pustules, lying near an open window where flies buzzed in and out between the little segregation ward and the kitchen. However, the wonder always is that so few doctors do so much.

The most thorough vaccination program I saw was conducted at Sonder in Celebes, a particularly enterprising community distinguished by the fact that no Chinese has ever been allowed to live nor trade there, which means that the people have plenty of gumption of their own. Sondor has a fifty-bed hospital, crowded, of course; lacking in equipment, of course; short on medicine, of course; enjoying only the part-time services of a doctor, of course; but the extension service was impressive for its homespun efficiency. Mantris went out to supervise small polyclinics throughout fifteen kilometers of countryside, keeping a sharp eye out for explosive typhoid, giving inoculations when needed, going twice a year into every home in the district to vaccinate every individual. Not even a newborn baby escapes for if it is not brought to the clinic it is caught up with inside six months.

In getting medicine to the places where it is needed, the chief difficulty is the shortage of personnel and the low salaries paid such workers as can be mustered. To an outsider it seems as if common sense and determination should be able to effect a solution, and so they might to well-fed Americans bursting with vigor, accustomed for generations to meeting exigencies with whatever resources are at hand. But the rank and file of the Indonesian people are not well-fed; they do not burst with energy, and they are not accustomed to over-all problem-solving. Once inside the Indonesian health service, every problem seems to hinge on some other problem equally pressing, equally tangled in personalities and precedents. As in other parts of the world, ineptitude breeds dishonesty; an inefficient system is the most expensive system.

Dr. E. Ross Jenney, in charge of American medical aid when we arrived in Java, was determined to see that American medicine and supplies contributed through whatever channel got to the outlying areas. He knew those areas from personal observation and he knew the difficulties involved in sorting out the vans in the warehouse and filling orders. So he contrived a way for the Indonesian medical distribution service to hire our American-trained Chinese-Indonesian friend with her Master's degree in hospital administration and an ample vocabulary in Indonesian, Chinese, Dutch and English, all of which she needed on the job. She did a spectacular job in reading the cabalistic signs on the vans, sorting invoices, matching needs to supplies, getting the penicillin to the places where the babies were dying of pneumonia and the sulfas where bacillary dysentery raged. As fast as Indonesians are trained they can administer these complicated services.

Just as pressing as the need for distribution of medicines is the need for sanitation. For instance, in Djakarta only 13 per cent of the 3,000,000 have access to city water and the wells and springs are often contaminated. Toilet facilities for the masses consist of ditch-streams running alongside the kampongs. When we lived in a suburb of Bandung, I often used to walk in the early morning and as I crossed the bridge over a neighboring stream I always saw three or four women from a nearby kampong squatting in the stream, their sarongs pulled up around their middles while they took care of their morning needs, the sun making lovely highlights on their coppery buttocks. They always smiled and wished me the pleasantest of good mornings. Certainly they were not immodest and definitely they were clean.

The basic health needs of the nation boil down to the fact that the common people, clean by nature and tradition, have to be taught the principles of hygiene. Who doesn't? Dr. Brock Chisholm, Director General of World Health Organization, reported to the World Health Assembly, "Three out of four men, women and children in the world still suffer from diseases spread by unsafe water supplies, unsanitary excreta disposal, uncontrolled insects and rodents, and inadequate protection of milk and other foods. . . . Sanitation is, after all, a way of life."

People who shiver with malaria, ache with yaws, lack energy from a bout with typhoid or dengue or dysentery or hookworm, cough from TB, squint from trachoma, cannot do a good day's work. So their exports languish, their currency is unstable, prices go up and wages go down. Sick and depleted children cannot even study what democracy is all about. The will to achieve is an earned capacity of the Indonesian people, but health to sustain the will is still to be won.

· 9 ·

The Religious Matrix

PERMEATING THE CULTURE, DOMINATING
the arts, conditioning law and custom, delineating the
outline of daily life, linking past and present, is the religion
of the people. All official acts of the government are con-
ditioned by the dominant religious cast of mind, which is
Moslem, but also by the Hindu-Buddhist fundamentals
which lie just beneath the surface, and by a still-hardy
animism.

Only an exceptionally philosophical Indonesian would
attempt to say which elements in his religion are uncon-
taminated Mohammedanism and which are legacies of the
older cultures. Except on Bali and Lombok, where the people
remain Hindus with Buddhist overtones, the average Indonesian thinks he is an orthodox Moslem. And so he is in the
sense of abiding by Moslem law, memorizing the Koran, quot-
ing Moslem authority and tradition, orienting his life toward
a trip to Mecca or at least toward those who have made the *haj*
to the Holy City. He does not know that he is different from
orthodox Moslems of other countries; that the fears and
wonders, obediences and taboos which are the inner cloak
of his religious dress are foreign to traditional Mohammedanism; that if the non-Moslem elements of his religion

158

were extracted he would be like a man with no marrow in his bones.

It is easy for a Westerner to see these layers of religious inheritance just as it is easy for an Indonesian scholar to sense the inheritances and admixtures in Christianity. To pare back nonessentials and find the core is more difficult. But one attitude we all hold in common—the inner conviction that *ours* is *it*, that our faith and belief however constituted are *the* will of God for all time. After we had lived in Bandung a few weeks we had as dinner guests four Indonesian educators, all men of parts, all Moslems, all interested in a philosophy of education for their new democracy. The conversation turned toward religion and I mentioned, chattily, my surprise some years back in finding that Mohammedanism had as many sects and divisions as Christianity. Then I asked which sect was theirs. The leader turned to me in pained surprise. "We represent the one true faith!" Just like that. "So do we," I confided to him. "Out of all the sects of Christendom we belong to the one true church. As of course do the adherents of the scores of other brands." Then he could smile—but not at the point I thought I had made. "Ah, yes," he said, "among Christians there could be this confusion as to which group held the central truth. But not among Moslems. Our particular sect, as you will call it, has the authority of the Koran, of tradition, and of Mohammed himself." And *that* was no smiling matter. And there is Indonesian Islamic conviction, more certain than analytical, a thing of allegiance rather than of spiritual sensitivity. Which makes it first cousin to Christian conviction.

The Hinduism below the surface, except in Bali and Lombok, where it remains dominant, is essentially the Hinduism of India but modified by antedating religious beliefs of the islands and by a loosening of the caste system. Hinduism came into the islands around the fifth century A.D. and flourished until it was displaced by Mohammedanism in the fourteenth century. The names of many of the Hindu deities of various echelons have been changed, although their chief characteristics remain more or less constant. Brahma, chief of the sacerdotal order, remains Lord of All, creator, sustainer, all-encompassing, as immediate as breath, as remote as an eternal abstraction of the universe. Vishnu, second of the Three in One and One in Three, remains the Maintainer. Siva, third of the aspects of the essence of being, remains the Destroyer in the sense of eternal alleviation and purification of life through death. All three are epitomized in "human" form, that is, given attributes, principles, actions. Two of the estimable consorts of Vishnu, Lakshmi and Saraswati, are particularly treasured for their nobility of nature. From the Indian Scriptures, particularly from the *Mahabharata* and *Ramayana*, ancient Indian epics which are the record of Hindu history and philosophy, come the stories which furnish the everyday fare of the people, not only on the two Hindu islands but also among the Javanese Moslems.

The merest child in those parts of Indonesia where Hindu culture once held sway knows the story of the five Pandavi princes who warred against their hundred wicked cousins, the Kurus. In painting, puppetry, song and dance the story is retold: how the dying King Pandu left his five sons in care of his estimable but blind brother, who brought them up faithfully as heirs to the throne, but who could not foster the same noble character in his own hundred sons, the Kurus; how the Kurus tricked the Pandavi into banishment, how the brothers returned and Arjuna entered the jousts in which the kings of many realms contended for the hand of the princess Draupadi by attempting to shoot with her father's bow; how Arjuna was able to lift the bow and shoot five arrows so rapidly that all were in the air at the same time, so accurately that all pierced the swinging ring and hit the target and thus won him a royal bride; how the Pandavi acted generously toward their wicked cousins who again and again cheated them out of their kingdom but were eventually destroyed in the battle which furnishes the background for Hinduism's greatest poem and scripture, the *Bhagavad-Gita.*

From the *Ramayana* come the many stories gathered around prince Rama, fathered by Vishnu at the word of Brahma, his twin brothers Lakshman and Satrughna, his youngest brother, Bharat, and Rama's lovely wife, Sita. In time of trial when Rama was exiled, Sita followed him into the forest and with them went the faithful brother Lakshman. There in the woods they were safe except that wicked *rakshas,* taking on various forms, attempted to molest them, repulsed only by Sita's purity and fearlessness. Once, however, when Rama went hunting for a golden-dappled deer Sita wished for a pet, he was betrayed by the deer—in reality a raksha—who cried aloud in Rama's own voice that he was wounded. Whereupon Lakshman broke their rule that Sita should never be left alone, went to the rescue of Rama, leaving Sita to be carried off by Ravan, most wicked raksha of all, King of the Demons. The long pursuit of Ravan by Rama and Lakshman, aided by Hanuman, noble king of the monkeys, and all his tribe, in search of Sita hidden in Ravan's palace on the island of Ceylon, forms the story basis for some of Indonesia's oldest and most beloved dance-dramas. Among them is the famous "monkey dance" of Bali in which 240 men taking the part of the loyal monkeys gather at night around a torch to enact a segment of the tale, their piercing ktjak-ktjak, their tremendous single-noted call on the gods, striking chill and wonder into the hearts of the listeners.

But most moving—and probably beyond measuring in its influence upon generations of Indonesians—is the story of the final quest of the Five Pandavi and Queen Draupadi when at the end of a long and worthy reign they decide to leave their prosperous subjects and set off across the desert to find the City of the Gods. With them goes the faithful hound of Yudhisthir, the oldest brother. Incredible distances, scorching sands, cold winds, hunger, privation, every hardship, these six who have long suffered and triumphed together bear with fortitude; more, with joy. And always with them goes the hound. One after another five die until only Yudhisthir and the hound are left. And then in the distance emerges the mountain of the gods. With renewed strength Yudhisthir begins to climb its slopes, when all at once comes the thunder of chariot wheels and in a blinding light Lord Indra himself appears. Trembling, the hound presses against his master as Lord Indra calls on him to mount the chariot and be carried to the gods' own dwelling where he will find his queen and his brothers waiting. Yudhisthir looks at Indra and then at the hound. Slowly he draws back from the chariot. "This hound has been my faithful companion," he says. At mention of the word *dog*, Indra's wrath is kindled. "Unclean, despised, lowest of beasts! Will you turn your back on the very threshold of heaven for a dog?" Whereupon Yudhisthir, remembering his long reign dedicated to justice, mercy and love of all creatures, looks at Lord Indra with level eye and elects to stay with his hound. As Indra listens to the pronouncement the light around him becomes glorious indeed. "Mount the chariot, my son! You have met the final test. You have not failed the least of the creatures." Then Yudhisthir takes the bedraggled hound in his arms, mounts the chariot with Lord Indra and rises to dwell among the immortals.

It is no doubt the upthrust of such Hindu legends which has tempered and mellowed and seasoned Islamic tenets and teachings, lending a pliancy, a gentleness of spirit, a tolerance, an empathy. One feels that the Indonesians were not made for legalism, that they have long known something fundamental to mankind's ability to dwell together in peace, unity in diversity, which does not need the legislation of minutiae which distinguishes much of Islam.

Buddhism as a religion apart from its Hindu progenitor scarcely exists in Indonesia today. At most ceremonies of any moment in Bali one finds a Buddhist priest among the Hindu priests, but his duties appear little different from the duties of the Hindu priests; indeed sometimes, at weddings and temple festivals one priest may officiate in both capacities. Buddhist and Hindu share alike the ancient awareness that the soul's development through time is a continuous progress, broken into stages by the sleep of death. Certain priests of both religions have the ability, in trance, to go back and pick up the thread of a young child's previous experiences upon the earth and to relay to the parents such data as may be relevant to the lessons he must learn in his present sojourn. All of this is taken very matter-of-factly by the Balinese, and, indeed, by many Javanese Moslems. I was surprised at the number of Moslems who never seemed to question the long-run sowing and reaping, the judgment at the heart of every choice, which characterize the doctrines of karma and reincarnation; they never thought of them as being non-Islamic; they were just "the way things are."

The Borobudur is the great relic of Buddhism. Situated

out in the country a few miles beyond Djogja, not far from the currently erupting volcano Merapi, this great stone monument rises in nine concentric circles. Said to have been built in one night by the angels around A.D. 800, it still seems a thing of supernatural beauty. Around A. D. 1500 the Moslems destroyed many of the statues and defaced the walls, but careful Dutch archaeologists later reconstituted the immense monument. Inside fifteen-foot bell-shaped pergolas are seated figures of Buddha in meditation while the largest statue of all fills the dome.

On the walls the whole story of Buddha's life is depicted in half relief—the dream in which his young mother, Maya, was approached by a white elephant who deposited in her open side the future Buddha; the thirty-two wonders which accompanied his conception, including such miracles as the blind being suddenly able to see, the deaf to hear, the lame to walk; his birth and its thirty-two further attendant wonders; the birth on the same day of his future disciple Ananda, his wife Yauthaudara, his horse Kantika, and the springing forth of the great tree Bodi under which he eventually achieved enlightenment. Also the incident of his having been taken to a festival by his nurses who laid him in the shade and forgot him, returning hours later in fright expecting to find the child dead of sunstroke only to see that the shadow in which they had placed him had stood quite still in their absence. Depicted also is the story of Buddha as a young prince wanting to go off as a monk in search of wisdom, his restraint by his father, his first sight of an old man, a sick man, a dead man, and his realization that the sorrow at the heart of life cannot be escaped by distraction or amusement; his decision to set forth on pilgrimage in search of life's meaning; his farewell to his sleeping wife and infant son;

his going forth on his horse and bidding the faithful animal good-by at the border of his kingdom; his years of wandering; his temptations; his further years of meditation, during which he subsisted on a grain of rice and a sesame seed each day; his five dreams presaging Buddhahood; his final struggle with the greatest of the demons and his oblivion of discomfort in the face of torrential rains, cyclonic winds, destruction of the forest; the transformation of impenetrable darkness to most radiant light; his wakening under a banyan tree to the four great truths and the necessities of the eightfold path; the choosing of his disciples; his long years of compassionate service among the needy; and finally his death and immortality.

But it is not only in carvings on a monument that the life of Buddha lives in Indonesia; he also lives in the minds of the common people, memorialized in their arts, their customs, their comprehension of the oneness of man, nature, and all forms of life. Here again are influences which were inextricably tangled into the roots of worship, wonder, and morality, modifying Islamic beliefs.

As for the animism coming down from no one knows how many generations of forebears, it is at once a kind of gentle nature worship, a fear of spirits, a continuing propitiation, an ordering of the calendar, a celebration of the chief events of life, an adjustment to the small exigencies of the day. Only the educated are aware that these taboos and celebrations are not taught by orthodox Islam; for the rest they are just the things one does.

Mohammedanism and Christianity both came into the Indies in the 1300's as accouterments of the spice trade. Neither the Christian traders nor the few Christian missionaries who followed made much impression on the native culture. On the other hand, the vigorous Moslem missionaries, militant in their ardor for Allah, swept formal Hinduism and Buddhism off Java and most of the surrounding islands. These two, Mohammedanism and Christianity, have led most of the world's religions in propagation by the sword and in proselyting zeal, but in the Indies Mohammedans had a sociological advantage in promoting plural marriage and in not disapproving matrimonial alliances with dark-skinned persons beneath their cultural dignity. Nevertheless, as has usually been the case with wholesale militant conversion, change was wrought slowly in the lives of the people. The greater Hindu deities gave way to Allah; the lesser deities lived on in daily life. Mosques supplanted temples; men took over public rites and prayers; women made their own peace in their own way with such supernatural beings as touched their lives and their children's. For the most part, the arrangement still holds. To be sure, there is an occasional mosque which welcomes women and there are Indonesian women with considerable understanding of Moslem law and tenets but they are few. Many, especially among the uneducated, have a passionate loyalty to Islam which is not separate in their minds from loyalty to clan and tradition. The unconscious eclecticism of beliefs and rites seems a part of their earnest endeavor to make things *right* for their families. They try to protect the young from threatened disaster, natural or supernatural, and to inculcate in them such principles of morality as they understand; and if the result makes the family happy, they give the credit to Allah.

In essence the Moslem belief holds the passionate conviction that God is one, that Mohammed is His greatest prophet, that salvation is assured to those who follow his teachings, and that the body of believers are the vessel of his holy will. It was A.D. 610, toward the close of the month Ramadan, that Mohammed felt himself overpowered by an angel and heard a voice saying, "Cry in the name of the Lord!" followed by the dictation of the Koran, a book approximating in size the Jewish-Christian Old Testament. To Moslems the Koran is an inspired book, significant to the last letter. To a Westerner it seems a tremendous book but inconsistent in ethics, bogging down in minute legislation of conduct which seems less than noble, then rising again in a call to righteousness, to dedication to the will of God, and to faithful prayer. Moslems who know Arabic feel that it is not amenable to translation since the language of its origin is an integral part of its thought; for this reason translations have not been encouraged and only recently have Indonesians had the Koran in their own tongue.

Mohammed was an orphan and knew hardship from his early years. At twenty-five he married a rich widow, Khadijah, with whom he seems to have lived contentedly. His was a keen mind and as he appraised his times he felt the terrific chasm between the conduct of the people and the righteousness of God. At first his fearless pronouncement of his message evoked the wrath of the political and religious leaders, so that in 612 he had to flee from his native Mecca to the northern city of Medina, a journey since known as the hegira, no doubt one of the most famous journeys of all time. Subsequently he gathered an army, established his authority both religiously and politically, vanquished his enemies, established his supremacy. When he died, A.D. 632, no provision had been made for a successor and so strife over the caliphate tore the body of Islam for centuries. But the teachings and tenets of the prophet gathered momentum, his admonishments became law, his acts the criteria for social and political behavior, his militant spirit the impetus which carried the Koran around the world.

In Indonesia it is apparent that orthodox Moslems lean upon three sources of authority. First the Koran; second, the accrued traditions about Mohammed himself and his teachings, which have become a solid theological structure; and third, the consensus of opinion both of Moslems as a whole and as an Indonesian national group. This consensus of the community, known as *ijma*, takes care of any of the minutiae of life not covered by Mohammed.

For practical purposes Moslem law has been modified in Indonesia by Dutch law, as well as by the exigencies of modern life. In one sense the strength of Islam is also its weakness: Mohammed legislated actions and relationships for practically all the daily events and responsibilities of his time; moreover, he thought in terms of his own time; he thought and taught as much through specifics as through principles. So now his followers have sometimes to choose between literal obedience and spiritual accommodation. If he had been less specific he might have been more universal, but also succeeding generations, with their conduct unregulated in detail, might have forgotten his great central teachings. It is a choice, a risk, which the founders of all the great religions have faced. Moses and Confucius likewise chose to legislate in detail; Jesus chose the other alternative, but many of his followers could not bear the latitude and set to work down the years to supply the missing documentation. Mohammedanism shares with all religions the task of lifting spirit from triviality, a task of which some Indonesian religious leaders are thoroughly aware.

From thoughtful Indonesians and from observant Westerners the question rises as to whether Indonesia can become both a democracy and an Islamic state. Historically democracy has deep rootage in the concept of the importance of the individual. Islamic thought does not stress the importance of the individual. Indeed, many Islamic tenets go contrariwise—as in the laws governing marriage and the status of women. A woman who is one of the four wives legalized by Mohammed, circumscribed by Moslem law in her prerogatives, can scarely be a democratic citizen. Nowadays plenty of women are aware of the predicament; they press at parliament to grant them their rights. Other women ignore the democratic experiment, preferring the ways of their fathers. These are matters which must be of intense concern to proponents of democracy. Furthermore, it does not seem native to Islamic thought to care for the helpless, to consider the least member of the social order important because he is a human being. Families care for those of their immediate group, but to consider the well-being of persons who have no personal claim is another matter. That the problem is not entirely one of low economic standards is highlighted by the way in which groups at the same economic level but with other religious motivation function with more universal concern. This is a thing one cannot help but note and ponder as he travels around Indonesia. Of course there is always the chance that a kind of leavening will take place, and that the insight of the few who understand the philosophy of democracy will quicken the understanding of the mass.

Then there is the matter of the insulation of Islam, the conviction that the plums and preferments belong to the faithful. In practical life it tends to work out that non-Moslems are second-class citizens. This is a fact of political life of which President Soekarno is keenly aware; from his early days as a nationalist leader he has affirmed his conviction that Indonesia has room for many faiths, just as it has accommodated many races; as a stalwart Moslem he feels that Islam can lead without legislating in religious matters. In drawing up the Pantja Sila, Indonesia's social and political Magna Carta, he stated his views firmly and reaffirms them frequently and convincingly. Many of the country's leaders agree with him and implement their tolerance in attitude and action, but most of them are European-educated. President Soekarno himself is Indonesian-educated but under Dutch professors. Increasingly the leadership of the country will have a modern education, which means grounding in democratic traditions of religious freedom. They will travel abroad. Certainly they will have to face the choice between democracy and old-line Moslem law—which is not a choice between democracy and Mohammed's spiritual intent.

The rank and file, however, do not see the problem. They are all out for democracy but they think about as far as the fact that they have a right to elect a parliament. In the choice of representatives in parliament many then take the stand that only Moslems should be allowed to run for office, while others advocate an all-Moslem state in which Islamic law and religion are politically supreme. These proponents of the all-Moslem state are divided into two camps—those who would like to see the government move in that direction by due process of law and pressure of public opinion and those who believe a Moslem state should be carved out by the sword if necessary. Many of this latter group have formed an organization with its own government, a state within a state, known as Darul Islam. This exclusively Moslem state is, they claim, the real state of Indonesia. Currently

Darul Islam is a terrific force and may have it in its power to wreck the democratic experiment.

Geographically Darul Islam stems out of Central Java, but has now spread into Celebes, Sumatra, Borneo and some of the lesser islands, setting up its rule in villages where the rightful representatives can be threatened or terrorized out of control. Historically it owes its genesis to an unfortunate political and economic situation in central Java during the struggle for independence. When the return of the hated Dutch seemed imminent, some of the dislocated peasants and many of the armed youth swung to its support along with bands of roving guerrillas, followed by certain Dutch ex-army men and officers who felt any means were fair if they served to displace the Republican government. And so the movement entrenched itself. Its methods have been the methods of terror—trains held up, busses looted and burned, villages razed, crops commandeered, people tortured and murdered. Disrupted villages now number many hundreds while the government estimates murders to average six a day for the past year. Whole areas of Java are so terrorized that communications, commerce, production and political life are completely disrupted, not to mention the psychological deterioration of the people as they find themselves and their government helpless before the assaults of organized fanatics. As its power has grown in Java, Darul Islam has spread into other sections of the republic, taking advantage of poor economic conditions, general unrest, resentment against the central government's poor performance in matters of security and general elections, and particularly taking advantage of troubles instigated by the communists. Although the two groups are ideologically in sharp opposition, still neither hesitates to use the machinations of the other to further its own ends. And their common end is to discredit the national government, instigate armed rebellion and then take advantage of the chaos. It is in this combination of communism and rabid Mohammedanism that the republic's gravest danger now lies. Moreover, there seems little hope of righting matters until the government is ready to take a strong stand against both groups. Obviously it cannot take a strong stand against communism so long as major parties keep on placating communist interests, nor go all out against Darul Islam terror so long as sizable numbers of Moslems all over the country share the conviction of the Darul Islam leaders.

If the threat of Darul Islam were a temporary matter rising out of the instability of a new government which is finding its way, the situation would be less significant, but the theory of an all-Islam state which Darul Islam advocates is inherent in Moslem teaching and modification in the direction of modern self-determination is contrary to the literal teaching of Islam. Nevertheless plenty of Moslem leaders, and among them some of the best minds of Indonesia, claim that Mohammed's social principles are amenable to the needs of any society and that modifications in form should be made as they prove necessary to the well-being of the people. Thus the struggle is on and the fate of Indonesia as a democracy is here at stake.

The vehement loyalty to Islam of educated Indonesians is a matter for international interest. I had a certain advantage in talking with educated Indonesians because I had long had a warm appreciation for the Koran, knew a bit of Moslem history, had a fair library on modern Islamic thought and had got around the country where I could see how Moslem tenets worked out in daily life. We had our arguments, all friendly, but often with no holds barred. After a time it was no astonishment to hear educators say that they were not going abroad to learn modern educational methods for the good of the Indonesian school system, nor for the furtherance of knowledge, nor for the advantage of the people, but for just one end: the glory of Islam. Intellectual power for Islam, economic power for Islam, armed might for Islam, international advantage for Islam. They translated their slogans for me: OUR MOON RISES; AFTER A THOUSAND YEARS OF ECLIPSE, ISLAM SHINES FORTH, and many others. The theory behind the slogan is that a third world war is imminent, that it will disrupt Western culture permanently, that the Western democracies will be eclipsed, whereupon Islam will come into its own. When I pressed the point that it might be difficult for democracy to survive in Indonesia if the Western democracies were obliterated, they answered that the form of government administered by Islam was of secondary importance to the power of Islam.

At that point in our argument I would customarily ask about the fate of the rest of the world when Islam took over. The answer was unanimous: the fate of those who do not turn to Islam does not matter. Aghast, I would point out that the philosophy of Christianity is different: the welfare of every individual matters, down to the least. And that, they said, was because Christianity has grown weak. In the Middle Ages Christianity was strong, they said; its armies were mighty; men fought as Christians and not as citizens of this or that country. When I suggested that that record is Christendom's present embarrassment, they felt that such a reaction was just another sign of decadence. When I pointed out that love of the least, including one's enemies, was the highest criterion of conduct, they responded that such a philosophy is also the product of weakness. In one discussion I recall an Indonesian educator asking me if a Christian would work as hard to save an Indonesian baby as his own. Fortunately I could point around Indonesia to the answer—schools, medical services, care of the unfortunate. So here we are again facing the fact that the present democratically oriented government is an empirical device toward an end not consonant with Islamic historical structure.

Once in a while I came upon an Indonesian who saw the danger in Islam's parochialism. Occasionally I met someone with a fine appreciation and knowledge of other religions—and of the two the knowledge is the rarer as it is in any country. I met humble and wise Moslems who believe that there are many paths to God, that all are steep, and that one who climbs far enough will see them converging. These persons are in the minority as they are in any culture but there may yet be enough of them to give democracy a chance in Indonesia. Then Indonesia will be able to make a large contribution to world society, carrying Islam's loyalty to the God who is One and its passion for righteousness into international relationships. The more I traveled in Indonesia the plainer it seemed to me that if young Indonesia is faced with a choice between democracy and Islam, then some sort of modification of Mohammedanism is on the docket.

As for Christianity in Indonesia—there are about 3,500,-000 Christians, 750,000 Roman Catholics, 2,750,000 Protestants, a total of over 4 per cent of the population. The dominantly Christian areas of Celebes, Sumatra and Ambon are characterized by high literacy, initiative in matters of health and social welfare, and concern for the whole of the country. Christians furnish a disproportionately high percentage of those who enter the service professions. But their ultimate contribution to Indonesian culture depends upon the people's decision as to what constitutes a Moslem state.

· IO ·

The Nation's Food

I F AN AMPLE AND NUTRITIOUS DIET IS THE
first step toward health, then Indonesia has scarcely
taken the first step, but at least all the people are aware of
the food problem and hunger is never far from the center of
concern. Doubtless food is the first concern of people everywhere, but when the wheat crop fails in a country with a
high standard of living there are other grains; when beef is
scarce there is mutton and pork; when one region suffers
shortages quick transportation soon evens things off. In
Indonesia, however, food has to be eaten largely where it is
produced; there are no granaries to tide over a lean year;
refrigeration and transportation are luxuries; the urban population is almost as dependent upon the current crop as
the peasantry.

About three-fourths of the working population are farmers, producing three-quarters of the national income, which
is one of the lowest incomes in the world, something under
$40 per capita. Not that each person or each family sees that
much cash, for all over the archipelago thousands of agricultural families seldom have occasion to deal with money.
"Tanah air kita," the people say—"our land and water."
Their land and water is their sustenance, their preserver,

the companion of their days. The only way into their minds is through the land and water gate. A newcomer may be more interested in the political scene or the rebirth of handcrafts, but he will not understand either, nor any other facet of Indonesian life, until he understands the basic concern for the land and the food it produces.

As in all of Southeast Asia, rice is the important food. Java-Madura, Bali, Lambok and south Celebes export rice for interisland trade; in Java half the 20,000,000 acres available for native agriculture produce rice; Sumba and Sumbawa, Timor and Flores, usually produce enough for their own consumption; the tin islands, the Moluccas, Sumatra and Borneo and many others have to import.

Rice culture, it seemed to me, was the heart of daily life, a gauge of the people's vitality of spirit. Living on the edge of Bandung, we had small rice fields for our front yard, except for a twenty-meter stretch of lawn, so that we could see the rice come and go, two and one-half full crops a year. Sometimes when the near field was planted with delicate chartreuse seedlings, the next field was celadon with half-grown rice, while the side field might be pure gold with man-tall heavy-headed ripe grain. When the time came for a new rice crop our neighbor would let in the water to soak the field for two or three days, then plow by driving his water buffalo round and round in narrowing circles, finishing off in the center of the field. His harrowing was done by wading around happily in the ooze squeezing the mud between his toes, often assisted by his wife and sons and not exceptionally by any foreign children whose mothers were not looking. Beginning at sunrise, women transplanted the seedlings, pulling the young plants from the nursery beds, wading out into the newly flooded field and rhythmically poking holes in the wet earth with the forefinger of the left hand while with the right hand they inserted three rice stalks in each hole. During transplanting time, the farmer who had trodden the mud sat himself comfortably on the narrow hard-packed abutment which cupped the field and fished in his little pond. Division of labor, he called it.

We watched the offerings and ceremonies which attended each season. Harvesting is a beautiful sight, with the women moving into the field, often two hundred of them, their kerchiefed heads or broad hats bobbing up and down like animated toadstools. Stalks are cut individually with a small broad blade, the woman saying a small and ancient prayer as she severs the stalk about fourteen inches from the head. This personal relationship of harvester to rice has added to the difficulty of introducing modern machinery. Usually by nine o'clock in the morning the cutting is finished and the women move off across the countryside in long rows carrying their bundles of rice on poles, as much as is their payment for harvesting plus whatever they may have bought. After a harvest great contentment settles over the countryside. The rice is *in*. People will eat. The land has bestowed its blessing. Life will move on in its great cycles. For home consumption the rice is then dried in the sun and hand-threshed, after which the kernels are loosed from the husks by pouring small amounts of grain into a scooped-out tree trunk where it is pounded by women holding long mallets. A difficult operation to the uninitiated—as I found to my undoing.

This wet culture of rice is called *sawah*, a word one hears continuously as the country people point out across their fields, up the terraced mountain sides, to the work of their hands. In Java-Madura 85 per cent of the rice culture is sawah. But there is also a dry method called *paddy gogo*;

much easier, it seemed to me, although the yield is less than half the sawah yield. We watched the dry rice culture on the outer islands—a mere matter of clearing a piece of forest land (although there is nothing so mere about that), then planting rice as long as the land is good, after which the land is returned to mother jungle and the rice-hungry move on to a new clearing job.

The two big rice problems are the need for selected seed, a matter in which rice experts from abroad are lending assistance, and the need of commercial fertilizer. Having seen the frantic way in which Chinese, Japanese, and Formosan farmers save every dribble of night soil for their land and the eagerness with which they buy commercial fertilizer when they can get it, it seemed strange to me to find the Indonesians so indifferent to feeding their precious crops. One reason may be that in volcanic regions the land gets a fair amount of mineral renewal from the volcanic ash, either air-borne or carried down by mountain streams in irrigation water. Mostly it is the European estates which utilize the million or so tons of fertilizer imported annually. I thought of going into the fertilizer business when our friends the rice experts explained that moderate phosphate manuring of 2½ million acres of poor rice land would increase the yield two-fifths, which would mean another million tons of rice. But it now looks as if the government's long-range rice program will include fertilization; indeed, I am sure it would if I, or any other foreigner, began to make money by importing phosphates.

The government program already operates through a Food Supply Board to control the rice market and keep the price constant in spite of the rising cost of living. When we first reached Java the rice market was jittery; all the servants could talk about—and the farmers, and even our more sophisticated friends—was the price of rice. Chinese middlemen were blamed for the price rise, as much the historical carry-over of an ancient guilt as a present accomplishment, but Indonesians have a constitutional proclivity for blaming the Chinese before they look into the real cause of any price increase—which often is the Chinese.

No one has yet got around to supervising the quality of marketed rice, an important consideration since rice furnishes close to 80 per cent of the people's diet. Unfortunately all Asians prefer white rice, which means highly milled rice with the outer covering containing the vitamins entirely removed. Lacking the vitamins, people develop beriberi. It was the Japanese who first recognized beriberi as a deficiency disease, but it was two Dutchmen in Eykman Institute, Djakarta, who isolated the first vitamin—vitamin B. Manual laborers require more B than sedentary workers and most Indonesians are manual laborers; pregnant women and nursing mothers require high B and most Indonesian women are pregnant or nursing; children through adolescence require high B and 40 per cent of the population is under fifteen years. Many of the other foods which could supply the missing catalyst are expensive. Recent analysis in typical Java markets indicates a meager amount of vitamin B left in the rice, while the high infant mortality, 300 per 1,000 live births, indicates undiagnosed beriberi, often fatal to infants in three days.

Fortunately it is now possible to extract the vitamins from the discarded husks, reduce the extraction to a colorless liquid and spray it over the polished rice. Only one part of this reinforced rice to 200 parts of ordinary white rice is necessary for health. Some countries, such as Puerto Rico, now require that all imported white rice be thus fortified. Japan is experimenting with fortification. The Philippines led the movement. Indonesia has made no move to date. To be sure, the addition of fortified rice raises the cost ten cents on every hundred pounds, but around twenty-five cents per person would foot the annual bill and pay handsome interest in increased energy.

Teaching people what to eat is a slow process where illiteracy is high, billboards few, electricity rare and hence radios, television and moving pictures scarce. The United States Educational Service has a few mobile units which take health films to the people. In Sumatra we went one night many miles into the jungle, driving through old rubber plantations largely discontinued because of insecurity. The cinema screen was set up in a cleared space near a village protected by soldiers. It was the first moving picture experience for most of the 1,500 people and they really buzzed over the life story of the fly in relation to typhoid and other filth diseases. We asked ourselves why someone couldn't make a like film on the advantages of unpolished rice.

Corn comes second as a carbohydrate staple. It is usually grown on upland dry fields where the soil is less fertile and the yield is not exactly up to Iowa standards. Experiments are currently under way on hybrid seed, but American varieties do not readily adapt to Indonesian conditions, partly because the day is shorter. Cassava is the potato of the Indonesian diet. Never a luxury and often a monotonous necessity, its food value is not high, but as a dry land crop it can take over soil too depleted for rice or corn. When preferred foods are plentiful there is cassava for export, largely processed as some form of tapioca. In the last two decades soy beans have been coming into their own. Following a crop of irrigated rice, they grow rapidly and close to a million acres are now planted, but the yield is only two-thirds the Manchurian yield and half the yield in the United States. Peanuts are the most popular pulse. Besides their wide consumption by all classes of people, they furnish peanut-cake fodder and peanut-leaf hay for cattle. Sweet potatoes, a cheap, filling and nutritious stand-by, are also grown on irrigated land following rice.

The Dutch have introduced many good European vegetables—onions, carrots, cabbage, a fragile-stalked green celery, eggplant shaped like thin cucumbers, small squash, small peas and lima beans, but neither the Indonesians nor the Dutch are great vegetable eaters. We never ate any vegetables raw unless we bought them directly from germ-conscious Dutch farmers—from whom we also got Plymouth Rock-sized eggs which looked like ostrich eggs alongside the usual Bantam variety—Bantam, Java, being the home of the famous little chickens.

Fruits are abundant but no longer cheap. Bananas come in all sizes and colors from the small *pisang rajah* to the two-foot plantain. *Djeruk*, a generic term for citrus fruits, include medium-sized rather woody oranges, sweet tangerines, small limes and sour lemons. Deprived of these vitamin-C bearing fruits, gangs of workmen fall prey to scurvy. Papayas are relatively inexpensive and rich in vitamin A but the people do not know it. The big thing about papaya is that it grows from a seed to a sizable tree producing fruit in six months. To stand beside the bed of a blind baby and realize that he could have been saved from decades of darkness if he had been fed the papaya growing around his door is about as much argument as one needs to get the Mothers' Schools spreading faster. Lack of vitamin A is also probably the predisposing factor in the formation of bladder stones and in Djakarta 10 per cent of all surgery performed on children is for the removal of bladder stones. The problem of food production constantly tangles with the problems of health and education.

Mangoes are abundant in season, the best ones coming from the Surabaya area. Mangosteen tastes as if it were the offspring of a peach and a pineapple. Pineapples can be had the year around, relatively inexpensively. Breadfruit, resembling a round six-inch loaf of bread, is a staple in many sections. Jackfruit, a kind of overgrown breadfruit, weighs up to thirty pounds. Rambutan are cheap and the pulp has a pleasant thirst-quenching acid taste; people can be seen on any road swinging a bunch of prickly red rambutan.

Durian is an experience in itself. A seller of durian passes the house and immediately one looks for putrid fish or rancid butter or a herd of goats or limburger cheese or rotten cabbage, but the evil-smelling fruit is forgiven and cherished because of its taste. In size it resembles the honeydew melon, in texture of rind a good stiff thistle, in taste pineapple ice cream with crushed cashews—but ask the next person and he will make some other comparison. As durian season approaches people begin to salivate. Unfortunately, no matter how the fruit is served, even in ice cream, it produces an unsquelchable belch, horrifying Europeans unaccustomed to its peculiarity but delighting the gourmand Chinese.

In a land where daily consumption runs around 2,000 calories and 1¼ ounces of protein per day is average for a manual laborer, production of good grains, vegetables and fruits is highly important. We saw a beautiful demonstration of the rise in energy effected by good food. When our cook and maid, a man of thirty-five and his wife of twenty, lived in their crowded kampong in Bandung, they were sweet and accommodating individuals with low energy. At work they were always leaning on something. If their willingness outran their lethargy and they toted and carried for a spell, they were breathless and spent. Then we moved to Djakarta where they were finally installed in our guest room, slept in good beds with mosquito nets, and ate our food, which included more meat, eggs, butter, vegetables and milk in a week than they were accustomed to eat in half a year. In two months they were different individuals, never tired, full of energy, ambitious and inventive. They took on the verve one finds among the well-paid, well-fed Indonesians but seldom meets in the working classes. Of course two individuals do not constitute a meaningful experiment, but . . .

Production of most foods could be increased by the use of improved farm implements. Customarily a man hoes his land, digs, chops down a bunch of bananas or chops up a rattlesnake with his *patjol,* a heavy hoe with a sharp iron blade. Traditional patjols are made from wood and iron by the local blacksmith, but machine-made imported hoes are preferred and currently the agricultural development program distributes them free to many farmers. However, the needy farmer is likely to sell his efficient new hoe for private gain and go on using his old patjol. The task of changing to more efficient implements is not the simple matter of providing better tools.

As for mechanization, it is used primarily on the estates and then only in a limited fashion. Some sugar estates use tractors for plowing a farmer's riceland in order to speed his crop and get the use of the land for cane; some wheel-type tractors are used for cultivation of tobacco, fiber and tapioca. East Coast Sumatra uses tractors for clearing land on oil palm and rubber estates, and ten tractors have recently been sent to Atjeh to open up new riceland. As the transmigration schemes work out, the large land-clearing projects will demand mechanization.

"Tanah air kita"—not only the land but the water is an indispensable source of food supply, for the chief protein in the Indonesian diet is fish. However, old-line Dutch policy discouraged large scale fishing on the part of Indonesians and withheld permits for motorized vessels until 1934 lest they become competition for Dutch-owned interisland ships. Even then they were restricted to operating close to shore where the small sailing craft also fished intensively. When the war broke in Europe there were exactly thirty-two Indonesian-owned motorized fishing vessels in all the islands. Realizing they were likely to need more fish, the Dutch attempted to motorize a fishing fleet large scale but the Japanese soon commanded Indonesian waters and regulated fishing for their own purposes, including development of a tuna fishery which American submarines then took care of. War and postwar struggle took heavy toll of fishing craft so that not a motorized vessel and very little fishing gear remained. However, after independence the new government formed a Sea Fisheries Service which began at once to raise Japanese vessels, to repair local craft and to expand the fisheries program in general.

Nowadays small craft, all kinds, all sizes, skim up and down the coasts and hazard waters which appear much too rough for them. Families are born, live and die on these boats. Until recently their ways and their days could have been interchanged with the habits and times of their ancestors. Indeed, watching them, I often wondered whether or not they were their ancestors.

Fishing is of four main sorts. *Majang* fishing is named for a particular kind of small sail or rowboat of which there are more than 4,000, scarcely 1 per cent of them powered. Out at dawn, returning in early afternoon, except for the larger vessels which carry ice and stay out for several days, they operate the coastal waters from fifteen to fifty miles off shore. *Pajang* fishing utilizes nets woven of *pinti* twine made from the skin of a certain palm, operating like purse seines. For trap fishing, thousands and thousands of craft go out in spawning season to catch sardines and anchovies, sprat, Spanish mackerel, horse mackerel, milk fish and the like in floating traps laid near masses of seaweed. In reef fishing divers drive the fish into fixed nets, cleaning out a given area quickly. Finally, but not least, there is tuna fishing. Indonesia's tuna fleet consists of around a score of motorized hook-and-line bait vessels. The season lasts around two hundred days and, since the tuna run close to shore, ice is not needed. Formerly most of the catch was smoked but now an increasing amount is canned.

We watched the canning process at the Canning Indonesian Products Factory in Denpasar, Bali. The factory was built by the Japanese but is now owned by Chinese and Indonesians, presently incorporated at R. 1,000,000 and employing around 500 workers, but expecting shortly to double payroll and output. Tin for the cans is a problem. Although tin is produced in Indonesia there is no rolling mill in Southeast Asia, so the tin plate is bought in the United States. Such processing plants are among Indonesia's great needs. At Macassar I also wondered why someone did not open a factory to turn out mother-of-pearl products such as buttons, knife handles and ornaments, utilizing the trochus shells at hand instead of sending them abroad to be made up.

Not only the ocean but lakes, swamps, rivers, ponds, paddy ditches—almost every waterhole as large as a dining table—contain fish. Nevertheless, fish stocking is greatly needed and millions of acres of swamp in Celebes, Sumatra, Java and Bangka are suitable for fish. At present Indonesia has the lowest average fish consumption of any maritime country, scarcely half the former fifteen pounds per person and only one-seventh the basic requirement estimated by nutrition authorities.

Inland fish culture is relatively a large industry. A quarter-million persons in Java-Madura engage in fish culture in salt water ponds called *tambaks*. Since fish will not spawn in the ponds, the ponds have to be restocked each year from young fry caught in the sea. The whole tambak industry needs a going-over, for many ponds are poorly built or too high or in a sad state of repair. Fresh-water ponds are usually small, but the equivalent of an acre of pond produces up to 1,000 pounds of fish annually, while the paddy fields yield around 350 pounds an acre. It takes an Indonesian to think of raising fish and rice in the same field and then eating them in the same bowl.

We became much interested in an experiment directed by an Indian scientist serving under American FOA as technical advisor to the Indonesian government. He set a village to making small earthen pots in each of which some two pounds of salted fresh fish were packed, the pot then sterilized in a food cooker, and dipped in a mixture of damar and paraffin. Thus preserved, the fish is good for six months. Some two thousand pots are out on trial, costing three rupiahs each as contrasted with six to eight rupiahs for two pounds of fresh fish. The project supports two small industries, pot-making and fishing; two fishes in one pot, the scientist observes.

Neither the million fishermen nor their ships are licensed, except a few foreigners. Conservation regulations are also few except that dynamite and poison are prohibited and in some areas coral fishing requires a local permit. Interisland fish trade is a two-way traffic except for Java-Madura which has no fish to spare. Foreign imports of dried and salted fish, canned salmon and sardines, and agar-agar are declining, primarily in order to save foreign exchange as well as because of a shortage on the part of exporting countries. Exports have also decreased.

The Sea Fisheries Institute has made a fine start at sponsoring public markets, largely owned by cooperative associations through which the fishermen make most of the profits. The fish market in Menado is typical in variety of fish sold, volume, smell, and slippery underpinning. I never saw so many kinds of fish even in China or the Philippines; every shape from the customary finned-oval to triangle and fan-shape; beautiful colors, opal-trimmed gold, purple-bordered pink, lapis and silver, besides ordinary fish color. Fishermen sell the catch direct from their craft; an auctioneer sells to anyone who wants as much as twenty pounds; buyers pay cash which is turned over to the fisherman minus 5 per cent commission, or maybe 10 per cent if there is a general savings account to be divided at Libarun (New Year). An official of the Sea Fisheries Institute stands guard and may bid in a catch if it appears to be going for too little. The fishery co-op extends loans, sells fishing supplies and issues salt. In some places the co-op even lends money for building fishermen's homes. A retail market alongside the wholesale market dispenses the fish to the people.

The problems of the Fishery Services are plenty—deciding what to do, obtaining funds, training personnel, dealing with insecurity; but branch administrative offices are being opened, technical knowledge disseminated, regional problems tackled. When I first traveled among the fishermen I thought of going into the fish business, but the instincts of an educator will out and I got more interested in the possible projects for research. For example, midwinter trawling might produce more kembung fish paste, dear to the Indonesian stomach; kembung are plentiful off the south coast of Borneo where waters are mixed from the deep Flores Sea and the shallow Java sea, but the area is distant from Java and motor boats few. In the Bali Strait sardine runs may be heavy for three or four consecutive years and then suddenly the fish are found only in the deep waters—why? At Pontianak, West Borneo, fish are especially abundant, supposedly because of the mixing of the waters moving south from the South China Sea and north from the Java Sea, a fine place to experiment with trawls for kembung and trolling for tuna. The Siamese are trekking off the fish from the grounds bordering West Borneo because the Indonesians lack motor vessels. A new station is needed at Bengkalis on Sumatra to study the miscellaneous small fish at the delta of the Rokan River, one of the most productive territories in the whole world. Additional projects include laboratories to study bottom configuration, research into water salinity, oxygen, temperature, currents and other particulars which matter to fish. New resources of seaweed must be found; hatcheries must be extended; model fishpond complexes set up for demonstration purposes. Each projected fishery station will cost from R. 200,000 to R. 1,000,000 and employ 30 to 100 persons. Education of the fishermen is basic. But where will the extension workers come from? No doubt from agricultural colleges, mostly still to be built. At present there are no fishery courses at university level.

Currently Indonesian Fishery Services are working closely with the Indo-Pacific Fisheries Council of the United Nations Food and Agriculture Organization. Recently a dozen fisheries officials left Indonesia for Hawaii and the United States. Foreign Operations Administration funds are helping to train the trainer as well as supplying certain vessels to get the fish business on its own bottoms.

That Indonesia's food problem is Indonesia's problem no one knows better than the Indonesian government. The Indonesian people have to bear the burden on their own backs, which, goodness knows, have become accustomed through the centuries to bearing burdens. The difference is that now their heads are up and that their neighbors in many parts of the world, variously initialed and implemented, are lending a hand.

Nothing exemplifies this will of the people to carry their own burdens more explicitly than the way they have put the philosophy and methods of the cooperative movement to work. Beginning with the small resources at hand, they have already put something of a foundation under their food economy. If a superstructure can be erected as soundly the country will have something unique among nations.

Father of the cooperative movement is Mohammed Hatta, vice-president of the Republic. A thoughtful lad was Hatta, growing up in the Bukittinggi and Padang area of Sumatra where the intellectual climate seems to produce long-range thinkers. A strong nationalist from his middle school days,

when he was at college in Holland and during the ensuing
years of his doctorate study, he became a kind of missionary-
at-large for the independence of Asian countries. While
Western imperialism was still in its heyday he knew it had
to go; he realized that its imperatives were outdated and that
for good or ill Asia had to fashion her own future. Returning from Holland in 1932, he began to talk cooperatives,
but under the Dutch any plan to modify the economic order
was an ax at the root of the political structure. Active also
in developing the Nationalist Party, PNI, he was the kind
of gadfly the Netherlands East Indies government could well
do without. And so at various intervals, the longest of them
eight years, he was imprisoned or exiled. In forced retire-
ment his economic and political philosophy matured. And
so did the man. After his release by the Japanese and all
during the occupation, he was a marked man. His office was
the only one in Indonesia where no Japanese was to be seen,
neither as clerk nor as head of a department. He stood where
he stood, too influential to ignore, too independent to push
around. Not an assuming man; not a go-getter, nor yet a
man who jumps from band wagon to band wagon strumming
for this cause and that. He believes that democracy is not
won once for all, that its implementing in days of peace is
more difficult than its initial achievement in time of war,
that economic democracy is the beginning of freedom, a
thing worth working for. Moreover, he believes that ordinary
people can and must understand the ends for which they
work and see some results in short-time achievement.

   To be the father of the cooperative movement is not
merely a matter of functioning as progenitor, attending the
christening and all subsequent birthday celebrations. It is a
day-by-day job, explaining, demonstrating, encouraging,

pointing out reasons for failures, inculcating a little more daring and a little less gullibility. Hatta is impatient with people at whatever level of authority who hunt an extraneous factor to blame for the low standard of living, although he is realistic about the fruits of colonialism. Nationalization of big foreign enterprises will come more easily, he feels, after the basic economy has been established on a cooperative basis. In the meantime "Private economy will fulfill in our society the function of developing economy and providing the thousands of have-nots with a means of subsistence. . . . We cannot but admit that the private enterprises, whether they are managed by foreigners or by our own compatriots, have still an important economic function in Indonesia's present national production." It is this abundant common sense of Mr. Hatta's which gives the cooperative movement its virility. "We need aid in the form of capital and expert-personnel from abroad." Few Indonesian leaders will admit as much in public. He also emphasizes increased production of food and daily necessities in terms of regional specifics; improvement of the smallholders' products so that they bring a top market price; improvement of distribution so that outlying areas can share in good markets and common people can exchange goods expeditiously. He needles the cooperative movement and the people in general to combat usury, to develop thrift, to set up communal rice storehouses, to get behind the village schools, to exercise their franchise at the village level where it exists as they push their demand for national elections.

Obviously one man does not make a movement nor furnish its leadership. Mr. Hatta has drawn about him some of the soundest minds in the land. No doubt they have helped to make him the leader he is and certainly they have given the movement its continuity and drive. At all levels the men who carry the ball for the cooperative movement appear a dogged, enthusiastic, open-minded group, as avid to learn as to teach and not above blaming themselves for their failures while spreading credit where credit is due.

In 1940 there were 624 cooperatives, of which 478 were credit co-ops, a few producers' societies and societies for the amortization of debt. The movement was dominated by government servants and other salaried classes; it was an intellectual experiment. Total assets approximated $1,000,-000. Postwar, cooperatives were encouraged by various political parties. PNI, with Hatta in a prominent position, was bound to further cooperatives. Masjumi organized cooperatives on a large scale in order to provide credit to small farmers at reasonable interest for purchasing and selling their produce, redeeming land in debt, underwriting small businesses. The government, almost from the beginning, utilized the cooperative movement in economic rehabilitation.

At present there are close to 8,000 cooperative organizations in Indonesia, Java in the lead, with a total membership of nearly 2,000,000 persons and registered savings of nearly R. 60,000,000. Comparative figures indicate both the growth of the movement and its spread into various aspects of economic life. Central cooperatives, village cooperatives, sheds, granaries, and the like, credit cooperatives, production cooperatives, consumption cooperatives, are on the increase. Behind each one of these cooperatives is an educational campaign and behind each campaign, individuals who have experienced the value of participation.

Problems—of course. For instance, the government votes money for allocation to the credit cooperatives and then pays over only a fraction of the amount voted. Cadres and key men have to be trained in duly authorized courses; the courses have to be built from statistics and procedures gathered in the field; experiments have to be tried but abandoned when unsuccessful even though their promoters lose face; new cooperatives which need trained personnel have to be begun without trained personnel; learning on the job must be accepted as the necessary although expensive method of progress. And all the time the movement must live up to its name—cooperative. Moreover, while encouraging adaptability to the needs of individual communities, the movement has to maintain tight organization.

The very form of the movement, especially of its training program both for leaders and for local groups, is a natural opening for communist infiltration. And communists infiltrate. They even advance to positions of leadership. But the number is actually very small, the chief reason being that the two movements are antithetic in principle. Classes in the cooperative movement could easily be transformed into out-and-out communist cells if it were not for the fact that the more level-headed of the cooperative leadership, who are for the most part the better educated, are ardent advocates of democracy. They know that democracy offers the only soil in which economic cooperation can flourish. They also know that the movement's success in local situations is probably Indonesia's best economic rebuttal to communist promises. The rank and file, however, are not inclined to think in terms of communism vs. democracy. They are anti-colonial, anticapitalist (as they understand the phrase in terms of Marxist teachings) anti-white domination and therefore open to leadership from their own people toward some kind of self-determination. Fortunately, in regard to the cooperative movement, the leadership is sound.

Perhaps the biggest contribution of the cooperative movement is not increasing the food supply, nor stabilizing the economy, nor even training leadership, but teaching the people how to work together toward democratic ends. For ordinary people to look right at the fact that they still lack sufficient food, clothes and homes, that national health is still low, that travel is difficult and insecurity widespread, and not blame the government, but realize that they are the government with the future in their own hands, is something of an achievement. An attitude not yet achieved by the masses, of course, but one which is spreading like a slow prairie grass fire.

The movement still lacks a certain amount of cohesion, but the much-discussed creation of an All-Indonesian Cooperative will strengthen it. Given time—and not too much of it—there is also a chance that Indonesia with its grassroots village democracy and a tightly knit cooperative movement may out-cooperate Sweden. And then the Indonesians might eat like the Swedes.

· II ·

The Nation's Industry

UNTIL MID-TWENTIETH CENTURY, WHEN IN-
donesia became its own master, practically all industry
was confined to the great estates, European-owned or leased
and managed. The estates developed the export crops which
formed the bulk of the wealth of the Indies and the bulwark
of Dutch economy. In the prewar days something over 7,000,-
000 acres, 1½ per cent of Indonesia's soil and 8 per cent of
the total cultivated land, produced three-fifths of the exports
and paid two-fifths of the government revenue. Mammoth
business. Europe furnished the capital and initiative while
the Indies furnished the labor. Pioneering ventures, the estates. Cinchona was brought in from the high Andes, cocoa
from Brazil, rubber from the Amazon basin, tobacco also
from South America, the oil palm from tropical west Africa,
coffee from the Belgian Congo, tea from India, China, Japan.
Imagination, foresight, dogged plugging, sweat, despair,
hope, triumph, profits.

Prewar some $800,000,000—Dutch, British, American,
French, Belgian—were invested in 2,400 estates providing
the livelihood for quite a segment of the native population.
One-quarter of the males of Java worked on estates. Earlier
Javanese feudal landlords frequently rented out portions of

their domain to include the labor of peasants so that a man might be forced to work up to 250 days for little or no compensation. Of course if he had not worked for the estate owner he would have worked for his native prince, but the common people have now forgotten that fact. In Sumatra as late as the mid-thirties, more than one in twenty of the coolies were under penal sanction codes. After passage of the Agrarian Law of 1870 conditions bettered but not fast enough to keep down a vast discontent. To be sure, some of the manual laborers profited by their employment, becoming skilled horticulturists, processors, foremen. Also specialized knowledge both seeped through to the Indonesians and was disseminated by the Dutch so that a growing number of farmers began producing the same crops the estates produced, seldom so scientifically, but increasingly. It is the increase in the number, skill and output of the small holders which offers promise in this time of disruption of the great estates. In 1910 small holders produced one-tenth of the value of all agricultural exports; by 1914, one-fourth; by 1935, one-third; immediately prewar, two-fifths. Throughout the war years all production was severely curtailed and all exports negligible, but by 1948 small holders and estates evened off and since then the small holders' exports have risen to two-thirds the total value.

From the standpoint of dollars earned rubber is the chief export. Beginning in 1882, when 33 seedlings were brought from Brazil, over the hump of the century when wild rubber was being tamed, taught to grow productively and give its milky white emulsion known as latex to the tappers, to 1907 when Indonesia supplied 5 per cent of the world's total production, 1912 when it outstripped production from all parts of the world, through the slump of the mad forties, on to the present with production at some 8,000,000 tons supporting 8,000,000 Indonesians, rubber has played a leading role on the country's economic stage.

A forest of rubber trees is a great sight, with miles on miles of the evenly spaced trees marching in formation. Although weeding is a considerable job when the trees are small, an estate of mature trees looks like a park laid out by a geometrician. Tapping begins just at dawn when the sap flows most freely; genie-like the tappers appear out of the morning mist and begin collecting the sap much as maple syrup is collected. A good tree gives about half a pint of sap on alternate days, which adds up to around 2,400 pounds of dry rubber from an acre of trees, an increase of 800 per cent in the past thirty years. Naturally I thought of going into rubber tapping along with the other bootleg tappers until one day I met a tiger, fresh-killed, on the very Sumatran plantation I'd thought of tapping. He had been lured into a huge cage by a poor little sheep and the estate manager explained that they had to get several like him before sheep and tappers would be safe again. Later the manager, too, was killed by a communist gang.

For the most part rubber is processed on the estates, the latex brought into the plant in buckets or barrels, poured into great containers, an acid added to promote coagulation; then the thickened rubber goes onto a rolling machine which turns it out in sheets resembling untrimmed hides, after which the sheets are hung on racks several tiers in height and rolled into the smoking room where they dry over a slow fire. When thoroughly smoked they are sorted, counted, stacked in bundles for shipping.

I enjoyed driving out to rubber estates to watch the latex process until one day in Plered, half a day's drive from

Bandung, when we met a friend who informed us that as he had driven into his nearby estate that morning he had met a funeral coming out of his gate; during the night his overseer had been killed by a Darul Islam gang. He advised us to get ourselves back to Bandung. On the way we met several truck-loads of soldiers, the trucks stopping here and there to disgorge their men into the jungle. Knowing how trigger-happy some soldiers are about targets which look Dutch, and thinking of my Dutch great-grandfather, I suddenly lost interest in rubber factories.

Practically anyone can grow a coconut tree and almost everyone does. Seed to fruit, it takes a tree about eight years to bear; full maturity is reached between the tenth and fifteenth year and then the tree maintains a constant yield until its three-score-and-ten, after which it works less arduously until it rounds out a century and calls it a day. Estate producers prune their trees; peasants let them grow. Estate trees produce from sixty to a hundred nuts a year; native trees twenty. Estate owners have the picking done at regular intervals; peasants pick a coconut whenever they feel the need of a coconut or the cash it brings. Expert among the pickers of coconuts are the Lampong monkeys of south Sumatra, trained to distinguish ripe nuts—but the monkeys are expensive fellows. An acre of properly spaced trees yields around 2,500 nuts, which means half a ton of copra. Copra is merely dried coconut meat, the ripe nut being chopped open and the good white meat scooped out and allowed to dry in the sun for five days. Kiln-dried copra is darker and has a smoky odor so that it brings a lower price.

Today copra is Indonesia's third largest export and in copra-producing areas around three-fourths of the population is dependent upon the industry. A Copra Foundation now functions as a central purchasing, storing and export organization, fathering the industry in areas where supervision is most needed, both for the sake of the crop and of the people who raise the crop. Because 95 per cent of the crop is grown by small holders and because so much of it goes for home consumption, it is difficult to appraise actual production. Besides, production jumps and slumps; when people have money enough to use their own coconuts, then export drops. Smuggling has almost become a trade in itself. At present the copra situation is complicated by the fact that the United States is purchasing almost the entire Philippine crop, partially for re-export, so that Japan has turned to Indonesia; but the Japanese offer is below the price paid by Western Europe, which, however, cannot pay in dollars. Copra manipulations become involved.

Besides being a fine raw food and furnishing a milky drink which tastes cool no matter how hot the weather, the coconut furnishes an important ingredient in many culinary masterpieces. Its fibrous husk, called coir, is woven into mats and rope; its plaited leaves made into hats, baskets, thatching for roofs, sleeping mats; its hard shell carved into utensils and ornaments. With coconuts, bamboo and an ingenious wife at his command, a farmer is really well set up.

The oil palm is an entirely different tree, with bright yellow-orange nuts growing in clusters. Prewar Indonesia produced a quarter of the world output of palm oil and exported 40 per cent of the total oil entering world trade, the oil being used largely for margarine, soaps, ointment and perfume base. After the war the oil-palm area had to be reclaimed, not a speedy process since trees require twelve years to reach maximum production. The proportion of export to production is lower than formerly because of increased uses at home.

At the height of its prewar economy Indonesia was the second largest exporter of tobacco in the world, exceeded only by the United States, but at present exports are curtailed by insecurity and by the need to use tobacco lowlands to produce more food for the increasing population. Large tracts of land are necessary for tobacco because after growing one crop a field needs to lie fallow for seven years. In Sumatra estates are owned or leased by Europeans and the workmen hired by the year or season. In Java estates rent from the local sultanates on a fifty-year lease, but plant tobacco only every second or third year; in the intervening years the sultan allows the local people to plant rice, corn or cassava. No fertilizer is used because of volcanic elements in the soil and the yield is half again as high as in the Deli area of Sumatra. The Besuki area of Eastern Java grows cigar wrapper, binder, filler and *krossok* (a native tobacco used in domestic cigarettes) on land leased directly to the tobacco growers, perhaps once every three years or when the owners feel like it. The peasant owner then becomes a sharecropper, using seedlings furnished him by the company. Nowadays he is paid in money, the price determined before planting, but if a drought comes along or an invasion of insects, then he is out of funds for he has no insurance against a poor crop.

The Besuki area was in turmoil when we were there, with local peasants demanding extremely high rents on the premise that European managers could stand any amount of bleeding if only the threats were dire enough. When the farmers forced production to close down, they sat back greatly pleased with their power while the communists patted them on their bare backs. During one season more than 400 drying sheds were burned and some 6,000,000 pounds of high-grade tobacco valued at $7,000,000 went up in smoke. To be sure, the tobacco would go up in smoke sooner or later in some part of the world, but here the $1,500,000 worth of sheds went too.

Export of kerf used for local cigarettes is now forbidden because the amount is insufficient for domestic needs. Home-consumption cigarettes, called *kreteks*, are aromatic with ground cloves and are paper-wrapped. Strootjes may also contain cloves, but are wrapped in dried corn leaves. Indonesia yearly uses around 11,000 tons of cloves (also called spice nails), approximately 90 per cent of the world output. A recent price war has prompted the government to appoint a Cloves Board to take over the cloves headache, but no funds have been allocated for the Board's activities. However, village cooperatives are beginning to lend an efficient hand in the cloves and tobacco difficulty. In all there are around 700 kertek factories employing 80,000 workers, turning out 260,000,000 cigarettes a day, netting the government R. 70,000,000 in taxes.

For almost 200 years Java shared with Mocha the traditional coffee honors. In contrast to the British, who drink one-eleventh as much coffee as tea, and the Americans, who drink twice as much coffee as tea, the Indonesians drink either or both impartially. Coffee consumption is estimated at 40,000 tons, drunk thick and black with sugar added. Coffee estates usually occupy hillsides for the sake of good drainage, the trees interplanted with some other crop, principally rubber. European-owned estates are now about one quarter the prewar number. Coffee statistics are hard to get because smuggling is so profitable. We heard fantastic tales from Dutch producers. Coffee is stolen off the trees and then stolen by the bag, deflected on its journey from estate to loading wharf, then disappears at the wharf. Sometimes it also disappears off the ship after being labeled, weighed and stacked. Comes a rainy night, comes a shift in loading coolies, comes the local police, goes the coffee. Smuggling is highly profitable in the direction of Singapore because the beans can be sold on the Malay market for Singapore dollars which bring a nice increase back in Indonesia.

In the peak prewar period when Indonesia exported the third largest amount of tea in the world, the plantations produced nearly six times as much tea as the native holdings on slightly more than twice as much land. Small holdings are now increasing, but only some 200 estates are operating, largely because of insecurity which deters capital reinvestment. The Penggalongan area above Bandung is the ideal tea country—high altitude with warm days and cold nights. As one drives up the mountains one finds Australian pine whose sparsely needled limbs grow in circles; mimosa announcing itself long before the lovely bloom comes into view; tree dahlias dug out of the jungles bulb by bulb and planted in gorgeous hedges; acres of cinchona, which usually grows close to tea. Then miles and miles of tea. Actually tea is not a bush but a tree and tea trees untended for ten years are 25 to 30 feet high, although usually tea is kept at about three feet.

Tea seedlings are planted close together under matting sheds and then after six months or so transplanted in straight rows, some 3,000 bushes to the acre. Both men and women pick the year around, the small fresh leaves near the end of the stem making the best tea. Women pickers wear the oldest possible clothes, patched sarongs or skirts of gunny sacking, their arms wrapped in strips of cloth. Baskets of tea are heavy and the women help each other with the lifting, as did their mothers and grandmothers before them. However tea picking does not go back many generations, for tea did not come to Java until 1826, although the Chinese have had it for 4,500 years. The Javanese say that Daruma, a famous tenth-century Buddhist monk who introduced Buddhism to Japan, once fell asleep at his devotions and was so disgusted with himself that he cut off his eyelashes, and where they fell the sleep-killing tea sprang up. The fact that tea existed long before Daruma bothers no one, for most Indonesians have a vague time sense and anyone who lived before their grandmother can be equated with Moses, or anyway Mohammed. Speaking of the Prophet, there was a time when tea and coffee drinking evoked the death penalty among Moslems, whose authorities placed it in the same category with alcoholic beverages.

All of the estates I visited had their own factories. We watched the tea being brought in, the leaves spread onto racks before being sent down chutes to be ground and fermented, put into huge containers for drying, and finally sorted. The final process consists in spreading the dried leaves on tables where women pick out the tiny white stems, which cannot be sorted mechanically. Many women sat on the floor, their bare feet in the tea. Some of them have scabies. The tea was merely swept up and put in with all the rest for packaging. One manager told me that before the war some American had found a black hair in a package of tea and had raised enough international commotion so that tea processors had to furnish nets for the heads of the sorting women, but now nets and cloth are so expensive that processors take a chance on Americans and hair in the tea. No sort of sanitary inspection is now enforced. The only place the law seems to come down on the processors is in the matter of wages; a tea worker must be allowed to make at least three rupiahs a day, about twenty cents at the realistic open-market exchange. Five rupiahs is a top wage for women, about ten times the prewar wage, but the price of rice and other necessities has risen accordingly.

The whole tea process, field to package, can be finished in 24 hours—withering, rolling, fermenting, sifting, drying, sorting, packaging. A white fluff said to be free caffeine collects on the floor; it is the caffeine more than the tannin which, together with essential oils, gives tea its stimulating effect. Thoroughly fermented tea is black; semifermented is oolong; unfermented tea is green; the leaves are the same. Chemical experiments have proved one thing formerly thought to be superstition: in making tea, water should be used the moment it comes to a boil; otherwise the best leaves will make a flat tea.

Outside the problem of security the big question mark alongside tea production is the blister blight, a devastating disease caused by a fungus which produces blisters on the leaves, changing them from green through red to gray. In the spring of 1951 the blight reached west Java, coming in from Sumatra where it had been brought from Ceylon on the clothes of paratroopers. In the Sukabumi area alone some 150,000 acres were infested in a matter of weeks. To bring this living fire under control means a drastically changed way of life to the small holders. Big estate owners understand that the carefully nurtured shade trees which stunt the weeds in the tea now have to be cut down so that sunlight can get at the blight, but small holders keep their haphazard banana and coconut trees for food and have no intention of cutting them down. The government furnishes the small holders with the Bordeaux mixture used on the blight, but for any kind of practical control inspectors are needed. In the first few months of its descent on Java the blight cost tea growers an estimated R. 50,000,000.

Cocoa is also a Java product; a premium grade too, practically all of it raised on estates in the Penggalongan and Semarang districts. Cocoa arrived in the country only in 1880, and in the postwar dislocation plant diseases got a foothold, but now about half the production has been recovered. Most of the cocoa is used in making chocolate candy.

Sugar came into the Indies more than a hundred years ago and between world wars dominated Java's economy, during its peak years furnishing some 15 per cent of the world's cane output. For a time there were a half-million acres in cane with an annual production of 3,000,000 tons of raw sugar. The cane is grown on irrigated land short-leased from the farmers. When the wet August days roll around the cane is planted by laying old cane along in furrows, allowing new plants to spring from buds at the joints. A field of full grown fifteen-foot cane is a pleasant sight. Harvest begins the following April and the harvest and grinding run through November so that sugar crews are never idle; indeed the crops overlap, for close to fourteen months are required to produce the finished sugar. The cane is brought into the sugar house, up an endless apron into a hopper and fed to huge rollers which crush it; then as the sap is extracted it runs in troughs into huge vats. After being purified and refined it comes to the barrel in white or brown sugar but not the fine white sugar of American consumption.

Life on the sugar estates used to be a special kind of life until the war, with the Dutch planters, chemists, overseers and their families, Chinese foremen, and Indonesian workers all geared to the sugar season's demands. During the depression the industry took a terrific beating, but production had started up satisfactorily when the Japanese invaded and, having Philippine sugar at their disposal, turned half the sugar lands into food and fiber plantings. Then after the war the sugar mills took the brunt of the Indonesian ire against the Dutch. Now insecurity militates against new investment of foreign capital and only about one-third the prewar estate acreage has been replanted. Trouble and sugar estates have become synonymous. Estate rents approximate thirty times their prewar level and communist-fomented strikes often close down the mills at the height of the season. Whether the workers will win out in the sense of closing the mills permanently or win in the sense of sharing in management and responsibility is at present unpredictable. In a sense it may be fortunate for Indonesia that at present world production of sugar is far outstripping consumption and that the International Sugar Conference has allocated Indonesia only about half her request. The government's current subsidy to sugar producers may not only save the farmers from the clutches of the money-lenders as planned, but also enable the nation to reach its cut-back quota.

Quinine is a saga of the Indies, a romance, perhaps soon a historical tragedy. In the early seventeenth century Jesuit priests learned from Peruvian Indians the antimalaria value of the bark of a certain tree, later named cinchona, and the demand for it soon spread over Europe. Seeds were smuggled from Bolivia to Java, but hundreds of thousands both of seeds and seedlings were lost en route or refused to adapt. However, by 1863 thousands of acres of mountainous jungle had been cleared and there were more than a million young cinchona trees in Java, although the quinine content of the bark remained so low that its cultivation was a financial embarrassment to the government. Nor had the British attempt to transplant cinchona to India met with better success. Then an Englishman named Charles Ledger brought back fourteen pounds of choice seed which the English government refused to buy. The Dutch government risked 100 francs for one pound, but by 1895 was paying Ledger an annual salary of 1,200 guilders. Out on the government cinchona estate in Java, most of that pound of seed spoiled, but 20,000 seeds germinated and 12,000 seedlings were set out in nursery beds. Eventually the Ledger trees were segregated in a small cleared area in virgin forest and all the other varieties destroyed except one low in quinine but high in quinidine and cinchonine.

But the problems of quinine culture were not quickly solved, for cinchona has its preferences of rainfall, temperature, elevation, freedom from wind. Terracing the mountains is task enough, but the care of seed beds is even more demanding: good compost is needed; the beds must be shaded with laths or cheesecloth and the watering done with the finest of mist sprays lest the seedlings fall prey to a fungus disease; weeding in humid tropics is serious business; and a good fifteen years growth is required before the bark is thick enough to be profitable. At maturity the trees are usually dug out roots and all, cut into short logs, the bark stripped by beating with wooden mallets, then loosened with bone knives and dried. Fresh bark has a water content of 70 per cent. Much of the quinine is processed in Bandung, bark to neatly stamped tablets bearing the Bandung trade mark. At present the output is one-tenth capacity owing to development of substitutes, wide use of DDT to reduce anopheles and consequently malaria, and increased production of quinine on the Congo.

Some of the less famous crops of Indonesia promise a bright

export future. Kapok trees, frequently 100 feet tall, their branches extending grotesquely at right angles from their trunk, are certain to catch the eye of a traveler new to Java where nine-tenths of the world supply of kapok is grown. The mature pods are harvested just before they are ready to burst by means of long poles with sharp hooks at the end. The big job falls to the pod-openers, who must separate the silky fibers from the little black seeds, after which it is dried in the sun, hand-baled by screw presses and shipped to a port where it is rebaled by hydraulic compression to save space. It is light, resilient, water resistant, sound-absorbing, heat-insulating, and when floated can carry thirty times its weight. The Agricultural Service has begun a long term replant program by distributing seeds to peasants.

Chief among the hard fibers is sisal, which looks like a large edition of a Mexican century plant. Usually it is propagated from suckers which form new plants in the same fashion as the hen-and-chickens of our grandmothers' gardens. At maturity the long outside leaves are cut two or three times a year for the seven years or so of the plant's life. On the small plantations the fiber is extracted laboriously by hand but the larger estates use machines. Cantala plantations are all on Java; abaca plantations on Sumatra; with sisal they make up the hard fiber production of the country. Such soft fibers as roselle and kenaf, known as Java jute, produce a useful, hemplike fiber.

Before the war 85 per cent of the world supply of both black and white pepper came from these islands, practically all of it grown by small holders but handled by European middlemen. Labor difficulties have reduced both output and profits. A Dutch acquaintance of ours in Java, middleman for a sizable area, customarily bought the entire crop for export, paying a percentage of wages in advance and generally acting as benevolent landlord—for good profit. Postwar, when he finally got his sheds rebuilt and business reconstructed, he found that as fast as he bought the crop it was stolen and sold to him again the next day. So he called the district police, who saw the pepper walking off through the woods and cheerfully shot over the heads of the pepper thieves, after which the thieves divided the profits with the police. Finally the Dutchman became so angry that the police captain took note and advised him to lower the price he was paying. That seemed a preposterous notion to the Dutchman because the chief complaint of the pepper growers had been the low price. But the police captain knew the answer. "Now the people know they can sell the pepper to you about three times and I think they'll be content with a lower price." Which they were. After the harvest the Dutch promoter went out of business, greatly to the perturbation of the pepper pickers.

Western Sumatra around Padang produces most of the cinnamon trees, known as cassia, growing above 200 feet tall. A close cousin produces a cheaper bark, called Chinese cassia, used to adulterate the higher priced cinnamon, and another cousin produces senna. Under the Dutch one-fifth of the world's cinnamon came from the Indies. Vanilla beans, formerly exported, are now largely used at home. The pods are sold along the street by vendors and I found that a slice of bean or even a stirring of a pod in a sauce furnished unadulterated flavor. From the flesh of the yellow pear-shaped drupe of the tall gray-trunked nutmeg tree, nutmeg butter and nutmeg oil are derived; nutmeg comes from the seed and from its outer covering comes mace.

In growing estate crops small holders are already beginning

to band together for the sake of more economical production, and as top-level technicians and managers become more plentiful and Indonesian capital more mobile, no doubt many of the fine old estates will pass into Indonesian hands. With the present tendency toward socialization of the means of production, some estate crops—or some estates—may be government-owned. Either way, the contribution of the estates to the Indonesian economy will continue to be enormous, but industry is no longer confined to the estates. It is spreading out, taking heed of the country's immediate needs, looking toward decreased imports.

One import which could feasibly be decreased is textiles. Fine muslin is the basic Indonesian material, but cotton is not grown on the islands and cotton specialists are only beginning to comb the archipelago for congenial cotton-producing areas. Development of a good stock will take some time. A more immediate first aid is to import raw cotton and spin the thread. Toward that end a 30,000-spindle plant is being set up at Tjilatjap on the south coast of Java, equipment from Japan and installation very slow. One such large unit in operation will not only turn out millions of yards of thread but train workers for future plants. Then comes the need of looms. New types being tried out in the interest of higher production and better quality include both the foot-powered Shanghai loom and small-power looms for decentralized small factories. Labor is as big a problem as looms. Textile labor is well organized and in some places where one operator can handle four or five looms the workers hold out for one loom per person if not for two operators per loom—and let the economy break down if it will.

Although current consumption is less than half the prewar annual per capita of 14 yards, some 5,000,000 yards a month are imported in addition to the product of about 60 "large" weaving mills with 100 or more looms each and 1,500 smaller concerns. How to import less? One answer is that Indonesians could wear, at least temporarily, a less fine grade of cloth; on a par, say, with that worn by the common people of India. An average Indian *saree* is figured at reed 40, pick 40, the "reed" being a device for compacting the weaving and the "pick" indicating the number of times the shuttle is thrown across the loom; weft 20, warp 18. In Indonesia the count is reed 60, pick 60, warp 30, weft 30. A reduction of reed and pick by one-fifteenth would save 23 cents per meter, while the use of 10 per cent coarser yarn in the annual requirement of 1.5 billion meters would effect another big saving. Altogether a reduction of 3.3 per cent in quality would net a savings of R. 87,500,000 in one year. If enough people could read the figures and translate them into public demand, the load of the cost of living could be eased.

A further textile poser is production of machine-patterned fabrics to meet the competition of cheap imported fabrics. Indonesians still prefer their sarongs and *kain* hand-batiked, but the hand dyeing has become too expensive for most of the population. With the shift to machine-stamped patterns the national taste is changing and ordinary Western designs may sometime supercede the traditional batik patterns. Where and how to get the machines for the new processes? A mechanization loan program is under way, equipment rather than money being furnished to selected industries by the government on a long-term basis. In order to train operators one of the best textile institutes in the Far East has been set up at Bandung, courtesy of Foreign Operations Administration, but a training program requires trainees and to date very few Indonesians with sufficient background plus desire have applied. The institute could be filled to capacity with Chinese, but few Indonesians have the equivalent of a high school education or have accommodated to the new concept of social standing for people who work with their hands. Moreover, the idea of popular responsibility for the country's economy is still vague. There are other textile quandaries: developing enough power to supply an expanded industry, granting systematic credit to the industry, dealing with insecurity, and the psychological matter of worker responsibility.

In Padang I visited a typical mill with 300 employees, mostly men except for enough women to wind the spindles. Cotton thread came from Japan, India and the United States; rayon thread from Japan. The big headache was the spasmodic application of the workers. Often weeks went into their training, after which they would decide to quit and live for a while on their earnings or get another kind of job or trundle back to their ancestral village for some sort of celebration. "Completely undependable in these days of freedom," said the Dutch manager who had lived all his life in Sumatra but was soon leaving permanently. "They expect the government to lay a golden egg which hatches their housing, food and guaranteed wages with no effort on their part." He spoke, of course, for one of the basic labor needs of the whole country: workers with a sense of responsibility. But responsibility, I reminded him, has to be taught; a baby is no more born with it than with breeches; give the Indonesians a generation. He snorted. "The communists will have them toeing the mark before then, and their short week at half production will go up in smoke where my capital has gone." He had a point, I thought, but not the whole point.

Cotton is not the only textile. The ramie industry is also beginning to walk on its own feet, although not rapidly. A fund of $10,000 from FOA supplies testing and pilot plant equipment, and a plant in Siantar, Sumatra, is almost ready to open. Nothing moves rapidly in Indonesia, but if anything could be rushed it might well be ramie for with its tough humplike fiber and silky luster it could carry part of the burden for cotton.

One of the most promising harbingers of a new industrial order is the Industrial Research Institute under direction of an Indonesian trainee returned from the United States. Indonesians who have studied abroad and returned to head their own projects have far greater success in training workmen and building an enterprise than do the most affable of foreigners. Foreigners can then work alongside the trained Indonesians with real success. Sometimes the trained Indonesian outthinks and outadapts his foreign coworker, which is a very satisfactory situation in a country where Indonesians have been expected to accept what they were told by Dutch technicians. Only a few Indonesian trainees have returned from technical study abroad. Working with them is an American chemurgist, directing the refining of damar resin for making colorless varnish and extracting tannins from local bark for the tanning industry, a French chemical engineer testing a more simple process for making certain basic chemicals, a New Zealand mechanical engineer. On the immediate docket are projects in resin purification, fermentation of vegetable wastes, vegetable oil processing, fiberboard manufacture, plus extension work to take the laboratory demonstration into the field. A Materials Testing Institute, headed by an Indonesian trainee back from the States assisted by a French technician, is also working to evolve new construction materials particularly suited to the tropics. At Bandung one fair-sized company has gone into production on impregnating wood in a fashion which increases the durability of teak and ironwood four to five times. Likewise a project is under way for the impregnating of coconut fiber with resin. Volcanic trass is being used increasingly for making bricks and mechanization of around a score of brick and tile establishments is under way.

Leather making is one of the most promising infant industries. At the Leather Institute, a government research and demonstration plant, a Yugoslavian leather expert has introduced new tanning methods. Already there are some seven hundred shoe and leather factories registered and probably another hundred beginning to operate. The total 1953 production of about 12,000,000 pairs of shoes and sandals takes care of some 10 per cent of the people and demand exceeds the output.

The other young hopeful among industries is ceramics. The model government plant at Plared, in spite of teething troubles, has done so well in its first two years that not only are increasing numbers of people in that old pottery section of Java making a better living but sales have scarcely scratched the surface of the demand. The pilot plant at Bandung, inherited from the Dutch, tests clays from all over the archipelago and trains a few workers. This pottery plant exemplifies a basic dilemma in industrial development—how to inspirit the worker. The Dutch manager told me that in Holland one worker turns out 2,600 saucers per day; in Indonesia one worker produces 150 saucers. The machines are the same. No doubt diet and living conditions have some thing to do with the difference, but so also has the more delicate matter of being geared to the machine age, not to mention the still more subtle Indonesian question constantly thrown at the foreign entrepreneur as to *why* anyone should work that hard and fast.

All over the country new industries, mostly small, are starting up and many more are in the planning stage, some of course to be still-born but some with promise of a long and healthy future. Fifteen bottle factories, for instance, are turning out glass bottles from cutlet and experimenting with making glass from sand and soda ash. A factory in Solo is making steel beds at the rate of 1,000 per month, price R. 287 each, and about to begin making wooden beds at a more modest price. A coconut desiccating factory near Menado is currently using 3,000,000 coconuts per month to produce 600 tons of desiccated coconut for American and European confectioners. A bicycle assembly plant is opening near Djakarta, able to market at reduced cost. A project is under way for making 3,000 bicycle tires per day at Banjermasin.

None of the contemplated new productions is more important than the making of cement. Building construction of all kinds is retarded for lack of cement at a price commensurate with other building costs. Also newsprint is so scarce and so expensive that the sight of a copy of the Sunday *New York Times* throws publishers into an ague; they could run their papers a year on the week-end supply of one sizable American paper. They also go into an understandable froth over the world's uneven division of paper, not to mention the price of certain imported machineries and chemicals and the scarcity of technicians.

Among the many factories I visited, the many technicians with whom I talked, the many theorizers on economic affairs with whom I swapped Big Ideas, none stands out in my mind more than the man who was in charge of the local department of economic affairs in Macassar. He had a practical imagination with a positive gift for hard work. In the villages around Macassar, he had got some of the ancient handcrafts going—the finely spun Macassar silverwork, basketry, weaving—and had developed a market so that it paid the young bandits to come down out of the hills and go to work. Also he had a papermaking plan worked out to the last detail, some kind of process for rice paper which I wished I understood for it was all very plain to him. All he needed was R. 5,000,000, and I was convinced that here was one locality where it would prove an investment. His spare time went into experiment with cement mixtures. He was obviously the sort who should go abroad for further training and had been picked to do so, but the government could offer no replacement in the Macassar area and he would not leave his present industries to collapse with the hopes of yesterday. Of such, I keep telling myself when I'm fed up with the good-natured procrastination of certain Indonesians, of such is the kingdom of tomorrow.

Technical assistance for Indonesian industry includes help from the Technical Assistance Board of United Nations, from American FOA, from the Colombo Plan, from such other specialists—European, Australian, American and probably Japanese—as are specifically invited by the Indonesian government. And now also from the Ford Foundation which has designated half a million dollars for a technical teacher-training program to be conducted by Dunwoody Institute in Minneapolis, with several American teacher-trainers to go to Indonesia and Indonesian technicians to come to America. Officially the program is set up as a part of the newly organized Indonesian Technical Teachers Training Institute at Bandung and is administered by the Ministry of Education, covering the fields of woodworking, machine shop, automobile and diesel mechanics, electricity, machinery maintenance, and printing.

Indonesian economy cannot be legislated into prosperity, as the government well knows, although better legislation would help; a feasible and profitable economy has to be built day by day, factory by factory, machine by machine, man by man. Each new undertaking means energy expended, and expending energy in the tropics is contrary to physical inclination. But as fast as the people catch on to what their needs really are, they are beginning to underwrite them with effort. Sometimes the catching-on process seems slow to an outsider habituated to the machine age, but when contrasted with the limited initiative allowed in the days before independence, it is heartening.

. I2 .

The Nation's Economy

WHEN DR. HJALMAR SCHACHT, GERMAN financial expert, went to Indonesia in 1951 to make a study of economic conditions and give advice, by invitation, on financial procedures, he wrote a report which still stands as a line-drawing of the nation's economic problems.

The first consideration he brought to the fore was that the country's basic difficulties originate in the fact that millions of people of divergent and often primitive background were torn by revolution from a soundly functioning foreign administration and left to themselves without sufficient trained administrators. Too fast a weaning, he might have said, and any mother knows what *that* does to a sensitive child. Holland and America, he felt, were primarily responsible for Indonesia's premature assumption of complete self-direction. "They have thrown a man into deep water when he could not even swim in the hope that he would help himself out; without considering the possibility that he might also drown. . . . They must grant this country considerably more aid . . . they should keep in mind that the development which they have started can never be curbed back."

However, to the new government with adult responsibility

too soon laid upon its shoulders, he also said a stern word about realizing that there can be no economic development without security; no security without reliable police and military force; no military force without a strong leader with authority over the whole country. If he meant to point the way toward one-man domination he certainly misread the temper of the Indonesian people, but otherwise his diagnosis was apt.

Dr. Schacht also made allowance for the psychological factors involved in economic development—a thing the Indonesians themselves are not always able to do. Speaking of the investment of foreign capital, he said: "The youthfulness of their freedom as a Republic makes it understandable that the Indonesian people are very touchy at present as far as preservation of their sovereignty is concerned. Yet . . . foreign co-operation in their future development is fully compatible with their sovereign rights. The only obligation connected therewith consists in treating all foreign capital in accordance with the same principles as apply to native capital, and without discrimination, as is done in all leading Western states. The United States of America . . . was before the First World War still a country in which eight to ten billion dollars of foreign capital were invested. Today all the foreign enterprises of the United States are in American hands. All the Argentine railroads have been built with British capital; they are now in Argentine hands. One hundred years ago the Rhenish-Westphalian industry of Germany was mainly started with Belgian and British capital. . . . Such a possible purchase is awaiting Indonesia as well. Indonesia should open her doors wide to foreign capital . . . but if the demand for 51 per cent participation by Indonesians in capital ventures is made of every enterprise newly established by foreigners, then this demand must scare away every decent foreign enterprise because participation . . . to such an extent can either not be put up at all by Indonesians, or it must be substituted for by unseemly camouflage."

Nevertheless, although Dr. Schacht's point seems plain enough to an outsider, it is easy to see why Indonesians look askance at every foreign investment and want a finger in every financial pie. Prewar, half the general import trade was in the hands of four Dutch houses; four-fifths of the technical imports were handled by five firms; three-fifths of the medical and pharmaceutical supplies by two firms; almost half of the books and periodicals by two firms; most of the motorcars by three firms. Not much left for the Indonesians. However, since the transfer of sovereignty the trend has been reversed and import trade has been nudged in the direction of Indonesian firms to whom special privileges are granted in the form of reserved commodities which include the more readily marketable consumer goods. Now the total economic planning for the country has been placed on the lap of a Planning Board functioning under the Ministry of Finance, assisted by experts from United Nations and such aid groups as the White Engineers, FOA and the Colombo Plan. At top levels, Indonesians appear to be getting over some of their skittishness about foreign investment.

A glance at the national budget is a good way to see the effect of the import-export trade upon the standard of living. During the first year of complete sovereignty, 1950, there was a deficit of R. 1.7 billion. In 1951 rising incomes and the favorable balance of trade brought demand for imports, while high income brought corporation and personal taxes zooming up, and consumer spending raised the yield of sales taxes.

The total summing up on the national blackboard disclosed a surplus of R. 1.2 billion.

But 1952 was a different story. Individual ministries, cash-happy, kept spending without effective checks by the Ministry of Finance. Most of the expenditures were needed in the interest of raising the country's standard of living and expanding its development, but they totaled more than the intake could support. Debits and credits were a continuing problem in cancellation; tax revenues fell, but increased export duties, which hit the exporters below the belt, brought up total revenues. Although in terms of tonnage, total exports increased, prices for exports dropped. Imports increased both in volume and value, but the real picture in terms of trade was not good, for Indonesia exports agricultural products and raw materials while importing manufactured goods. Therefore, a drop in world-market prices meant that a given volume of imports cost more in terms of exports—ultimately, in terms of man-hour labor. If the year 1948 is taken as par, 100, then in terms of trade—ratio of export to import prices—1950 rates 149; 1951, 110; 1952, 88; 1953, 108. The year 1953 showed a deficit of R. 478 millions in the trade balance. At such a rate of decline both the standard of living and the foreign exchange reserves must drop.

In view of the figures, Indonesian's financial picture could be somber but is saved in part by its fine sense of perspective and highlighted by a kind of stubborn realism. To be sure the perspective is the product of only a few minds but they are strategically placed. Prices for most major foodstuffs have been held down, including strict price fixing for the poor man's staple—rice. The price of luxury goods has risen, but that is helpful rather than otherwise, even though articles rated as necessities in the United States are semi-luxury and luxury goods in Indonesia. Indonesia financial experts know where their economy stands; they know what measures must be brought to bear upon its weaknesses, what burdens the people must shoulder, what sacrifices must be made and what economies must not be made. Current means are matched to long-term ends. Attitude is as important as action and the two are currently standing shoulder to shoulder.

One of the highlights is the government's determination to block inflation. Lacking legislation on credit control which more advanced countries have, a check on the expansion of the money supply has been effected by requirement of a heavy down payment on applications for foreign exchange. Also foreign firms are now prohibited from transferring profits until their indebtedness to banks operating in Indonesia is paid in full. Determination seems evidenced to hold the deficit budget within its agreed figure. Apparent also is the intent to increase production and export. Income taxes, particularly in the lower brackets, have been reduced; export taxes are reduced; the Dutch-owned Java Bank, the bank of issue, has been nationalized with 98 per cent of the stock in government hands and a gold reserve covering 25 per cent of the paper in circulation; foreign investment is at last said to be about to be encouraged—insofar as investment without promise of security can be encouraged.

In any long-time economic appraisal, the present deficit budget and low standard of living needs to be balanced against the country's richly stored earth. Indonesia's natural potential is tremendous. Traveling over Sumatra and Borneo, looking down on jungle stretching as far as the eye can scan, I used to try to reckon the lumber possibilities. Having lived in the big pine area of North Wisconsin, I naturally thought of going into the sawmill business and did sums on my cuff:

65 per cent of the country's total land area is forest, a million acres for every day in the year. But actually only some 9,000,-000 acres are immediately available for lumber production because lumber needs export facilities. The rest of the uncut timber serves a purpose, however, in protecting river sources and preventing soil erosion; and after all those trees are deposits of centuries of sunshine.

I also went into the reforestation business—from airplane, launch or motorcar. Around Lake Toba, that fabulously deep crater-cup of indigo water in Sumatra, mountain tops are covered with a thick growth of pine planted by the Dutch. On the other hand, Java hills denuded by the desperate Japanese, have not been reforested and are now failing to hold the water supply at its source so that rice irrigation and electric power are cut back. Behind the need for reforestation is the need for trained foresters. The same story everywhere —lack of development for lack of developers.

Among the untapped resources the need for water power reduces itself to simplicities the people understand: no water, no rice. In many areas new reservoirs are under construction, or at least contemplated. The Tjitarum in West Central Java should provide 100,000 kilowatts of current; the Darmo guarantees 50,000,000 cubic meters of water. Government officials reel off figures and total the nation's wealth in terms of hydro-electric stations; when three important lakes in Celebes and three in Sumatra are harnessed to generate current, the government will net 18,000,000,000 rupiahs. But they know that their figures are pie in the sky until some kind of security is guaranteed and foreign investment made profitable.

Among the development projects the Kalimantan (Borneo) Polderplan—polder meaning a tract of low land reclaimed from the sea—is perhaps the most exciting venture in all Indonesia. A wise and brilliant Dutchman with an Indonesian heart, Engineer H. J. Schophuys, married an Indonesian wife and, with her, her land and her people, their impoverished present and their problematical future. He looked on Borneo, an expanse of poor earth with islands of good soil, and saw that the fertile sections had to be extended if the livelihood of the people was to be sustained, not to say improved. Great sweeps of South Borneo are covered by marshes so unfertile and forbidding that the local people migrate rather than struggle with the unproductive land. Redeemed, this marsh land could furnish all the rice Indonesia customarily imports and plenty for export. So Dr. Schophuys began on the marshes. He began with the people at hand and the implements at hand, primitive people without a written language, and primitive hand tools. He educated as he went, both the people and such government officials in Java as could be interested in drainage canals, wet rice cultivation, the need of pumps for ditches and dredges for the banks of silt deposited by the tide at the deltas of important rivers, in floating workshops and training schools, in trainees going abroad and specialists coming from abroad. As he promoted, he trained until there are now some 200 more-or-less adequate technicians at work.

Moreover, the work is being done under a carefully thought out 15-year plan which breaks down into three 5-year plans dealing in the most immediate and practical terms with such large problems as soil mechanics, hydraulics, phytopathology, mechanization of agriculture, social hygiene, statistics, land law, transmigration, farm management and the like. Obviously, machinery and machinists are the *sine qua non* of success and both are acquired slowly and at great expense. However, 1,500,000 people of South Borneo have already reclaimed nearly half a million acres of marsh for wet rice. The first 5-year plan, begun in 1953, should reclaim 75,000 acres, half to be cultivated by the local population, and the remainder opened three years later for transmigratory families.

Indonesia is said to have great quantities of mineral deposits, but actual surveys have been spotty, and an adequate appraisal would require trained prospectors with apparatus, time and budget. Coal deposits are said to be only scratched. The present output of coal is not large because of general unrest and poor management, which is now under the government. A couple of figures struck me as instructive: in 1940 some 7,000 miners produced 2,000,000 tons of coal; in 1952 some 10,000 miners produced only 792,000 tons, a typical illustration of production shrinkage since Dutch oversight has given way to Indonesian merdeka. Coal illustrates another national dilemma—the failure of various ministries to get together. In 1952 export of coal was prohibited lest there be a shortage, so a large Japanese order was not filled. Then Indonesian industry got worried and hastily imported from India a considerable quantity of coal which was never needed. In 1953 the Japanese orders went to India, so the Indonesian government reduced production tonnage. Finally the railway and coal-mine dignitaries got together to pool recriminations and start over. The amount of coal and wood the railways would need per year was agreed upon and production promised, but in the meantime the government had been slow in ordering machinery for the mines so that production has had to wait upon delivery of machinery which means men out of work.

At present no iron is being mined but instead is imported

in the form of bars, plates and sheets, reinforced rods, iron and steel pipes and tubing, household articles and structural steel.

Tin is important to the country's economy. Indonesia furnishes about one-fifth the world mine production, exceeding Bolivia but exceeded by Malaya. At the beginning of the Korean war the price of tin dropped to a new bottom. The United States, formerly a good tin buyer, has an ample supply on hand but now lends support to the price in order to keep production open. Most of the tin is produced on the islands of Bangka, Billiton and Singkep off the southeast coast of Sumatra where it furnishes the livelihood of a large share of the population. The miners are largely Chinese, originally snared into the islands by ships' agents who combed the China coast offering false promises and small advance payments. Delivered at the mine a skilled Chinese craftsman brought fifteen dollars. But these imported workers, often little better than slaves, learned the business, prospered, and eventually took over so that now the Chinese communities are relatively well-to-do. Craftsmen, who make by hand the beautiful tinwear bought by Europeans and wealthy Indonesians, are as artistic as they are skilled. I watched them by the hour using their hand bellows at a charcoal fire to produce exquisite articles from pure heavy tin which does not tarnish. And if it develops a lackluster look I was instructed to spit on the tongue of my shoe and rub hard.

Nickel mines were under construction before the war, and during Japanese occupation the Celebes mines employed 4,000 workers. Currently the Macassar Regional Economy Council is trying to raise capital with which to reopen the mines. Diamonds are mined in Borneo and the Dutch-trained Borneo diamond cutters are famous for their precision work. The largest bauxite mines in Southeast Asia are located on Bintan Island in the Riouw archipelago just south of Singapore. Three gold mines are in partial production, one on Benkalis island, one at the seaport town of Bengkulen in Southwest Sumatra, and one at Bantam, Java.

Salt is a government monopoly. Production varies greatly, as much as 500 per cent in three years. During the Japanese occupation salt nearly passed off the scene because the Japanese would not listen to Indonesians experienced in their particular process. In 1947 the country was salt-hungry, but now production is up to standard and practically fulfills the country's need, only a small amount of fine table salt being imported. We went to see the national salt works in Madura where the salt is processed from seawater. The wet salt comes into the factory from vats eight miles distant, dark brown in color until washed to pale caramel shade, then shoveled into small carriers on vertical belts and taken to a centrifuge which slings out the water. After being dehydrated, it is pressed into cubes, baked, cooled and packed. Most of the machinery is 1890 vintage and some workers have been tending the same machines for thirty-five to forty years. Formerly the 2,200 workers had one day off every fortnight, but now the whole salt works closes down from six A.M. Sunday until Monday noon. The loaders from warehouses to the small freight cars carry 120-pound packages of salt and are paid 3½ rupias a day (about 20 cents) for their labor. I thought of organizing a salt-loaders union until I realized that a salt-union boss could squeeze very few Cadillacs from those wages. A small amount of salt is rewashed in a special pool until it is white enough for table use but nothing like as white as the American variety. Some salt is iodized, the iodine also extracted from sea water.

To say that clamor for nationalization of the oil wells wracks Indonesia would be an overstatement because millions of Indonesians scarcely know there are oil wells and further millions do not care who owns the oil just so they can light their little lamps. But there is noise enough about nationalization. The pro-nationalizationists work up a big head of steam —fuel furnished in part by the communist rabble-rousers— about Indonesia for the Indonesians, and knowing little about the art of attracting capital or the impossibility of developing resources without it, they produce the high-sounding argument "Somebody gets rich, why not us?"

Against nationalization at the present time, facts stack up like this: Indonesia has eight oil companies, five in current operation, the largest being the Dutch company known by its initials as BPM; then Standard Vacuum and Caltex-Pacific. Together they dominate the crude oil reserves, estimated at a billion barrels, 1.05 per cent of the world reserves and 1.84 per cent of present world production. Beginning with BPM in 1889, 75-year concessions were granted over an area of some 750,000 acres. After World War I, a new policy went into effect offering leases with a maximum currency of 40 years on a land grant area of something over 5,000,000 acres, and granting five-year permission to explore new oil bearing areas. All the land under any kind of oil concession totals five per cent of the whole Indonesian territory, and fifty per cent of the profits of the oil industry go to the Indonesian government in the form of company taxes, mining taxes, export duties and a device called "fixed rate." The companies are permitted to manage their own foreign exchange under supervision, a permission granted them in order to speed reconstruction after the tremendous war losses. But the total effect of private ownership is production of larger revenue for the government than if the government took over the oil.

Says the great Nationalist Party, PKI, and some others, "Oil must be nationalized at once." Many newspapers echo, "Yes, it must." But, say some of the more far-sighted officials in the Ministry of Economic Affairs, if Indonesia nationalizes, then delivery of oil apparatus may not be affected in the near future, if at all, because such materials now fall under control of the United States Control Commission for Strategic Materials, and besides, with which dollars would the government buy equipment? They also point out that since 1945 the BPM oil wells of North Sumatra have been run by the government or its deputies, production small scale and operation at a loss, while at Balikpapan, Borneo, BPM production is in the hands of BPM, with production large scale and profit steady. Other localities show the same divergence under like conditions. All in all, with the oil companies furnishing the new investment and carrying the headache, the national budget now profits $60,000,000 annually, while internal needs for oil and oil products, both for economic and strategic purposes, are guaranteed by the companies. To be sure, the companies must increase their social provisions for the welfare of laborers and train more technical staff. But could the government move toward these ends any faster? It had better, say some political leaders, and if the present Ali cabinet wants to live long and gain the confidence of the people, it must settle this dispute on the side of immediate nationalization.

As important as developing the untapped resources is improvement of communications. As an island republic intent upon balancing the budget and raising the standard of living, Indonesia has to concern herself with the movement of food and other necessities. Indeed, the movement of goods is quite as important as the investment of capital or the co-operation of labor.

The Indonesian government is now in the process of buying the Dutch shipping monopoly known as KPM which formerly owned the railways, although KPM is reluctant to relinquish either its stock or its share in management, the latter of course to guarantee profits on the former. However, management has been transferred from the Hague to Djakarta and the rest of the transfer is a matter of time. Most of the equipment, including some 4,000 miles of track, is in Java. Wartime losses are rapidly being replaced by diesel locomotives, passenger carriages, various types of goods vans and restaurant cars arriving from Europe and America and other countries, but capital investment is curtailed by the ever-present problem of security. A passenger never knows when he boards a train whether he will reach his destination safely or be held up en route by bandits, and the same uncertainty conditions the movement of freight. Many of our friends had hair's-breadth tales to tell, but I never traveled by rail and my husband's only trip was third class, where he made some wonderful student friends. In spite of banditry, passenger and freight service increase by the month, as does income.

The railways have their difficulties: heavy equipment bought abroad has to be paid with dollar equivalents; personnel has to be trained from scratch; freight and travel costs have to be kept within the wage span of the public; trucking and shipping competition must be reckoned with. Nevertheless, service and morale are improving steadily, credit to be divided between the government, management, and what is possibly the best labor union in the land.

Prewar the Dutch also had a monopoly on shipping, owning and manning all craft of any significance, and they still dominate the shipping interests although the government is intent upon buying out the Royal Navigation Packet Company, shipping division of KPM, as rapidly as feasible. The government is definitely alert to the problem of ships. Since 1946 some 300 small ships have been built, the largest 600 tons, and coastal vessels, motor boats and fishing craft are being purchased from abroad. Bids are also open on a fleet of civilian ships up to 10,000 tons, delivery in two years with five years to pay, while assistance for private concerns wishing to buy ships is being contemplated through a special shipping bank.

From the traveler's point of view, these Dutch ships have their points, such as the ubiquitous larger-than-life paintings of Queen Juliana which smile down on all dining saloons; the solid Dutch breakfasts of perspiring cheese, limp cold meats, ample slices of bread, but fruit only by special conniving with the steward; the giant cockroaches which come on—and on—when the lights go off; the cold baths which are dipped from great jars or tanks ladle by ladle; the old-line Dutch entrepreneurs, now retired but with free passage, who always seem to have a pocketful of uncut precious stones and a tongueful of personal encounters with wild elephants (and what a boon an American listener must be, notebook in hand); the sea captains who know where all the ships of yesterday are sunk and walk their uneven sea gait with one foot on yesterday's peaceful decks. The most incredible stories prove the true ones: the lane leading out of Surabaya harbor is still mined and mine sweepers cannot make the way safe, at least not by the American twelve-year standard, so the coastwise ships do pick their way with great care and do occasionally make a miscalculation.

But for shipping, harbors are quite as necessary as ships.

Java has three excellent harbors: Tanjung Priok for Djakarta, Semarang and Surabaya; Sumatra has Belawan in the north and Padang in the west; Celebes has Macassar on the west and will soon have a new R. 45,000,000 harbor at Bitung near Menado in the north. All of the large harbors and many smaller ones are currently under improvement except Surabaya whose facilities remain adequate since the drop in sugar trade. Priok in particular is expanding. Formerly, chiefly ocean-going and KPM interinsular vessels docked at Priok, but recently a variety of coasters have so complicated facilities that additional quays and warehouses have become necessary, along with a dock to handle timber and more space for lighters and oil tankers. The harbor is also being deepened and extended, and sunken vessels are being removed. Draining the swamp between Priok and Kemayoran, congested harbor flank of Djakarta, adds around twenty-one square miles of new land.

More efficient harbor labor would pay dividends to Indonesian shipping. Because of the short working day and the unusual number of holidays, turning around time averages five days in Indonesian harbors, against two days in Japan, slightly less than three days in an average European port, reportedly one and six-tenths days in China. A general clean-up in the interest of order would also expedite shipping. Recently the *Times of Indonesia* reported an official inspection of Djakarta's godowns by the chairman of parliament's communications committee who found them "bursting at the seams with a staggering array of articles in various stages of rust, decay and obsolescence. As no inventories exist, no accurate valuation can be made, but an estimate approaches U.S. $2,000,000." Part of the overlooked cargo was left by the Japanese occupation, part is American war surplus purchased by the Dutch, part is "junk acquired in the Philippines" by the old United States of Indonesia. "Loitering about the godowns were a large number of government workers, hard at work idling strenuously as they did not know what was expected of them." Personally I was fascinated by the open pilferage and the insouciance of the light-fingered dockhands but appalled by the waste in tying up valuable storage space for years. Now old stock and supplies are being distributed to the various ministries and the remainder sold at auction.

In extenuation, there is always the lack of trained personnel. No doubt, help might have been had for the asking through some branch of United Nations, but Indonesia still leans toward a hands-off policy, preferring to bungle at great cost to her people and economy rather than ask for foreign aid. The attitude is partially understandable for the Dutch specialists hired to help untangle some of the postwar snarls sometimes managed to increase the complications. Paucity of trained Indonesians is indicated by the fact that only six harbor masters were ever allowed master licenses under the Dutch regime. One of them told me tales of the way he was battled down as he climbed up which I did not believe until I checked and found the tallest tales were understatement. If their own history seems bitter to the Indonesians, it wasn't they who brewed the tea.

Napoleon was the causative factor behind Indonesia's first good roads. When he conquered Holland and the Dutch became enemies of England, the British advantaged themselves by taking over the Dutch East Indies, and as part of their defense plan began to build roads where before worn tracks, transformed into bogs during the rainy season, had served for transport. It was then that much of the Great Post Road was constructed, running the length of Java. Driving on this excellent highway today one remembers the forced labor which built it, with casualties exceeded only in the building of the Burma Road. But then one gets off the good highways into the back country where the Dutch forced no roads, where Indonesian lag-and-sag still operates in hereditary manner, and the advantages which have accrued to the Indonesians from being pushed around by the Dutch are apparent. No wonder the Indonesians themselves have a divided mind about the Dutch.

It was a bad road which almost got me an adventure. On a day of drizzle, rain, downpour, we were coming back from the forsaken leprosy colony 28 kilometers outside Jakarta, when our car—lumbering along like an elephant with an overload of teak—got stuck in mud which had been sucked to a deep sticky mash by a truck an hour ahead of us. This booby trap was located smack in the center of a village of Blackshirts, revolutionary extremists, who had vowed never to cut their hair until every foreigner had been driven from Java; the vow says nothing about not combing the hair but they made that sacrifice also. The men looked like a musical-comedy chorus; sarongs didied into shorts with no other gesture of clothing but a few fine large earrings and a kris in each belt. Seeing us wheel deep in mud they jeered raucously. Pearl Cheng, an American-trained Chinese-Indonesian, offered a good price for the help of four men to push us through, but they only laughed and shouted. My impulse was to sit it out and let the chauffeur plow off to the nearest telephone to lay our difficulty in the Embassy's lap, but the little chauffeur, his eyes bigger than his steering wheel, was shaking too hard to make it out the door and the young California doctor with us could not leave two helpless women in that spot. Finally the headman, a sinister-looking villain with large incisors, who probably raised rice and was kind to his family, said eight men would push us through for a fee higher than the entire amount we had with us. He would not bargain but motioned his men to close in. I ran down my window to add a little persuasion but Pearl felt all windows should be kept shut and locked. Our situation was definitely not good but we looked so melodramatic that it was impossible to take it seriously. So I just got out laughing and said to the headman, "Sajah sudah tuah tape kuat," which means, "I'm already old but I'm strong." The *tuah* part was plain enough, what with my white hair, but the *kuat* struck them funny as I sloshed through the mud and pushed at the car so they also came sloshing and laughing and we whooped her right through. Pearl paid them amply and fast, and the way we sped down that jiggle-jogglety old road hanging onto our teeth was not slow. I felt very noble because customarily I cover my head when a bat flies in, but when I reached home, looking like a beachcomber, my husband thought I had taken a careless, needless, pointless risk. What kind of risk would it have been to sit there through the rainy season till the mud dried up? That's Indonesian roads for you.

Prewar there were about 43,500 miles of roads good enough for motorized traffic, some 16,000 miles in Java with about one-third of the distance asphalted. Sumatra came second; then a big drop to Borneo, Celebes and Bali, about 22 miles in the Moluccas and 10 in Timor. That was it, sum total. Under the Japanese, maintenance was poor, asphalt disappeared from the market and wore off the roads. Sumatra suffered most heavily. Cyclists had hard going, with pneumatic tires reserved for the Japanese and their cohorts. After the war the Dutch made repairs in their occupied areas; the Indonesians had no equipment. Mechanical equipment for roadmaking has been hard to get and when obtained is not very useful without trained operators. Occasionally one still sees roadscrapers being driven merrily back and forth on a perfectly good road with nothing to scrape, the drivers having a wonderful time waving off traffic while they turn around. One also sees an occasional rusty bulldozer lying by the roadside as useless as a sleeping dinosaur. But now mechanics are being trained under various FOA, United Nations and Colombo Plan arrangements, and machinery is both respected and appreciated.

The one completely new road job turned out since the war is the asphalted highway between Djakarta and its new suburb Kebayoran. In these days of motorized transportation such practical four-lane highways should probably take precedence over railway expansion, for the expense in terms of foreign exchange is much less. However, modern road-building costs ten times the prewar rate. The government's five-year plan for 2,500 miles of new road will cost R. 656,-000,000 with an additional outlay of R. 400,000,000 for the repair of 75 miles of old road. Cost is the reason why some five-year plans require ten years to mature. But then that happens in our family, too.

Since independence, the number of cars has almost trebled and trucks more than doubled but the number of auto-busses has risen only slightly and motorcycles have dropped by half because of insecurity and prohibitive import taxes. More busses are needed and thousands more motorcycles could be used advantageously and immediately if the price could be brought down and if it were safe to go about without armed escort.

The small European cars which predominate suit the slenderly built Indonesians but seem a mite incongruous

when weighed down by the generously built Dutch. Still, it
was a very large Dutch woman in a very small car who gave
me about the pleasantest welcome I had in two years. I had
landed at the airport of Menado, northern tip of Celebes, not
knowing a soul within a thousand miles, and had waited an
hour and a half for the little springless bus which should take
passengers the twenty-five kilometers to town, when I heard
my name called in the sweetest voice this side of Paradise. My
name! Then a very, very large Dutch woman with gentian
blue eyes came lightly across the waiting room. An Indonesian friend—may she be a rajah in her next incarnation—
had cabled her to look out for me. My new friend took me to
her midget car whose front seat she entirely filled except for
a thin slice of chauffeur; my bag and I filled the back seat.
Well into the jungle, she turned and said, "Mrs. Bro, you
shouldn't wear that dress; it has all the wrong vibrations and
brings out your old trouble around your gall bladder and
stirs up your old amoebic dysentery." My Indonesian friend
hadn't wired her *that*; did I wear my maladies mapped on my
face? Later that car took me on all sorts of jaunts and one
night it brought another guest to my sweet friend's home—
which was an ex-Japanese teahouse on a riverbank. The new
guest was a Jehovah's Witness missionary, a tall Canadian,
who had heard I was interested in religions. He began at
once to set forth the position of his sect on the Second Coming, explaining that the righteous would be raised from their
graves to live for a thousand happy years right on this earth.
My Dutch friend, who was a theosophist, listened raptly.
Then when he paused for breath she asked, "And which body
will be raised up? The body from the last incarnation or the
favorite of all the bodies the soul ever used?" He was taken
aback. "And what age will the resurrected man be when he

rises from his grave?" He knew that answer. "He will be in his prime." "And what is his prime?" she pressed. "Maybe he was in his prime at forty but maybe his son was not in his prime until he was fifty-six, so then the son will be older than the father, and the grandson may be older than both!" After that they both talked at once, but we wound up the evening amicably by admiring the Witness's excellent new translation of the Bible, and the little car took him back to his hotel. And if this car trip seems a digression the answer is that that is the way one travels in Indonesia—by digression.

Garuda Indonesian Airways provides the domestic air service with flights scheduled to twenty-eight points in Indonesia, as well as to Singapore and Manila, and additional points in prospect. International airlines also utilize the Djakarta airport. It will be a boost to public morale when the bucket planes, ex-transport World War II items, can be replaced. I would have promptly got off the first one I got on if my husband had not assured me that he had made many trips by bucket plane and lived to regret them. Seats run along the sides, every alternate person sitting with his back bowed against a small low window, but at least he can double over with a half-twist and see out, which is more than the others can do. Both ends of the aisle and most of its middle are piled with baggage more or less strapped down. The long flight from Macassar to Menado was my Test of Determination to see Indonesia. But there are also wonderful Convair two-engine planes on which one has excellent meals with chewing gum and all the trimmings. "Djangan naik di sini" is lettered on the wings—"don't climb here"—but underneath in English, "Don't stand up here."

Postal service, telegraph, cable, radio and telephone service are all government owned and from the consumer's point of view they all appear to operate with average efficiency, except the telephone service. The entire archipelago has approximately the same number of telephones as does Lincoln, Nebraska, and until the purchases of 1953 the latest equipment had been bought in 1925. However, automatic phones have now been installed in government offices and before seven years and 70,000,000 rupiahs have spent themselves, the capital city will have an entirely automatic system. It is even hoped that some of the 6,000 accumulated applications—half again the present number of subscribers—can be acknowledged. In Bandung, service is picking up; Macassar already has automatic service. Furthermore, highly placed members of the telephone service staff are now abroad acquiring advanced training for advanced equipment.

I tried the trans-Pacific telephone service a few times until the unfortunate day when our daughter in Nebraska asked what she could send us and I answered, "Garlic salt and catgut," meaning violin strings. The operator to whom I paid the toll thought garlic salt and catgut were code words; she probably suspected H-bombs and smuggled twenty-dollar gold pieces, both much respected in Indonesia, because I never could get another clearance for a call. And I did understand her point of view a little better when I discovered that garlic salt could be had in any grocery if one just knew the Dutch word. That phone call brought us a great deal of garlic salt.

At the moment nothing is more relevant to the health of the nation's economy than the contribution of labor. Of course labor is a large factor in any economy, but in Indonesia from the beginning of the nationalist movement, labor has exercised its power both on the political and economic fronts. In America political democracy came ahead of economic democracy, and the labor movement sprang into being as the working man's effort to bring the two in line. But by the time Indonesia was ready for the great experiment, it was plain that the two nags, politics and economics, had a better chance to pull the chariot of state free from the dragging weight of colonial imperialism if they teamed up. Prewar, labor was useful in keeping them in line but of late has begun to fancy itself the charioteer.

Trade unions came about naturally in the days of conscript labor on Sumatran plantations and forced road mending in Java: one man was impotent against colonial policies, but a group of men could exert pressure. The leaders of the movement were all ardent nationalists, but they frequently differed as to the best method of achieving freedom. Some advocated widespread education of the workers not only in literacy but in the principles of government, at the same time pressing for political representation and economic rights. Others felt that revolution was more practical than evolution, force more effective than pressure. In this latter group were the leaders of the new communist movement, some of them already indoctrinated in Europe; from their point of view nationalism, trade unionism and communism could travel together and all reach their goal more rapidly. There is no doubt but that they sped the cause of nationalism. Some of the democratic leaders sensed the threat in this fellow-traveling, but desperately needing all their friends they trusted that once independence was achieved and a democratic government installed, then the radical elements could be controlled.

Looking back it is easy to see that eliminating the communists and turning to the West for help in organizing Indonesian labor would have been a more profitable course. But at that time Indonesian labor leaders knew little about the organization of Western labor. And many of those who were aware of the growth of the International Confederation of Free Trade Unions thought syllogistically: colonialism is evil; it is of the West; the Confederation may have accomplished a great deal on its home ground but it is also of the West; therefore it is evil; we will have none of its help. More than a trace of this syllogistic thinking remains today. The rank and file, now as then, knows little about labor conditions in other countries; they are harassed men and in the early days they were isolated with their own problems. They tended to demand their rights through any means available.

During the war the labor movement was disrupted and the communist party went underground, but as the Republican government began to function, the labor unions were reconstituted, and their growth accelerated. Also communism again came into the open and again offered funds and leadership and although democratic leadership had grown in power and understanding, it did not have sufficient experience to hold the communist elements in check. The big problem has always been the ignorance of the workers and their susceptibility to big promises, catchy slogans, and tricky analyses of the political-economic system. But throughout all vicissitudes the labor movement has continued to grow.

At present a few facts are patent enough so that labor in general, as well as the democratic leadership, begins to take them in. It is plain that communism means to keep up labor agitation, preventing estates and factories from operating profitably, no matter what the country's economic needs may be. Strikes, demands, and close-downs must follow each other; differences must be magnified; disruptions pushed to cabinet proportions. Ostensible opponents of communism contribute to the success of such tactics through lack of a sufficiently wide and effective program of their own; plantation managers, who still see the new day as a temporary concession to postwar unrest, contribute to the communist success by continuing to pay low wages and doing little about poor working conditions; the government aids the communist cause through vacillating and conciliatory action. However, there is the workers' own awareness of their losses due to constant strikes, especially as the unions are too new, too poor, and too loosely organized to build up relief funds; there is opposition on the part of the stronger political parties; there is the record of the government's firm and successful stand in the Maduin *coup d'état* of 1948 and in the clean-up of 1952 when widespread arrests of communists were made, including among the convictions six members and two assistants on the labor mediation board. At that time almost everybody in Djakarta seemed to know about the infiltration of the labor ministry by PKI and SOBSI (large communist-dominated union) before the government wakened to the fact, but once awake the government acted effectively.

At present the labor movement appears to face two fundamental necessities. First, the need to divorce the unions from politics so that they may be responsible only to themselves, working out their own programs without political hamperings and commitments. Second, the need for clear understanding within the unions on their relation to communism, a need shared by a sizable segment of the general population. Everywhere one hears people say proudly or apologetically, "I'm not anti-communist, you understand; just non-communist." They seem to fear that if they are anti-communist, then they will be taken for pro-West in a partisan sense and therefore in opposition to their country's neutralist policy. What communism actually is, they do not know. I was constantly surprised at the lack of knowledge of the communist record outside Indonesia. The general attitude even of educated persons is one of Marxist dilettantism. A classless society sounds fine and the dictatorship of the proletariat appears a pleasant next step in democracy, something which will automatically raise the standard of living and abolish all inequalities. The real meaning of a dictatorship, whatever its brand, is seldom considered; it is a thing the Indonesian people have never experienced aside from the tyrannies of petty princes. Nor do they realize how thin the layer of entrepreneurs and families of wealth is in their society. Nor are they conscious that the fundamentally democratic character of traditional desa government around which their lives are oriented would quickly disappear under communist domination. With their entire future as a nation at stake, the semi-educated continue smilingly to announce, "Not anti-communist, just non-communist." It is like the common attitude toward smallpox and cholera: if they are not *for* these diseases, why should they then be expected to work against them? Just a hands-off, middle-of-the-road policy as becomes gentlemen.

There are few authentic figures in the labor movement. Most unions have no definite membership lists; many claims are fantastic. Roughly there are 3,000,000 workers on the plantations and in the related factories; perhaps two-thirds of that number have union affiliation. Plantation employees form the largest section of organized labor. Next in size comes the organization of oil workers; workers in communications including post and telegraph; white-collar workers, including teachers, government and municipal workers, business firm employees; employees of smaller industries such as textile, shoes, printing; technicians; finally the unskilled workers. A rough line is drawn between SOBSI, definitely communist-dominated, and non-SOBSI, but the division does not have the significance it would have in Europe or America as thousands of members of locals affiliated with SOBSI have no ideological convictions while thousands in both camps are swayed back and forth. SOBSI, popularly called *sobsi,* currently claims around 1,250,000 members and may have as many as 850,000, belonging to some 36 trade unions. SOBRI, at once the enemy and the henchman of SOBSI, is said to be the creature of Partai Murba, many of whose members claim to be Trotsky-Titoist followers operating independently of the accepted communist authority, but reportedly SOBRI leaders are of late supporting the party line.

Among the non-SOBSI organizations, the local area federations are strongest. Some of them and of their constituent unions have thrilling histories which are really biographies of stout-hearted pioneers determined to effect democracy among the masses in terms of individual worth and group rights. To work intelligently among illiterate persons and not sway them to new demagoguery, to assuage their hurt pride without making them cocky over their corporate strength, to demand honest work from depressed groups—all these objectives require phenomenal patience and integrity. Most important of these groups in GSBI, made up of nine trade unions, including 100,000 teachers, the largest single union, and at least as many government workers, postal, bank, radio, and other white-collar workers, plus the association of judges. GSBI is influential beyond its size because of the high intellectual caliber of its members. It has no SOBSI counterpart.

In Bandung some hundred thousand workers, including employees in municipal offices, police, textile mills, and teachers, as well as workers on sugar plantations, are banded together in a union which is currently attempting to organize the metal and machine workers, office workers, employees in the shoe industry, printing, hotels and restaurants. It impressed me that the Bandung area is well organized in the main, and has sound leadership and public support.

In Djakarta, workers in the airport and harbors, in export-import companies, in hotels, restaurants, and printing establishments, are well organized. Some 20,000 of the 75,000 railway workers are members of a genuine national union with branches in many sections of Java and Sumatra, with a social service department, a credit union, a food and clothing co-operative, insurance for accident, sickness and death, and a real educational program. In North Sumatra the federation of estate workers, numbering close to 150,000, has recently reached into Java estates. A movement to fuse these area federations is making excellent headway and the result should soon be a national federation of half a million members.

There is also SBII, an out-and-out Moslem organization created by the Masjumi party, attempting to combine Islamic ethical ideas with functioning labor practice. Its usefulness lies in its potential mass (for anything bearing the name of Islam will draw members), in its registered membership which stands currently around 40,000, and in the fact that it is overtly and unmistakably anti-communist. Unfortunately the opinion of its leadership is divided as to whether the economic advantages of trade unionism should be emphasized or the religious and political usefulness of the organization, but it is definitely a conciliatory group, stressing adjustment between labor and management. Outside these sharply defined unions, North Sumatra has around a hundred thousand workers in nine trade unions which remain independent of SOBSI, SOBRI or SBII.

With which group does the future lie? In spite of some excellent non-SOBSI organizations, the future lies with communism unless the non-SOBSI trade unions quickly get a national point of view and realize that labor cannot progress without a democratic, non-political, dues-paying membership. Most of the strong unions agree with these aims, but are likely to walk out of the very meeting in which they agreed, and begin to drum up partisan loyalty to a certain political party, or to draw up a request for government support. Formerly some government support was probably necessary and may not immediately be completely withdrawn, but the general attitude of the workers that the government should subsidize their union to look after their multitudinous interests is self-defeating. Labor leaders themselves argue that their time has more important use than drumming up dues. They grant that the members of a strong union might be willing to pay dues, but that a union becomes strong through the regular financial support of its individual members is inconceivable. These are the same unions which look to some successful lawyer or politician for their leadership, for a leader in popular eyes must be an educated man in terms of book learning; the fact that he has no experience in a given trade and no experience in labor organizing is immaterial.

Definitely new strength is coming into the non-SOBSI unions as labor leaders return from their trips abroad for study and observation. When these leaders look and listen for themselves in a democratic country, they are doubly convinced. No doubt, observation teams also go abroad to communist countries, returning with improved ammunition. The race is on to see whether the labor unions can democratize rapidly enough to effect industrial stability before SOBSI and its supporters completely disrupt the economy. There is a point of no return visible on the socio-economic horizon. If labor can free itself, and be freed by the political parties, then it may actually effect the industrial democratization of Indonesia.

And so the national economy is pillared on a great many *ifs*. If a feasible fiscal policy can be maintained by such government leadership as is not easily bent by party control, if more of the abundant natural resources can be developed speedily and without corruption, if communications can speed distribution of necessities, and if labor can augment political democracy with its own democratic organization and principles, then the nation's economy can support the nation's ardent ideals of freedom, equality and opportunity.

· 13 ·

Foreign Policy

ROM THE BEGINNING THE INDONESIAN SHIP
of state has had to chart its course as it sailed. Having
set to sea, and heavy seas, as soon as the keel was laid and
enough superstructure plated together to support the bridge,
it has met local typhoons and heavy fogs sweeping in from
far shores with alarm bells sounding, but it now moves with
a certain dignity. In foreign waters it appears to maneuver
with confidence.

Indonesian foreign policy has always been motivated by a
realistic determination to further the interests of the country
and not to become involved in the struggle between democracy and communism. The first aim is self-evident; the second
seems to an outsider a bit of wish-thinking. Dr. Ali Sastroamidjojo, the present prime minister, expresses the minds of
his people: "My country's refusal to align herself with either
camp of controversy in this troubled world is based upon the
profound belief that such action could only serve to further
unbalance the already teetering balance of power." That no
alignment will throw power into hands which have no
interest in the well-being of Indonesia is a fact still more
profound and one with which Dr. Sastroamidjojo is increasingly having to deal.

On the matter of using foreign policy to further Indonesian interests, the government is feeling its way concurrently on at least half a dozen fronts. First, along the Dutch-Indonesian border where the terms are fairly well outlined in the Draft Union Status. Article 1 of the Draft stipulates that provisions of the union shall not "prejudice the status of each of the two partners as an independent and sovereign state," yet it appears that the financial and economic agreements limit the activities of the Indonesian government in order to safeguard prerogatives of Dutch companies and individuals remaining in Indonesia. They see themselves penalized by the outflow of profits toward Holland, by the safeguards for present and future Dutch investments, by the transmission to Holland of pension funds, expenses, and allotments for Dutch citizens working in Indonesia. Test case number one in foreign policy is what to do with existing Dutch-Indonesian agreements.

In the no-man's-land of economic interests, Indonesia's relationship to the Japanese comes second. The signing of the San Francisco Peace Treaty by Indonesia was not met with acclaim by most of the country's press, nor has parliament ratified it. Popular interest in doing business with Japan has risen very slowly and official overtures have been hesitant. The first commission to go to Japan to work out details of reparations felt baffled by the intricate simplicity of the fact that regardless of moral responsibility Japan could not pay what she did not have or could not earn without bankrupting or starving her own people. Currently Indonesia insists upon $8,000,000,000 in reparations. Whatever the amount decided upon, Article 14 of the treaty fixes payment in the form of services, but Indonesia insists upon services plus capital goods, calling attention to the testimony of four different American commissions that Japan could pay in part in capital goods and yet maintain a viable economy.

Japanese firms have offered, indeed pressed, to co-operate in developing various resources in Indonesia—industrial, commercial, agricultural, technical, communication, mining and fishing, transport—but Indonesia's cagey policy about infiltration of foreign capital has so far defeated both nations. However, a joint oil field venture is projected, including the building of a fleet of oil and ore carriers for Sumatra-Japan trade. One hurdle in goods exchange is the high price of Indonesian products necessitated in part by the low man-hour production of Indonesian workers. Matching man-hours, Japan far outproduces Indonesia. To date the two countries have exchanged diplomatic representation only at consular level, an unrealistic state of affairs soon to be rectified by diplomatic agreement.

The third front faces the United States. To date, diplomatic relations have been cordial in Djakarta and Washington, and both countries have been ably represented in the other's capital. Trade has done very well and American oil investments net profits to both parties. The people of America are disposed to admire the island republic and as the record shows, America has given technical, medical and educational aid under a variety of initials. All seemed well if not chummy until February, 1952, when the Indonesian Foreign Minister, Dr. Subardjo, signed the United States Mutual Security Administration agreement. Immediately both the Indonesian press and public accused the foreign minister of forsaking his country's neutrality program, to which the Minister replied that the pact, as clarified through conversations and exchange of letters between himself and the American ambassador, was substantially an extension of former aid and nothing to get hot and bothered about. However, so volatile was Indonesian reaction that Dr. Subardjo resigned and the cabinet fell. In time the tempest subsided, aid was continued under a new but similar pact, the United States concurring because the important thing is to get the technical aid to Indonesia so that she can maintain her economy. Bystanders looked for spoils and found some. Wrote a British correspondent in *Antara News Bulletin* published in Djakarta:

> Indonesia's resurgence of neutralism has already benefited Britain. Like Burma, which turned toward the Colombo Plan because it thought that accepting USA aid would commit it too much in the "cold war," Indonesia too is turning to Britain as a "smaller devil." Although a substantial contract for training Indonesian civilian pilots, involving £1,000,000 a year, was originally intended for an American firm, it has just gone to a British company.

Thus is trade the creature of foreign policy. Criticism of the United States continues, especially of American support of the French in Indochina, and the common accusation is made that the whole Middle East and North Africa would be free if United States aid were not on the wrong side. All in all, Indonesia is not different from other countries in expressing appreciation—but not too lavish—when a course of action fits her specifications and in expressing disapproval, vehemently, when actions are contrariwise. Which is another way of saying that the country is feeling its way in a difficult situation with a foreign policy as new as the republic.

Fourth, Indonesia presents a friendly frontier toward the Moslem states because of the militant conviction of solidarity which Moslem states share. Pakistan, as the nearest Moslem neighbor, is particularly influential on Indonesian policy, partly because Pakistan's current budget-balancing is held as a model for a newly independent country; partly because it was Moslem countries which gave the first Republic of Indonesia her first recognition abroad when Hadji Agus Salim made his trip in behalf of co-operation with the government. Indonesians follow the oil controversies and other involvements of the Arab states with close attention and are outspoken in behalf of Arab rights.

Curiously Indonesians seem to have small use for the Arabs in Arabia. Returning from *haj* (and more Indonesians make the pilgrimage than any other national group) they almost universally rail against the cut-throat Arab practices, and some even aver that Islam can never come into its own so long as it must drag the weight of the Arabs. But let an outsider cast aspersions in the direction of the Arabs and suddenly all Moslems are brothers—which proves that Indonesians are as human as anyone else when their religious affiliations are attacked from the outside.

On the question of an international regime for Jerusalem, Indonesia voted for appointment of a committee to study protection of all "the spiritual and religious interests of the Holy Land," under United Nations, as did the Arab states. Indonesia also voted $30,000 to the budget of United Nations relief work for Palestinian refugees.

Fifth, because of its cultural impact and political influence, India is important to Indonesia's foreign policy makers. It was the Indian prime minister, Pandit Nehru, who called the New Delhi Conference on Indonesia in 1949 and led fourteen other nations of Southeast Asia to take a firmer stand on its previous cease-fire-and-arbitrate resolution. It was India which led out in withdrawing transit facilities, both air and sea, from the Netherlands during the Second Police Action. Later it was India which, with Australia, introduced the resolution of approval that made Indonesia the sixtieth member of the United Nations. Obviously Indonesia had sufficient reasons of her own for wishing to join the United Nations, some of which were stated as a sense of mission in these troubled times, desire to enhance her own prestige, gratitude for the Security Council's having speeded international recognition of the fact of the Republic and for help received through UNICEF and WHO on a tremendous yaws campaign. But no doubt India also wanted Indonesia in the UN so that Indonesia might support India on occasion. However, during the first years of Indonesia's membership Indonesia and India voted together in only 25 out of 42 important cases where the voting record of both countries is known, while the other 17 cases involved abstentions by one country while the other was expressing a positive or negative position. The ensuing record has been similar although documentation is not available. Pro-Indian feeling remains strong in Indonesia. What the reaction may be in case of a sharpened India-Pakistan dispute remains to be seen. But at least foreign relations involving India begin with a favorable emotional and cultural cast.

Sixth, although perhaps first in importance, comes the Indonesian-Russian relationship. Economically Russia is still of negligible importance, but politically Russia has sown the seeds of calamity in Indonesia and the current tendency of certain political leaders to take advantage of communist backing for their own advantage may bring forth a harvest of tares and tears. The degree of reciprocal diplomatic representation between the two countries has long been an argument in Indonesia, but parliament has voted a full ambassador for Moscow, failing however to appropriate the money. Evidently Russia anticipates having an ambassador in Indonesia because a request for forty houses came through some time ago and did not set well with the housing authorities administering crowded Djakarta. There is definitely a tightening of the bonds of brotherhood, amply publicized by sections of the Indonesian press, including much of the influential Chinese press, and patently fostered by certain cabinet members and others high in political authority. Whether or not another Maduin is brewing is a matter of open speculation.

Subsidiary to Indonesian-Russian relationship, and of much more importance economically, is Indonesia's relationship to Red China. Indonesia has an ambassador in Peking, and the Chinese People's Republic has an embassy in Djakarta which looks after the interests of as many Chinese citizens as care to be looked after, attempts to foster trade, and does foster an immense amount of communist propaganda. All over Indonesia, in almost every remote village and certainly in book and magazine stalls in every city, communist periodicals can be bought. On the whole their format is attractive; they make ample use of pictures; enough of their content is authentic enough to catch the eye of readers who may also be listeners to *Voice of America* or Australian and Philippine broadcasts, and the rest of the content is the usual propaganda and twisted facts. These magazines, brochures, pamphlets, books, are cheap; they underprice almost every other kind of available literature; the common people buy them. They are slanted toward all levels, the newly literate, the moderately educated, the young, the old. This wide and thorough distribution does not come about by chance nor yet by popular demand; there is planned penetration of Indonesia. Nor do the communist parades spring up by popular demand. If the Indonesian government is aware of this insidious taking over of the minds of the people, certainly no move has been made to stop it. The hands-off attitude of the government is part of the Indonesian policy of fence-sitting.

Indonesia's day-by-day policy of making room for communism in ordinary affairs is much more consistent than her record of voting with the communist bloc in the UN. In the first year of participation in United Nations, Indonesian delegates nine times opposed resolutions introduced by the USSR and on numerous occasions voted contrary to the Russian stand. Noticeable is the tendency of the Indonesian delegation to safeguard and support the UN machinery. Indonesia opposed the USSR proposal to disband the UN Commission for Korea and corollary proposals. Primarily, of course, Islamism opposes communism on religious grounds and currently the religous moderates and right-wing parties still outweigh the left-wing parties in foreign affairs, although a shift to the left would take few observers by surprise.

In the Security Council Indonesia has spoken strongly in behalf of the rights of colonial peoples, working for the protection of Eritrean autonomy after incorporation with Ethiopia, concerning itself with the future of Libya, Somaliland, and of course with the Union of South Africa. Desire to co-operate internationally is shown by membership in a large number of international bodies beside United Nations. Indonesians work well with international groups.

Moreover, their view of the world is inspiriting. Perhaps because their own problems are so many and yet their zest for tackling them so keen, the problems of the world in general do not seem insoluble. Instead of radiating a sense of impending calamity, they radiate equanimity. After all, their history is a long one; they have buffeted many storms. They have resilience which is often more useful than might. And a kind of eagerness about tomorrow which may get them further than the grim determination which marks some of the more militant nations.

After living a year and a half among the Indonesians, my impression was that here is a people whose will to rise to full stature cannot be easily thwarted; here is a people who, technologically, are making so much of so little that they put older, more wasteful democracies to shame; here is a people pledged to education and willing to pay for it; a people concerned for the world predicament. If at times they seem uncertain, touchy, over-proud, even self-defeating, these shortcomings stem from a dignity and determination which presage maturity. And the whole world will profit by the contributions of a mature democracy in this strategic archipelago.

INDEX

Set in Linotype Baskerville
Format by Katharine Sitterly
Manufactured by The Haddon Craftsmen, Inc.
Published by HARPER & BROTHERS, *New York*

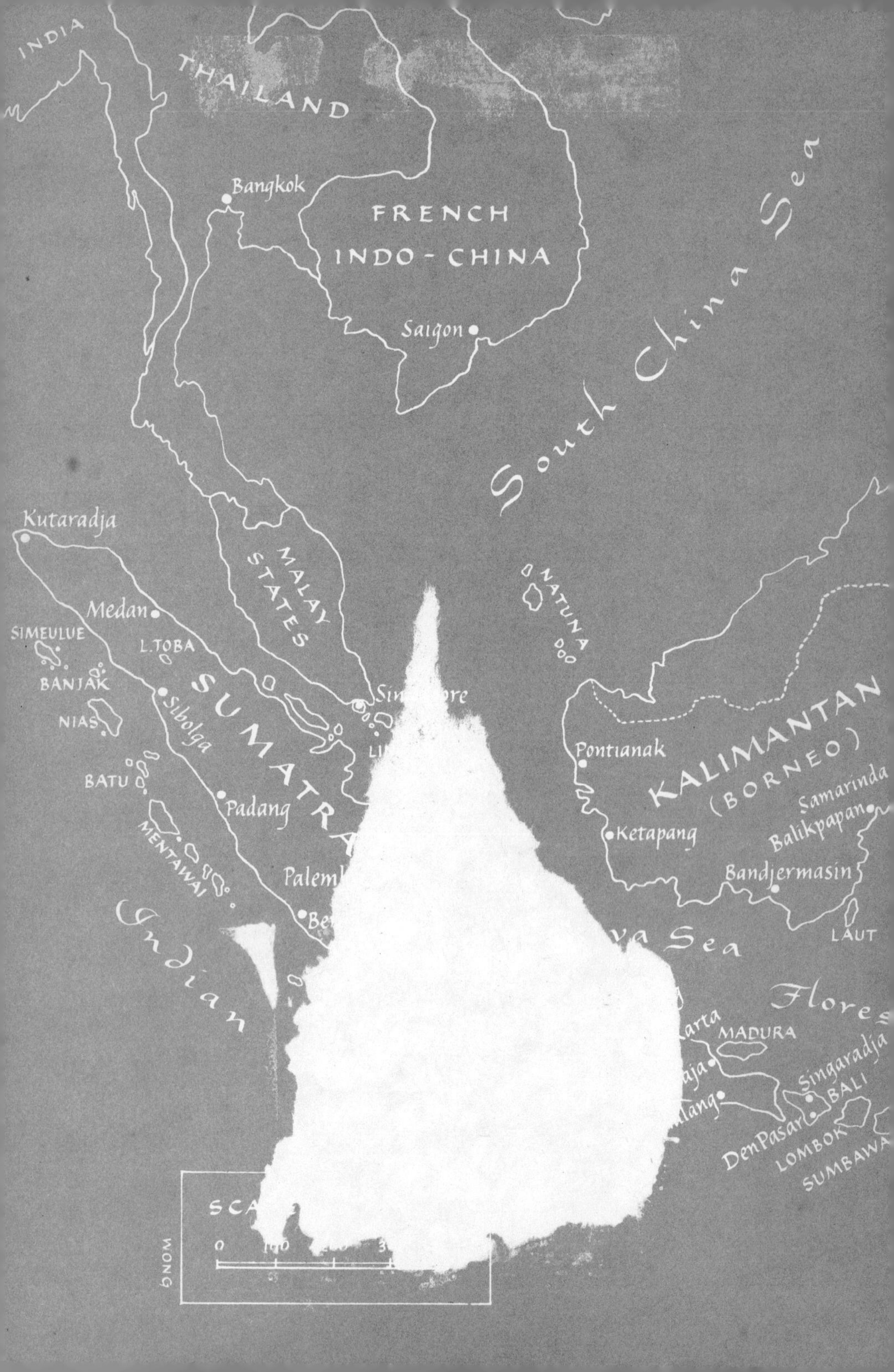

INDIA
THAILAND
Bangkok
FRENCH INDO-CHINA
Saigon
South China Sea
Kutaradja
MALAY STATES
NATUNA
Medan
SIMEULUE
L.TOBA
SUMATRA
BANJAK
Sibolga
NIAS
Pontianak
KALIMANTAN (BORNEO)
Samarinda
Balikpapan
BATU
Padang
Ketapang
MENTAWAI
Bandjermasin
LAUT
Indian
Flores
MADURA
Singaradja
BALI
DenPasar
LOMBOK
SUMBAWA
0
100
WONG